POLITICAL MANAGEMENT IN CANADA: CONVERSATIONS ON STATECRAFT

Second Edition

Allan Blakeney has been identified with Saskatchewan politics and government for forty years as a public servant, cabinet minister, premier, and leader of the opposition. A Rhodes scholar with an intellectual's perspective on governing, Blakeney brings a unique and valuable perspective to this study of political management.

Presented in the form of a dialogue between the authors, the book provides a thorough examination of the roles of politicians and public servants and techniques of management in Westminster systems. What emerges is a sophisticated philosophy of statecraft that recognizes both politics and management, and underlines the importance of balancing the two.

First published in 1992, *Political Management in Canada* is now available in a revised and updated edition. A new appendix shows how the book can complement the major political science and public administration texts currently in use in Canada.

ALLAN BLAKENEY is a former premier of Saskatchewan and former professor at the College of Law, University of Saskatchewan. He is presently Visiting Scholar, College of Law, University of Saskatchewan.

SANDFORD BORINS is Professor of Public Management and Chair, Division of Management and Economics, University of Toronto, Scarborough.

ALLAN BLAKENEY
and
SANDFORD BORINS

Political Management in Canada: Conversations on Statecraft

SECOND EDITION

UNIVERSITY OF TORONTO PRESS
Toronto Buffalo London

© Allan Blakeney and Sandford Borins 1998
Published by University of Toronto Press Incorporated
Toronto Buffalo London
Printed in Canada

ISBN 0-8020-4290-2 (cloth)
ISBN 0-8020-8123-1 (paper)

Printed on acid-free paper

Canadian Cataloguing in Publication Data

Blakeney, Allan
    Political management in Canada : conversations on statecraft

    2nd ed.
    Includes bibliographical references and index.
    ISBN 0-8020-4290-2 (bound)   ISBN 0-8020-8123-1 (pbk.)

    1. Federal government – Canada.   2. Canada – Politics and government –
    20th century.   I. Borins, Sandford F., 1949– .   II. Title.

    JL75.B53 1998   320.971   C98-931122-8

University of Toronto Press acknowledges the financial assistance to its publishing
program of the Canada Council for the Arts and the Ontario Arts Council.

Contents

Conclusion: A Philosophy of Statecraft and Some Directions for Inquiry 240

Preface

This is not the type of book you would expect either a former politician or a practising academic to write. Politicians usually write memoirs that deal with momentous decisions they made, the innovative policies they developed, and the fascinating, if not difficult, individuals they encountered along the way. Academics approach the same material to write histories that are based on a wide range of sources and that attempt to sum up in an objective way the strengths and weaknesses or contributions and failures of a government. However, this book is not a biography of Allan Blakeney, nor is it a history of the government and political party he headed.[1]

One of the hallmarks of Blakeney's political stewardship was his interest in and concern for the organizational structure and administrative processes of the Saskatchewan government and its public service. Among politicians, this is unusual. Many are content to work with what they have inherited; others, like Pierre Trudeau, had managerial interests and oversaw structural change, but left it to the public servants and academics to analyse and explain the organizational reforms.[2] A reductionist might say that Blakeney's interests are not surprising, given that he was a public servant before he became a politician. However, other politicians who came to politics from the bureaucracy have shown little interest, during or after their tenure, in management or organization.[3] Lester Pearson is a good example.

Our approach begins with the basic assumption that a premier or prime minister *ought* to be concerned about the quality of public management. We believe this for several reasons.

First, the ultimate agenda of any government is its policies, and these policies will influence whether it will be reelected or defeated, and whether it will be remembered for good or ill. However, it is management and organization that make policy development possible. It is difficult for good policy development to happen in a climate of organizational chaos. For instance, when ministers approach day-to-day operations as though they were major crises, ministerial time is monopolized, with the result described by the old adage, 'When operations rise to the top of the organization, policy sinks to the bottom.' Second, the essence of public sector financial management is the freeing up of discretionary resources for new priorities. When financial management is ineffective, this will not happen, and government will be locked into the practice of unimaginative incrementalism. Third and finally, good public management enhances the public's respect for and confidence in politicians and the institutions of governance.[4] Canadian governments bear the constitutional – indeed, moral – responsibility to provide 'peace, order, and good government.'

No individual, not even the most creative among us, develops ideas and techniques in a vacuum: we all have teachers, mentors, and precursors. The CCF (later NDP) government that ruled Saskatchewan from 1944 to 1964 was always interested in effective and efficient public management. Blakeney worked for that government, first as a public servant and then as a minister, learning his craft from political mentors such as Tommy Douglas and Clarence Fines, and public service colleagues such as Al Johnson, Tom Shoyama, and Tommy McLeod.

Later, the Saskatchewan NDP tradition of effective public management became well-known nationally, as embodied in the 'Saskatchewan Mafia' – the many senior public servants who left Saskatchewan for Ottawa or other provinces after 1964. This was the legacy Blakeney could build on when he took office as Premier in 1971.

As an academic, Borins works within a tradition that classifies information in order to build comprehensive systems. As Borins listened to Blakeney expounding his approach to public management in a course we team-taught and in many conversations, Borins came to feel that it was important to present Blakeney's views as a comprehensive system of theory and practice. In addition, Borins felt it was important to draw linkages between Blakeney's approach and the academic literature on management, both public and generic.

In this book we deal first with the political side of public management: cabinet, the caucus, and the political machinery. We then turn to the public service, discussing methods of co-ordination, financial management, human resource management, and intergovernmental relations. Finally, we tackle a number of special topics, such as lobbying, public consultation, the management of change, crisis management, media relations, and changes of government. It will become apparent that there are a number of fundamental principles that give coherence to the entire book; they are reviewed in the conclusion. We have given equal weight to the political and bureaucratic sides because much of the literature emphasizes one or the other, with politicians more likely to write about the political and academics studying public administration to write about the bureaucratic. We see politics and bureaucracy as two faces of the same coin, which must necessarily be discussed together.

We envisage two groups of readers of this book: practitioners and students. Practitioners include politicians, such as the opposition leader who has just been elected premier, and the first-time cabinet minister. They also include public servants who are interested in the general question of what drives their political masters or in studying specific administrative practices in Saskatchewan that might be adopted in other jurisdictions. Finally, we are writing for private sector managers, who would like to understand how public sector management is both different from and similar to private sector management. Greater knowledge of the public sector may benefit private sector managers in their dealings with government. Indeed, we include a chapter about the Blakeney government's experience dealing with private sector firms in the potash, oil, and uranium industries.

We are also writing for students of political science and public administration, who themselves may aspire to careers in politics or the public service. We hope they will find this book a useful supplement to their textbooks in that it illustrates the tasks and techniques of politics and the public service – how to chair a cabinet meeting, or devise a media strategy for a crisis – and offers general principles arrived at through the specific experience of the Blakeney government. To make clear the relationship between our work and the standard curriculum, we have included an appendix that shows where our discussions correspond to topics presented in a variety of commonly used public administration and political science textbooks.

In keeping with the unusual nature of this book, we have chosen a somewhat unorthodox manner of presentation. Most co-authored books are written by melding two or more voices into one common voice. For example, political autobiographies are often written with the help of a ghost-writer, who transcribes and then shapes the politician's words. In a co-authored academic work, the authors reach a common point of view, delegate different sections to one another and then check to ensure that all sections are consistent with that point of view.

We have decided not to merge our individual voices into a common editorial plural; instead we have kept our two roles and points of view distinct throughout the book. We have done this by presenting our material as a dialogue between the two of us. Blakeney writes as a former practitioner, explaining what he did and why. Borins structures the discussion by posing questions to Blakeney and by relating Blakeney's answers to general principles of private and public sector management as well as to the experiences of other governments. We would remind the reader that a dialogue is not the same as a transcript of an interview or a conversation. Interviews and conversations are spontaneous, but contain tangents, blind alleys, and dead ends. These dialogues are a distillation of the class we taught and the conversations we have had; they preserve the essence of our lectures and conversations while eliminating the prolixity of everyday speech.

Finally, we must acknowledge the circumstances under which this project was conceived and the people who have supported and assisted us along the way. After he retired from politics in 1988, Blakeney was invited by then Dean (now Mr Justice) James MacPherson of Osgoode Hall Law School, York University, to spend two years there, initially as the Laskin Professor of Constitutional and Public Law. When making the arrangements, Blakeney indicated that he was interested in teaching public administration in addition to his law courses. Borins had already been teaching a graduate-level public management course in the Faculty of Administrative Studies. The logical thing to do was to pool our efforts – that is, to team-teach the public management course. We thank James MacPherson, and Alan Hockin, then Dean of the Faculty of Administrative Studies, for supporting this cross-faculty project. It was while teaching this class that we began to compare our ideas and approaches.

Thanks are due to many people who assisted this project in various ways. The students in our public management course at York in 1989 and 1990 stimulated us with their interest and their questions. To have a record of our course, we taped our lectures. To transform the tapes into a book, we needed some resources; a generous grant from the National Centre for Management Research and Development at the Faculty of Business Administration at the University of Western Ontario provided them. Gordon Osbaldeston, former Clerk of the Privy Council and later senior fellow at Western, was particularly supportive. Our lectures were transcribed by two of the students who heard them, Valerie Jaeger in 1989, and Daniel Barkin in 1990. Their accurate and clean transcripts provided the initial raw material for the first edition of this book. During the preparation of the first edition, Greg Argue, Grace Bhesania, Russell Isinger, and Tania Sarkar served as our research assistants.

This second edition of our book received financial support from the Division of Management and Economics at the University of Toronto at Scarborough. Russell Isinger, Ilya Shapiro, and Sandy Wong served as research assistants. Our editors at the University of Toronto Press, first Robert Ferguson and then Virgil Duff, and Matthew Kudelka during the production phase, have been supportive all along the way.

Without all these different types of support, this project would not have come to fruition.

Part One

The Political Dimension

1

Making Collective Responsibility Work

This chapter begins with a discussion of the fundamental principle of cabinet government, which is collective responsibility. Blakeney presents his approach, which is built around an answer to this question: Who is the general manager of a government? This approach is contrasted with the private sector style of general management. We sketch the implications of collective responsibility for ministers and senior public servants, compare Blakeney's approach to that of two major British students of politics, and look at various ways of preserving cabinet solidarity.

Borins: Let's begin with first principles. Allan, many of those who served in your cabinets or worked in the Saskatchewan public service refer to a talk they heard you give so many times that they call it *the speech.*[1] In the course of our academic collaboration, I've also heard it more than once. Could you deliver it one more time? Let me prompt you with two questions: Who is the general manager in a government? And is the general manager of a government similar to general manager of a corporation?

Blakeney: A provincial government does not have a general manager or a chief executive officer in the sense that a corporation has. Although management structures are never as direct and uncluttered as they appear on an organization chart, it is generally accurate to say that a corporation has a board of directors that gives general direction to the corporation but does not involve itself in management. What it does is engage a chief executive officer, to whom it entrusts the management of the enterprise. It may involve itself in the appointment of a few senior officers besides the CEO, and it may have direct contact with them, but that contact is always limited. In general, the board deals with the corporation's

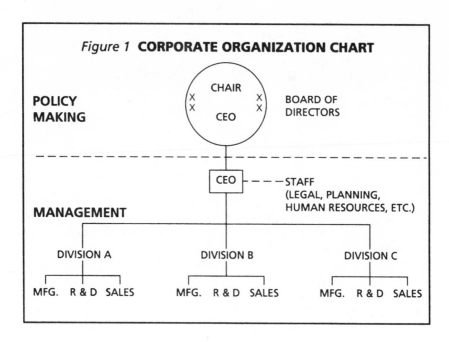

Figure 1 **CORPORATE ORGANIZATION CHART**

management through the CEO and his or her immediate staff. A simplified organizational chart for a corporation often looks something like the one shown in Figure 1. The contrast with the organization of a provincial government is stark. Consider a simplified organizational chart for a provincial government, like the one shown in Figure 2.[2]

The first point to understand is the distinction between an organization's direction and its management. It is easy to overemphasize the difference between policy making and management, since the effective discharge of each function requires some consideration of the other. But it is still useful to distinguish the functions. Within the typical private corporation it is clear that the board is involved almost solely in policy direction. The management may be involved in policy making, but the board is not involved in management. This is true even when the board has a number of management staff as members. It is as management staff that they are involved in policy making, not as directors that they are involved in management.[3]

A look at the government organization chart makes it clear that ministers in a cabinet have a very different function than members of the board of a private corporation. Both are members of a policy-making body, but ministers assume

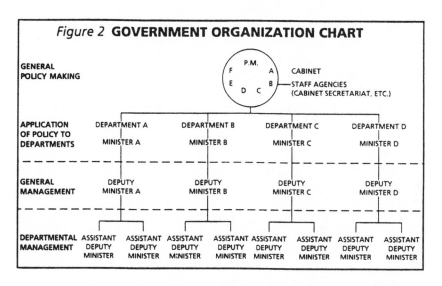

Figure 2 **GOVERNMENT ORGANIZATION CHART**

responsibility on behalf of the premier and the cabinet for the policy direction of a part of the entire enterprise; in a policy sense, they administer a department of government. I take the view that the minister does not become the CEO of the department. The permanent head of the department, the deputy minister, is the CEO of the department. Thus, on the governmental organization chart, when we draw a line between policy making and administration, we draw it between the individual ministers and their deputies, not between cabinet and the ministers. In Chapter 5 we'll have an opportunity to consider why I think this is important and how it affects the way ministers perform their duties.

The point that I make now is that the deputies, as the general managers or CEOs of their departments, are at the top of the management tree. There is no government-wide general manager; it is the deputies, as a group, who must assume that function. It is not as unpromising a structure as it sounds: departmental lines answer most questions of who makes which decisions. Where the policies of two or three departments interact, it is up to the deputies to sort out what steps should be taken to carry out what they understand to be overall government policy. (In Chapter 8 we will have an opportunity to refer again to what a government organizational structure means for deputies.)

This means that ministers are not the administrative heads of departments. Their job is to be a member of cabinet – to be part of the team that shapes the overall policy of the government, to defend that policy in public forums, and to interpret and flesh out that policy for the deputies and other officials of the departments for which they are responsible. Put another way, their principal function is not to carry the views and interests of the department to the cabinet table; rather, it is to carry the views and interests of the cabinet to the departments. It is the minister's job not only to carry the cabinet's message to the bureaucracy (a term I don't regard as pejorative), but also to carry to the bureaucracy and to cabinet a perception of whether the policies being pursued by the government – and particularly by his or her department – are being well received by the public.[4]

While the minister carries the government's message to the public, he or she must also carry the public's message back to the government, and in particular to the department. A minister who becomes too involved in formulating the department's plans develops a sense of loyalty to the plans at too early a stage. The minister is co-opted by the bureaucracy, and loses the ability to assess the plans on the basis of their public acceptability. And that's the minister's job. I found that ministers who had been co-opted by their bureaucracies sometimes defended the department's plans at cabinet without giving full weight to warnings from colleagues that the public was grumbling.

In speaking with ministers, I stressed the fact that what the bureaucracy felt was the best course of action from a technical point of view was only half the picture. We live in a democracy, not a technocracy. If a course of action is technically sound but is not acceptable to the public, then it is a poor course of action. Ordinarily, a minister who feels that a large percentage of the public would reject a course of action, even after solid and reasonable efforts to explain it, should not accept the bureaucracy's advice and should not recommend it to cabinet.

Public acceptance may not be immediate, and some policies may call for a pitched battle to win public acceptance. This must be recognized at the outset. But at the same time, a government cannot afford to spend its political capital fighting with large numbers of the public on unimportant issues. The minister's job, then, both as a departmental minister and as a member of cabinet, is to remain sensitive to the public mood – a job that is made much more difficult when the minister's time is taken up by, and his or her political sensitivities are dulled by, too deep an involvement in departmental management issues.

Borins: Your position puts you in some very good company. For example, Sir Ivor Jennings wrote the following in *Cabinet Government*, his classic study of the British system:

The minister's task is to bring an independent mind to the questions put before him, to be convinced by his experts that they are right, or to settle in the light of common sense the disputes between the experts. The wider his vision, the easier it becomes to grasp the implications. The dangerous minister is he who fails to see consequences, not merely in relation to his own department, but in relation to the process of government as a whole, and especially in relation to its impact on the House of Commons and upon public opinion ... The real reason for having ministers at the heads of departments is that this is an effective method of bringing government under public control ... It was no doubt this idea, and not merely a suspicion of military experts, which impelled a French prime minister to say that war was too serious to be carried on by generals and admirals.[5]

More recently, Richard Crossman, who was a minister in the Wilson government from 1964 to 1970, and became famous for his diaries, summed up the task of a minister in the following way:

The greatest danger of a Labour Cabinet is that its members will be corrupted from being a team of socialists carrying out a collective cabinet strategy into a collection of individual departmental ministers. The greatest temptation is that I should be too interested in the praise of the department and too pleased at being told how well I am doing ... Therefore, the battle is really for the soul of the minister. Is he to remain a foreign body in the department, inserting into the departments things they don't like, a political dynamo, sparking off things they don't want, things he wants and the party wants? Or is he to become *their* minister, content to speak for them?[6]

I would add that if you substituted 'Conservative' for 'Labour' and 'believers in the market' for 'socialists,' Margaret Thatcher – also a radical politician – as well as her successors John Major and Tony Blair would likely agree with Crossman.

I think Crossman was right to emphasize the danger of not being a team. There is a scene in a *Yes Prime Minister* episode where Sir Humphrey Appleby and some of his fellow permanent secretaries (or, in Canadian parlance, deputy ministers) are discussing policy and one of them cynically says, 'Isn't it a curious notion that the government would have a policy. Don't people realize that government is really a loose confederation of warring tribes?'[7]

What intrigues me about this statement is that it is an abbreviated reference to Graham Allison's classic study of government decision making, *Essence of Decision: Explaining the Cuban Missile Crisis.* Allison suggested that besides the co-ordinated and unitary 'rational actor' model of government behaviour, two alternative models exist: 'organizational process,' and 'governmental politics.' Together, these lead the analyst to view government as a loose confederation of warring tribes.[8] I can see the applicability of this approach to the U.S. government, with which Allison is most familiar. After all, the Constitution of the United States, with its system of checks and balances, was intended to *ensure* that government would operate as a loose confederation of warring tribes. In his recent memoir, former Labor Secretary Robert Reich described a cabinet meeting in the following terms: 'I've been in many meetings with [President Clinton], but few with the entire cabinet. Cabinet officers have nothing in common except the first word in their titles. Maybe Clinton is going through the motions because he thinks presidents are *supposed* to meet with their cabinets and the public would be disturbed to learn the truth ... I gaze around the room. Even the formal titles belie reality. Each of us has special responsibility for one slice of America.'[9]

However, the parliamentary system was designed to concentrate power in the cabinet. The conclusion to be drawn is that a cabinet always has within it centrifugal forces, and that it is the premier's responsibility to keep the ministers all moving together in the same direction.[10]

Blakeney: In some sense, any large organization is a collection of warring tribes. Just as there are territorial imperatives, there seem to be organizational imperatives that affect any large organization, public *or* private. Two examples: the modern university has been described by Robert M. Hutchins, former president of the University of Chicago, as a series of separate schools and departments held together by a heating system, and by Clark Kerr, former president of the University of California (in a warmer climate) as a series of individual faculty entrepreneurs held together by a common grievance over parking.

Borins: But universities were designed to be chaotic.

Blakeney: On the other hand, as the political theory of collective responsibility would mandate, it was our objective in a small provincial government to reduce the level of conflict among the warring tribes and to make sure that the tribes were not led into battle by ministers – or by deputy ministers either.

I felt that in a small province like Saskatchewan with a politically aware public, a cabinet that had a common policy and presented a united face to the public was essential. Our government had a program it wanted to put in place. Parts of it would need to be sold to the public. Some members of the public would be unhappy. If, for example, we had to curtail a highway construction project, we could tolerate the local member of the legislature expressing his or her unhappiness, in measured terms, but we could not tolerate the Minister of Highways questioning the cabinet decision in public. If he did so, other ministers would be under pressure to defend 'their' projects. Carried further, the only defenders left of the government's financial decisions would be the Premier and the Minister of Finance. A government loses credibility and loses the public perception that it is 'in charge' if cabinet members disagree in public on major issues of policy.

There are further problems in such public disagreements. When cabinet ministers question cabinet decisions in public and thereby put other ministers in the difficult position of having to dispute with a colleague in public, it is more difficult to keep the group working as a team in making tough decisions. Every government faces some difficult times, some troughs in public acceptance, and it is important for each cabinet minister to feel that all his or her colleagues will be firm allies in public. Stress from long hours and overwork creates enough problems without more being created by colleagues taking public positions that contradict or seek to pre-empt cabinet decisions.

Another consideration is the comfort level of the Premier. If cabinet makes a decision to curtail a highway construction project, and the Minister of Highways publicly dissents, the Premier, when next in the affected community, is going to be met with protest against the decision, reinforced by the argument that 'even your own Highways Minister disagrees with your decision.' That is an unfair position in which to put the Premier and his or her cabinet colleagues.

I found also that cabinet solidarity was valuable in dealing with a special public – the Saskatchewan New Democratic Party. At conventions, the delegates were often aggressive in demanding to know why this or that piece of party policy had not yet been implemented. Since everything a party seeks cannot be done at once, and some things cannot be done at all, cabinet ministers have to resist any temptation to curry favour with delegates by breaking ranks. Such playing to the delegates will not only set minister against minister but will likely set delegate against delegate and thus damage the party's internal harmony. And it is one of the jobs of the Premier to keep the party united and its ire directed at its political opponents. A party, like a cabinet, has within it centrifugal forces that must be tamed.

Borins: The literature about the government of Tommy Douglas – Saskatchewan's first socialist government – makes the point that his government's main responsibility was to the province, so his government's policies sometimes differed from the party's preferences, which resulted in occasional disappointment for party zealots.[11]

On reading through some of the material we gathered from your government's archives, I came across one memorandum that conveys the importance of cabinet solidarity in a slightly different context. Treasury Board, as we will discuss later on, is the committee of cabinet that deals with spending decisions. Walter Smishek, the Chairman of Treasury Board and Minister of Finance, wrote a memo dated 18 August 1977 to all ministers and deputy ministers. Part of it read as follows:

Recently several incidents have come to my attention in which program departments have referred to decisions which are 'before Treasury Board' or 'pending Treasury Board review' in relating to outside groups or agencies. This clearly tends to focus the interest of such groups on Treasury Board and the Treasury Board process rather than the program department and its minister ... Public reference to the Treasury Board process tends to weaken the Treasury Board's ability to objectively examine the merits of a given proposal, and to set it in the context of other priorities.[12]

Allan, any comments about the point Smishek was making?

Blakeney: Mr Smishek was making a point similar to the one I was making earlier. Just as ministers may sometimes say in public that they agree with what an interest group is asking for, and allow cabinet to take responsibility for the negative response to the group, some public servants – and sometimes ministers – will say to an interest group that the proposal for which the group was pressing is before Treasury Board.

Treasury Board is, as you know, a committee of cabinet. The clear implication is that the public servant or the minister, as the case may be, has made a favourable recommendation to Treasury Board. If the proposal is rejected, the villain is not the public servant or the minister but the Treasury Board. This puts pressure on the Treasury Board, particularly if it is a minister who has suggested that he or she has recommended the proposal. For reasons similar to those for insisting on cabinet solidarity, we tried to insist that public bodies not be advised that a proposal was being considered by Treasury Board. If the proposal was rejected, then it was the job of the minister and the public servant to defend the rejection as government policy. In dealing with the public, all ministers and senior public servants were required to maintain a common front, and not separate themselves into white hats and black hats in an effort to placate persistent interest groups lobbying for particular proposals.

I am making here the classic case for a cabinet that puts forward a common policy and presents a united front to the public. There are other models of cabinet government. Some cabinets are 'advocacy' cabinets, or at least have advocacy ministers. These are ministers who speak on behalf of given interest groups and say very openly that they agree with the proposals of, say, interest group X and that they have recommended to cabinet that the government act on those proposals. When cabinet does not accept the proposals, the minister simply goes back to interest group X and says that he or she fought for the proposals but that the cabinet turned them down. I remember how Eugene Whelan, a Minister of Agriculture in the Trudeau government, used to play this role.

Borins: This sounds like Sheila Copps in her role as Heritage Minister in the Chrétien government.

Blakeney: This mode of operation can probably be made to work at the federal level, where the Prime Minister and Minister of Finance are less likely to encounter the particular interest groups who have been adopted by advocacy ministers. Cabinet government is a flexible tool, but at least in small provinces there are real limits to a cabinet's ability to tolerate ministers who purport to support proposals from specific interest groups that have already been rejected as government policy.

Borins: One thing that interests me about *the speech* is how often you gave it. The management literature on leadership emphasizes that one of a leader's responsibilities is to repeatedly articulate the essential values of the organization. So if you sounded like a broken record, there was a reason.

Blakeney: I fully realized that I had only intermittent opportunities to warn ministers against being co-opted by their staff. Some ministers faced daily pressures from their staff to 'discuss some problems the department is facing.' Some public servants like the security of dealing with policy questions along with the minister. This avoids the difficulties inherent in making a firm recommendation for the minister to assess. It also makes it harder for ministers to assess the quality of their management skills. Delegating upward is a finely honed art. Ministers need to be reminded of this.

Also encountered often is the temptation to take a position in favour of an interest group, when the minister knows the decision will need cabinet or Treasury Board approval. The perils of appearing to commit cabinet or Treasury Board, and possibly being left out on a limb if one of these bodies does not agree, need to be emphasized whenever the opportunity arises. I often made *the speech* at a new minister's first cabinet meeting, so that the new minister could hear it and the entire cabinet could hear it *again.*

Borins: I am sure you used other techniques besides *the speech* to keep cabinet ministers and public servants playing on the same team. Let's deal with them in the chapters on cabinet, ministers, and co-ordinating mechanisms.

2

Choosing a Cabinet

In this chapter we discuss how to choose a cabinet that will unite the party and ensure diversity in government with respect to region, ethnicity, religion, occupation, and gender – not to mention ability. We then discuss the qualities a minister needs to be successful and show how the system can compensate for the occasional weak minister. We then consider how cabinets change over time – for example, the rationale for naming a very small cabinet when first taking office, the logic of cabinet shuffles, and how a cabinet can be rejuvenated.

Borins: Politics, like the rest of life, is organized in cycles, so we can begin the discussion at any point in the cycle. Let's start with the moment you were elected and were preparing to take office. One of your first tasks was to choose a cabinet. Let's discuss some of the considerations that influenced your choices.[1] In the chapters that follow we will talk about the management of cabinet and the political work of cabinet and individual ministers. In Chapter 7 we will complete the political cycle by talking about getting elected.

To begin, I understand that the 1970 leadership race in which you were chosen to head the Saskatchewan NDP was hard-fought. Dennis Gruending's book discusses in detail the resignation of your predecessor, Woodrow Lloyd, the factionalism of the Waffle group, and so on.[2] Your strongest opponent was Roy Romanow, who actually led on the first two ballots at the leadership convention. How did you decide what role Romanow would play in your government?

Blakeney: That decision was easy. Roy had shown surprising strength, he had run a good campaign, and he had lots of ability, so he had to have a key position in cabinet. Deputy Premier was the obvious choice.

There were other reasons why this choice made excellent sense. Clearly, it would help heal any wounds that might be left after a hard-fought leadership campaign. Roy was from Saskatoon and I was from Regina, so together we represented the two main cities in the province. It might have been better if he had had a rural base; it would have been difficult if he had been from Regina. I was particularly fortunate that Roy and I had complementary skills.

I have often said that a provincial cabinet needs at least one high-profile mouthpiece and one bean counter. I had been a public servant. I had an interest in financial matters and administration. I was not a charismatic speaker. So I was the bean counter. Roy was a charismatic speaker with a great capacity for reaching out to almost any audience. He had worked in the media and knew the media. He was the mouthpiece. By further good fortune, my roots were English-Welsh Protestant while Roy was Ukrainian and Catholic. He spoke Ukrainian.

In 1971 there was still a residue of tension in the party over the circumstances in which Woodrow Lloyd had stepped down as leader. I was a Lloyd loyalist, while Roy was one of the new guard who had been restless with Mr. Lloyd's style of leadership.

Between the two of us, we covered most of the bases in the caucus and, to a lesser extent, the party. Roy was the obvious number-two person in the cabinet.

Borins: The practice of having one high-profile mouthpiece and one bean counter seems to be quite firmly established in the Saskatchewan NDP and other governments. In the Douglas government, Douglas was the mouthpiece and Clarence Fines, the Treasurer, was the bean counter.[3] In the present government, first elected in October 1991 and re-elected in June 1995, Roy is once again the high-profile mouthpiece and Janice MacKinnon, the Finance Minister from 1993 to 1997, has generally been the acknowledged bean counter.[4]

I imagine that the electorate naturally expects the Premier or Prime Minister to be the high-profile mouthpiece and the Finance Minister to be the bean counter so that, if the Premier tends to be the bean counter, then the high-profile mouthpiece becomes indispensable to the Premier. The current federal government presents an interesting variant on this theme. While Prime Minister Jean Chrétien is usually the mouthpiece, the priority of reducing the federal deficit in the government's first term meant that Finance Minister Paul Martin had a higher profile and greater popularity than most finance ministers. It will be interesting to see whether his role will change now that the government has achieved a balanced budget.[5]

The practice of giving your main rival a key cabinet portfolio is often followed in politics, one example being Joe Clark's role in Brian Mulroney's government. In the private sector, defeated aspirants for senior executive positions – especially CEO –

often leave the company. One difference, I suppose, relates to alternatives. In the private sector there are many other firms, often in the same industry, that a dissatisfied senior executive can go to. In politics there are fewer alternatives.

Blakeney: But Roy certainly had alternatives. It was clearly open to him to seek an NDP nomination for the House of Commons, and I'm sure he would have been elected in the federal election of 1972 or 1974. I did not consider for one minute not including him as a key member of our team, and I wanted him specifically as Deputy Premier.

Borins: After accommodating Romanow at the cabinet table, who came next?

Blakeney: As I noted, neither Roy nor I had a rural background. This suggested that the third choice for cabinet should be a high-profile farmer. John Messer was just such a person: able, hard driving, a successful young farmer who came into the legislature in 1967. He was from northeast Saskatchewan and had supported Roy in the leadership campaign.

The next choice was Walter Smishek. He was from Regina. Ideally, he would have been from another centre. But he had close links with the trade union constituency and had supported George Taylor, another leadership candidate. Taylor was a labour lawyer with strong trade union support. In addition, Smishek had better links to the left of the party – the Waffle-minded people – than did Roy or I.

The next choice was Everett Wood. He was a farmer from southwestern Saskatchewan who had been an MLA since 1956 and a cabinet minister in the Lloyd government. He had spent many years in rural municipal government and was respected by these people across the province. He was also an active member of the Pentecostal Assembly and represented some of the social gospel roots of the CCF and NDP. He was decent and shrewd.

Next came Gordon Snyder, a locomotive engineer. He represented our third-largest city, Moose Jaw. He had an abundance of good sense, a wry sense of humour, and the respect of the railway unions, who were a large group in Saskatchewan at that time and who did not readily identify with the Saskatchewan Federation of Labour and the people Smishek represented.

Representing north-central Saskatchewan was Ted Bowerman, a farmer from the constituency immediately adjacent to Prince Albert, our fourth-largest city. He was a former public servant, recognized as a good head, and from a well-respected family. His father had been an MP, having defeated Prime Minister Mackenzie King in the 1945 federal election.

About one-third of the caucus were teachers. The next choice was Neil Byers, a teacher from east-central Saskatchewan who had won a key by-election in 1969. Then followed Gordon McMurchy, a farmer who had no legislative experience but who had been provincial president of the party. He had also been chairman of the board of a large rural school unit, and I had in mind a particular role for him.

The final choice for our small first cabinet was Eiling Kramer, who had been in the legislature since 1952 and who had enormous political skills. He was a rancher and auctioneer and represented the northwest part of the province. I'll digress and give you one example of his political gifts. On one occasion when he was in opposition, he was pressing very hard to get a stop sign erected by the Department of Highways at a dangerous intersection on the outskirts of his small city of North Battleford, with no results. After writing letters to the local newspaper laying the groundwork, he had a standard stop sign constructed. Then he dug a hole, alerted the media, and proceeded to put the sign in place.

That presented the Department of Highways with a problem. They could remove the sign, but what then? If the department left the intersection unsigned and a serious accident occurred, they would be faced with public hostility. If they put up their own sign, they would be admitting their earlier error. They elected to do the latter, to the amusement of the community.

You will note that I tried to see that the cabinet represented the main geographic areas of the province. That is key. I also wanted the various wings of the party to be represented. That was important in 1971, when we assumed office, but it became less of a factor as time went on and the divisions in the party accentuated by Lloyd's retirement and the leadership campaign began to dissolve.

Ethnic representation was a consideration of lesser importance. Almost without effort, our cabinet represented the province's main ethnic groups. I had hoped to get a minister of Jewish origin – the Jewish community is small but influential. The NDP has an enviable reputation for opposing anti-Semitism and welcoming Jewish people in leadership roles, as the careers of David Lewis, Dave Barrett, and Stephen Lewis will attest. I wanted to build on that. Later I appointed Norman Vickar to cabinet, and he served ably in building links with the Jewish community, and the small-business community generally.

I wanted occupational groups to be represented. There is a public perception that the best cabinet would consist of lawyers, accountants, and businesspeople – that is, people who have experience in making the types of decisions that governments face. Not so. A cabinet needs farmers, working people, people from many other groups – people who see the world from a perspective outside the business mainstream.

An apocryphal story might help illustrate this. While visiting another province,

I remarked that I thought a particular cabinet minister was not exactly a rocket scientist. The reply from a fellow cabinet minister in that province was, 'Yes, I agree. A is not a rocket scientist. But I'm sorry to say that about 25 per cent of the people in this province are decidedly not rocket scientists, and they deserve representation, too.' And that story is only half in jest.

Cabinets must recognize that while the processes of analysis and logic are the way to deal with most problems, many citizens do not govern their lives by analysis and logic. They hold illogical opinions and are often inconsistent. A cabinet must be tuned in to these currents – to what people are saying at the curling rinks and the sports days. It is not that cabinet necessarily responds to these trends. But deeply held sentiments and convictions must be taken into account. Oliver Wendell Holmes, the great American jurist, said that the life of the law is not in logic but in experience. The same is true of political decisions. And if these decisions are to serve all the people, then every cabinet must have access to the experiences and feelings of a broad spectrum of the public. In Canadian politics we are only now grappling with what 'representation' means. For a provincial cabinet it means membership that reaches beyond the business and professional élites to include ministers who have a very different view of the world, or who can readily relate to those who do.

If I were engaged in the exercise of choosing a cabinet today, I would be considering gender and visible minorities. There were no women in the Saskatchewan legislature in 1971, nor were there any visible minorities. Surprisingly, this was not an issue in 1971. Later in the 1970s we began trying to elect women and people of aboriginal origin to the legislature, but this effort did not bear much fruit until the 1980s. This means that no women or people of aboriginal origin served in any of my cabinets. Nowadays representation of these groups has to be an important consideration in cabinet building. The Romanow cabinets since 1991 have included a Cree-speaking aboriginal minister and women in high-profile positions such as Deputy Premier, Minister of Finance, Minister of Health, and Minister of Education.

Borins: You haven't yet mentioned ability. Where does that come in? What abilities did you look for in a minister? Also, I find it curious that you mentioned the individuals, but not the portfolios to which you appointed them.

Blakeney: Clearly, ability is the first requirement for a cabinet minister. A minister should be able to handle written material, to speak clearly, to answer questions in the legislature factually rather than confrontationally, to listen to the public and to advisors, and to exercise independent judgment as an individual minister and as a part of a collegial cabinet. Some natural caution is an asset.

Sometimes a premier will have to accept lesser skills if the member's ability to represent an otherwise unrepresented group is particularly strong.

Some cabinet ministers, but not all, must have superior administrative skills, and some, but not all, must have superior political and media skills. But with a little assistance from public servants, many people could do the job of a cabinet minister.

Just as any provincial cabinet should have a high-profile mouthpiece and a high-profile bean counter, so it needs five or six able administrators and five or six people with real political gifts. Sometimes these attributes are present in the same person, sometimes not.

Note that I gave very little consideration to the specialized knowledge of the potential ministers. The public holds the misconception that what is being sought is specialized knowledge. This often stems from the notion that the minister is the general manager of the department. As I suggested earlier, I don't agree with this role for ministers. I regard the minister's role as more like that of a director of a private corporation. As you know, many major corporations select their directors for their broad knowledge of affairs, and for their ability to maintain links with other organizations, and even because of where they live, rather than for their specialized knowledge of the corporation's operations. That's why I thought in terms of who should be in the cabinet *before* I thought about which role each should play.

In any case, sometimes specialized knowledge is a liability as much as an asset. In a small province, a road contractor who becomes Minister of Highways will know the business but will almost certainly find himself or herself in situations of real or perceived conflict of interest. The same is true for a medical doctor as Minister of Health, and so on. That is another reason why I looked for generalists rather than specialists.

However, a premier will sometimes seek out a person with particular skills for a ministry. In 1971 there was a high level of tension between teachers and school trustees. We proposed to deal with this by making legislative changes, which we feared the trustees' organization would oppose. I therefore wanted a minister who had unquestioned stature with trustees generally. I chose as Minister of Education Gordon McMurchy, who had been a visibly successful chairman of the board of trustees of a large rural school unit. Gordon was a generalist and later became Minister of Municipal Affairs and then of Agriculture.

Borins: Concerning the abilities required of a good minister, Jennings emphasized 'the art of rapid digestion ... the ability to seize the gist of a long statement by a single reading.'[6] Harold Wilson stressed 'the great and unteachable quality of being able to handle the House of Commons.'[7] Another ability of increasing

importance is that of handling the media. We discuss handling the legislature in Chapter 6 and handling the media in Chapter 17, both of which we think are teachable skills.

The misconception that ministers are chosen for specialized knowledge is certainly with us still. To illustrate, I include a cartoon from 'Back Bench.'

Some years ago, in one of my more unconventional moods, I put Sir Joseph Porter's song, 'I Am the Ruler of the Queen's Navee,' from Gilbert and Sullivan's *H.M.S. Pinafore,* on an examination, and asked my students which principles of management it illustrates. The song, as you'll remember, tells us that Porter went from a career in law to Parliament and then to the Navy, 'guided by this golden rule – stick close to your desks and never go to sea, and you all may be rulers of the Queen's Navee.' Sad to say, very few advanced that notion that generalist skills might be excellent training for the political ruler of the Queen's Navy.

Let's assume that in any caucus, ability is not distributed evenly across all groups. Doesn't that mean that some less able people will be put in cabinet to represent given groups, and that other, more able people will be bypassed because their groups cannot be overrepresented?

Blakeney: Yes, that is the result of attempting to choose a representative cabinet. But the best cabinet is not necessarily the one that has the ablest people, as we have just defined ability or as Jennings or Harold Wilson defined it in the comments you have just quoted. To use an extreme example, the people who appeared most able, considered singly, might all be academics and lawyers from Regina and Saskatoon; but together they would not make the best cabinet. The best cabinet is one that balances individual ability with the ability to represent, in a visible way, the various constituencies whose support you seek to maintain, both for your government and for the system of representative democracy.[8] The different regions, shades of opinion, ethnic and religious groups, minority interests, age groups, and so on should all be represented in cabinet.

Borins: So you will have some weak ministers in cabinet. Is there any way you can accommodate or compensate for their weaknesses?

Blakeney: There are several techniques. The obvious one is to have a strong deputy minister. I do not agree that ministers should choose their own deputies. Many ministers do not know how to do this; it is simply not within their range of previous experience. Sometimes they look for the wrong qualities – for example, personal loyalty or political compatibility – rather than administrative competence and knowledge of the work of the department and the procedures of government. Nor are ministers necessarily familiar with the pool of talent from which to choose. Our practice was for the Premier and the minister to agree on a person for deputy. With a new minister, the initiative almost always came from me. My 'government deputy' and the cabinet secretary knew who the promising candidates were, which deputies were strong and which could work with particular ministerial styles.

If a minister's weakness was an inability or unwillingness to push the department to deliver a policy agreed upon by cabinet, my staff dealt directly with the deputy. On one or two occasions I got involved personally. The problem was usually that the deputy was raising obstacles and that the minister was not sufficiently determined in requiring action.

Borins: Your first cabinet in 1971 was very small – just ten ministers. In addition, some people had multiple portfolios – you were also Minister of Finance and Minister of Industry. Why the sudden burst of workaholism? What was your intention?

Blakeney: I had a particular problem in 1971. The large caucus had four people besides me who had served in the Lloyd cabinet before our defeat in 1964, and a number of able people who had been elected in 1964 and 1967, as well as some new members – some of them very young – who I thought were able. I did not want to appoint two of my four former cabinet colleagues, on health grounds; and I also felt that some of the new members would make better ministers than some of the more experienced MLAs. I knew there would be disappointed people, and there were. I hoped to lessen the disappointments and show the caucus why I was doing what I was doing. I therefore started with a small cabinet. Everybody knew that more would be added. So for caucus members, there was still hope. Meanwhile, we had many caucus meetings in the early months of our term, and several new members began to show their grasp of issues and ability to make points. After six months, I filled two spots with experienced members. At the end of the first year, when I rounded out the cabinet with three of the newly elected members who had shone in caucus, there was less grumbling from caucus members than I had feared. Meanwhile, I had had an opportunity to test my earlier judgment of the abilities of the newly elected members. Of the new members appointed, one was thirty-six years old and the other two were under thirty.

If a premier knows the members of the legislature well and can make his choices, or if he wishes to make a point when selecting the cabinet – for example, by building a well-rounded cabinet in terms of geography, gender, ethnicity, occupational group, and so on – then appointing a full cabinet at the outset may make sense. That was not the case for me in 1971. I well knew that it is difficult to drop a minister once the appointment has been made, so the appointment had better be right.

During our entire term in office, the most disappointed MLAs were the ones who were not overly disappointed at not being selected until caucus member X was selected for cabinet. They felt they were every bit as competent and deserving as X. So the problem of disappointed MLAs is not over when the initial appointments are made; it reappears every time a new face is added to cabinet. Dealing with human nature is part of the job for any premier. I was well aware of this when I appointed my first cabinet in 1971.

Borins: Roy Romanow's selection of a small cabinet of eleven ministers in 1991 – he has since increased the number to seventeen – is another instance of this approach. Conversely, Bob Rae decided to start with a full-size cabinet, and in his recent memoir he recounted the consequences:

Allan Blakeney gave me some advice in the early days, which I should have followed. He urged me to keep the cabinet very small, and enlarge it only if necessary. I listened instead to others who encouraged me to make the cabinet as inclusive as possible, and give people a chance to learn on the job. I appointed more women to the cabinet than anyone in the history of Canada. I also threw a great many rookies in at the deep end. Many excelled. Others did not, and there is no quiet failure in this business. Learning to play the violin in front of ten million people is not the easiest thing in the world. I gave Blakeney's firm advice to both Kim Campbell and Mike Harris, and they both took it. Too soon old, too late smart.[9]

Over the years, you shuffled your cabinet from time to time. Media pundits analyse whether a certain minister's stock is rising or falling by comparing his or her old portfolio with the new one. Do the analysts get it right? Do they read the right signals? Is the notion of an individual's stock rising or falling even a useful way of thinking?

Blakeney: Cabinets are shuffled, and some of the shuffles do indicate that a certain minister's stock is rising or falling. But it was my experience that the media and many other analysts read the signals incorrectly. They concentrated on the departmental duties and not on the more important duties performed by the minister as part of the collegial team. They missed three key points. First, many of the most important government decisions are made not in the context of particular departments but by cabinet and its committees. Second, important government initiatives are launched through Crown corporations or other agencies that in normal circumstances do not require direct ministerial involvement. Third, whether an appointment as the minister of a particular department indicates rising or falling fortunes depends on the emphasis that the government intends to give to the work of that particular department after the appointment is made. Let me try to give examples.

Suppose I moved a minister eighteen months before a proposed election from the Department of Education, which is a high-profile and prestigious department in our government, to the Department of Revenue, Supply and Services, a much lower-profile department, but also made him the vice-chair of the cabinet's planning committee charged with mapping out our strategy for the next election. The public might perceive this as a demotion, but cabinet and caucus would view it as a sign that the minister was in favour with the premier and his colleagues.

In another case I moved a minister from Finance, a prestigious and important portfolio, to Provincial Secretary, a very low-profile portfolio. This was promptly announced in the press as a demotion. What had not been picked up was that that minister had also been put in charge of a major new policy – a move to acquire up to 50 per cent of the potash industry and to organize its operations as a provincial Crown corporation. Cabinet and caucus knew that the fate of our government hung on the success or failure of this highly controversial move. I appointed the person I thought best qualified to perform that crucial task. It was anything but a demotion.

To give another example, suppose the government of Ontario in 1998 proposed to do a complete analysis of the advisability of privatizing Ontario Hydro – an analysis that would include not only technical and economic issues associated with electric power generation and transmission and distribution but also issues of how to deal with the outstanding debt of Hydro and how the privatization would affect the government's financial standing. And suppose a senior minister, say the Minister of Finance, was transferred to a minor cabinet post but given the job of guiding the Hydro privatization project. In this situation it is quite likely that the minister's transfer would be described as a demotion. Yet if the government was intending to proceed with privatization on the basis of the study, and if the success or failure of the privatization initiative would have a huge impact on the economic life of Ontario, on the financial position of the government, and on the political success of the governing party, then the minister given the job of guiding the study would be a key person performing a key role. No demotion there.

I'll turn now to the third point that the analysts and the media sometimes overlook. It is quite possible that to be Minister of Mineral Resources when no new programs are being planned is to be regarded by the premier as a minister of only medium importance. But at another time – say, when a wholesale review of resource royalties is being proposed, so that a battle with the industry is likely to start – it may well mean that the premier regards the minister as a key player on the team.

So there will be ups and downs in a particular minister's standing in cabinet, but you cannot call them correctly by simply looking at the departmental labels.

Borins: Mike Harcourt told a similar story about a cabinet shuffle involving Glen Clark, who eventually succeeded him as Premier of British Columbia.

Glen Clark was surprised when I told him he was being moved from finance to a new post as minister of employment and investment ... I also put [him] in charge of Crown corporations and infrastructure spending under our new BC21 programme ... Moving Glen had nothing to do with 'putting him in his place,' as some people thought. I saw Glen as a star in our cabinet. He was young, clever, and, as far as I could see, had a great political career ahead of him. He had been a very effective minister of finance, carrying out our government's health and education spending priorities and working hard to eliminate that Socred deficit. He was a bit controversial at times, but as I saw it, the move would help him politically. It would reduce the chances for controversy and distance him from the property surtax gaffe [introduced by Clark in a budget shortly before the cabinet was shuffled].[10]

As the years pass, cabinets age. Given the demands of public life, ministers get burned out and lose their energy and their capacity to develop new ideas. Is there anything you did to rejuvenate your cabinet?

Blakeney: You raise an important point. Some cabinets come to depend on a core of key ministers. In our case, this core included those who joined in 1971 and 1972. In 1972 the average age of cabinet ministers was just forty. But as the years rolled by, the average crept up and the need for rejuvenation became clear. Rejuvenation required both adding new people to the cabinet and finding some new challenges for ministers who were too valuable to be replaced. Over the life of our government the average age of the cabinet was never below forty or above forty-five.

To appoint new ministers, a premier must increase the size of the cabinet or replace ministers. We started with a small cabinet and gradually added ministers, and this provided an element of rejuvenation that was very useful. But clearly, the scope for this was limited.

The much thornier question is how to replace ministers. As ministers were appointed after the initial group, I advised them that we had to present new faces in cabinet from time to time and that I proposed to shuffle the cabinet after each election, which meant that I could not guarantee that each present minister would find a place in the new cabinet. The appointees assured me that they understood this fully. I found that when the time came to make changes, they understood it less well, and there were some disappointments. In particular, it was suggested to me that I should have told them before the election what I intended for them so that they could have considered whether to run for election again. I tried to explain that I could not know before an election what I wanted the post-election cabinet to look like, because I didn't know which ministers might be defeated and which new candidates would be elected. There are enough variables in trying to shape a cabinet when you know who its potential members are. It is quite impossible to factor in possible losses and gains of legislative members and say with assurance that a particular MLA will or will not be in the cabinet after the election.

Of course, a premier knows with a good degree of certainty who some of the members of the post-election cabinet will be – that is, to the extent that he can be certain about the election result itself. But a premier does not know who all the members of the post-election cabinet should be, and it is clearly hazardous to give assurances to some and not to others. So dropping ministers produces some wounded feelings and limits the use of this tool. New faces must be added to reflect the changing electorate and to deal with the aging of core ministers. So ministers must be dropped. I dropped some and I expect that there are one or two who were dropped who even today are unhappy that they were victims of the process.

There is another way for a premier to rejuvenate the cabinet, and that is by giving new challenges to existing ministers. I found that a few ministers were right for a particular department and were best left there. I had a Minister of Labour who was well accepted by the groups with which he dealt, and transferring him might have created a political problem with the labour movement. At other times, ministers wanted a change after a few years in a portfolio. I doubt whether there is an optimum length of time for a minister to serve in a particular department. Other things being equal, I would favour a period of four to five years, but other things are not often equal. If a new initiative is being launched and a particular minister is needed to launch it, a shuffle of three or four ministers may be necessary. As a generalization, a minister should stay with a department long enough to become familiar and comfortable with the interest groups that deal with that department, but not so long that he or she loses a sense of challenge, and not so long that he or she has had to refuse the requests of some of the interest groups too often.

Deputy Premier Roy Romanow remained as Attorney General during our entire eleven-year term. On a couple of occasions I suggested that he might move to the Department of Education or some other large service department. I was totally satisfied with his performance at the Department of the Attorney General, but I saw him as one of my potential successors and I felt that experience in a large service department would be useful for him. He chose not to move. But I continued to call on him for many different challenges – House Leader, Minister of Intergovernmental Affairs, minister in charge of negotiating rail transport issues with Ottawa, and so on. He was also part of the team that shaped our moves into ownership of potash, and was heavily involved in piloting the potash legislation through the legislature. He rarely lacked for challenge, and I believe that he preferred this challenge-a-month career to one of directing a major service department with a large and varied public.

We used service on Crown corporation boards as a way to provide new stimulus for ministers. And we tackled particular problems through ad hoc agencies, which we called secretariats. We created these to deal with oil and gas issues, potash acquisitions, uranium royalties and ownership, and relations between the government and status Indian and Métis organizations. (I will say more about these secretariats in Chapter 4.) Work with the secretariats provided variety and stimulation. I do not mean to suggest that we created these ad hoc agencies solely to provide job satisfaction for ministers. My point is that the activities of our government, at least during the 1970s, were sufficiently varied and changing that it was not difficult to accommodate those ministers who wanted new challenges. Not all wanted new challenges: some simply wished to play their role in cabinet and master the work of dealing with their department and its publics. Getting the best out of cabinet colleagues involves dealing with different personalities in different ways.

3

Managing Cabinet

This chapter starts with a discussion of cabinet meetings in the Blakeney government: the agenda, the format required for cabinet documents, the context for raising political concerns, and ways in which cabinet solidarity was maintained. A key participant in cabinet is the person sitting off to the side taking notes – that is, the cabinet secretary – and Blakeney describes the characteristics of the ideal cabinet secretary. We then look at cabinet retreats as an extension of regular cabinet meetings. The rest of the chapter deals with cabinet committee systems. Blakeney outlines the committee structure he used and the traits of effective members of the different committees, and Borins compares Saskatchewan's cabinet committee structure with those of the Canadian and British governments. We explore why in recent years there has been a trend in Canada back toward smaller cabinets and simpler committee structures.

Borins: Now that we have a cabinet in place, I'd like to deal with some of the issues involved in your managing cabinet and cabinet managing the public sector. Let's begin with cabinet meetings. How often did your cabinet meet, and for how long?

Blakeney: The full cabinet met weekly for the equivalent of a full day. When the legislature was in session, the cabinet met Tuesday mornings and continued with several hour-long meetings at midday for the rest of the week. When the legislature was not in session, the cabinet met all day Tuesday.

Borins: How did you structure the agenda?

Blakeney: During the first hour we dealt with routine matters. These were really reports from cabinet committees. A cabinet committee would have reviewed all orders-in-council appointing, say, notaries public or a deputy minister, or promulgating new regulations dealing with fees for getting a fishing licence. The committee would have identified items it wanted to draw to cabinet's attention for information and perhaps for decision.

Similarly, the legislative review committee would have reviewed the drafts of any proposed legislation that had already been approved in principle by cabinet. This group would now report on any specific points in those drafts that cabinet should consider. As an aside, I might add that cabinet ordinarily dealt with legislation by first reviewing a memorandum in narrative form from the agency promoting the legislation. This memorandum outlined what the legislation was intended to do as well as its general contents. If cabinet approved, the legislation was then drafted by the agency's lawyers and forwarded to cabinet's legislative review committee, along with detailed explanations of the provisions. That committee then reported to cabinet.

The cabinet's chief financial committee, Treasury Board, dealt with spending and staffing decisions that involved changes in the approved annual budget, and dealt also with miscellaneous organization issues – that is, which agency should do a particular job. The board produced minutes of decisions, which were sent to all members of cabinet for information. Cabinet ministers could appeal to cabinet to revise a Treasury Board decision. Cabinet usually supported Treasury Board. Ministers knew that if they became involved in many of these decisions they would be overwhelmed with trivia. In any case, the appeals were often attempts to overturn decisions made during the annual budget process. Many ministers were unhappy with some of the decisions made during the budget finalization process but were prepared to live with them, and they did not take kindly to their colleagues having another go at getting approval for their pet projects. I usually supported Treasury Board. Even so, a minister sometimes won an appeal. This gave ministers the assurance that they were not completely dominated by 'those bureaucrats at Finance.' Ministers harboured suspicions that the ministers on the Treasury Board were unduly influenced by their staff, the faceless minions of the Budget Bureau (a part of the Department of Finance). In any government there will be continuing tensions between the financial controllers and the people who deliver programs.

We tackled the committee reports first. They needed to be dealt with to keep the bureaucratic wheels turning. Also, by dealing with them first we were providing a period during which a minister's late arrival was not troublesome, and starting ourselves off on a relatively noncontroversial note. Right afterwards, I often brought forward a few relatively uncontentious issues that could be dealt with quickly and harmoniously.

We then had a period for unstructured discussion, which we called 'state of the nation.' This period allowed ministers to raise issues of political concern. We had a political committee of cabinet that would sometimes report on the sale of party memberships, the state of constituency organization, and other matters of organizational interest. Then we had a more freewheeling discussion on how we were doing with the public. This allowed ministers to question how the public was reacting to programs of departments other than their own. No matter how often it is stressed that a minister is a member of cabinet first and a departmental minister second, ministers tend to get defensive about their own departments, so it is important to provide a forum in which the public acceptability of any government activity can be questioned without it being regarded as a reflection on a particular minister. Putting a specific item on the cabinet's agenda about another minister's department could raise hackles; raising the matter during a state-of-the-nation session was less threatening.

It is easy to get caught up in and overwhelmed by the problems of administering government programs. It has been said, only half in jest, that there is nothing more dangerous to a government than giving too close attention to Her Majesty's business. Even though we were all politicians, we found it necessary to structure occasions for political discussion.

Often nothing specific was decided during a state-of-the-nation discussion. If it dealt, for example, with how we were getting along with people of aboriginal origin and how we could get more progress on, say, treaty land settlements without generating more backlash among non-aboriginals, the decision might be to ask an individual minister to come up with some ideas or strategies that cabinet might consider again. Discussions were sometimes preludes to fuller discussions at a caucus meeting or a cabinet retreat, where we brainstormed about larger and more amorphous questions.

Borins: You've just taken a cabinet meeting through the preliminaries. Now you get down to the hard decisions. Were there any procedures you followed to make sure that cabinet had the right information to make good decisions? How did you ensure the quality of the briefing notes?

Blakeney: We had a formal agenda, with almost all agenda items having backup material. The material was in the ministers' hands the day before. All material had to come from a cabinet committee or a minister, had to have a brief one- or two-page summary, and had to have a firm recommendation. The question was always, 'What do you want cabinet to say yes or no to?' Recommendations of the upward-delegating variety, that asked cabinet to 'consider' or 'advise on' a problem, were firmly discouraged. If ministers needed to talk to me or the Minister of Finance or another minister, I asked that they do so and formulate their own position before sending the matter along to cabinet.

Later in our term, we asked that all submissions carry a brief report on financial implications – for example, a note saying, 'This is not a budgetary question,' or 'Any expense covered by budget already approved,' or 'The issue is raised in principle, and will later be submitted to Treasury Board,' or 'The matter is important and I want cabinet to instruct Treasury Board to accommodate additional expense, subject to our sorting out with Treasury Board how to keep expense down.' These reports allowed cabinet to know what the financial implications were. Sometimes they apprised cabinet that it was being asked to end-run Treasury Board.

We also developed what we called a civil rights report. This applied mainly to proposed new regulations and legislation, but to other matters as well. Each report required a statement that nothing in the proposal represented any unusual or unreasonable invasion of civil rights. Most often, the issues these reports addressed related to regulations that gave park officials, or game conservation officers, or highway patrols, or liquor inspectors, the power to search premises or seize automobiles or boats or the like, without a warrant. We wanted to be sure that if regulations or laws contained such powers, the powers were circumscribed, and that cabinet had had the issue drawn specifically to its attention.

I liked to get the agenda material in a form that allowed cabinet simply to accept or reject the recommendation. If the recommendation was rejected and the reason was not obvious, I tried to state briefly what I felt cabinet's reasons were, so that the minister had a sufficiently clear idea why his recommendation had been turned down.

Borins: How quickly did cabinet make its decisions?

Blakeney: For some cabinet ministers, not quickly enough. We took longer than was necessary simply to arrive at the sensible decision. I felt that the major decisions were collegial decisions and that it was therefore desirable, and sometimes necessary, for all ministers not only to acquiesce in decisions but also to understand them and why they were made. I wanted all the ministers to be able to explain cabinet decisions and defend them with caucus and the public. This often involved identifying all the reasonable options and reviewing each before choosing one. Some ministers found this tedious – and I sometimes did, too – but I felt it was necessary. The ministers I knew well would kid me privately about running a seminar, but I think they understood my desire not to have cabinet too obviously divided into an inner group that knew why we were making certain decisions and an outer group that did not fully understand.

If cabinet is to be a cohesive group, at any particular meeting, it is sometimes better to discuss and not decide than to decide and not discuss.

Borins: A cabinet operates on the basis of consensus. How did you work toward a consensus on difficult issues where there were divisions in cabinet?

Blakeney: Getting consensus is sometimes not easy. If it was a contentious issue, I usually asked each minister to give a brief opinion. The classic method is to ask the most junior ministers to speak first so that they are not intimidated by the expressed views of the senior people.

Borins: Isn't that the practice in appellate courts?[1] I imagine it also provided an opportunity for you to assess the quality of the junior ministers' advice.

Blakeney: Yes, but I didn't always do it this way – who spoke first could also depend on the issue. After we had gone around the table once, there were usually some ministers who wanted to make rebuttal points. If the issue concerned one department – for example, the size of the fee increase to be negotiated with the medical association for services delivered under the medical care plan – I some-times had to ask the Minister of Health to stay out of the discussion for a period so that it did not degenerate into a battle between him and four or five other ministers. Usually, I then tried a straw vote. This was understood to be a vote on where each minister stood at that stage of the discussion. If it looked as if the minister had little or no support but was clearly unwilling to concede the issue, I usually asked him to reconsider the matter and come back with another proposal, keeping in mind the views expressed.

Sometimes the issue was contentious but no minister had much emotional capital tied up in it. In these cases we could take a vote. Sometimes the vote could be allowed to stand, sometimes a compromise position was possible. Nobody ex-pected to win all the time, not even the premier. A premier has a reserve power to make an opinion stick. But he or she is unwise to exercise that power except in very pressing circumstances. I recall reading in Premier Mike Harcourt's remi-niscences that he had eighteen cabinet ministers besides himself. Each of them had one vote, and he had nineteen votes. I suspect that he cast his nineteen votes very rarely indeed. There is always some deference to the premier's views. There was one time we had a discussion in cabinet on an issue – not a major one, as I recall. I had not expressed a view, although I think most cabinet ministers knew what my position would be: of two possible choices, I would favour A. I called a straw vote starting with the junior minister. Around the table we went, every minister favouring not A, but B. After the vote I said, 'Well ...' and paused. Before I could continue, Jack Messer chimed in 'Oh, oh – another tie.' It was not a tie – the B's had won. The comment not only livened up the meeting but implicitly acknowledged the special role of the Premier.

Our objective was to leave cabinet meetings with as few bruised feelings as possible and with firm decisions to work from.

Borins: Cabinet solidarity was vitally important to you.

Blakeney: Yes, very much so. Cabinet members have to give more than grudging support to a government's policies – they have to give enthusiastic support. The opposition is out there, trying every day to embarrass you, to prove you are unfit to govern. And the media are also there, looking for incompetence and weakness. Politics is a world of rough-and-tumble competition. To survive, your team must be united and enthusiastic.

It is part of the system that quite a few major decisions come to cabinet only for information and an almost pro forma approval. In some styles of cabinet government a minister may launch a major initiative after consultation with the premier and perhaps the Minister of Finance. I did not favour this approach. Even when the departmental minister, the Minister of Finance, and I as Premier all approved, I still liked it to go to cabinet. Primarily, I wanted to know that all ministers were informed and would be able to defend and promote the initiative. But I also wanted to know whether we had missed some point about how the public would react to the initiative.

If a cabinet has some members with particularly well-honed political skills, it is wise to give them a chance to comment on a new policy before it is announced. Often the result is not a change in policy but a change in public presentation.

Borins: In their recent history of the first Chrétien government, Greenspon and Wilson-Smith included the following story of a conflict within cabinet and the Prime Minister's role in managing it. The nub of the conflict was that Lloyd Axworthy, then Minister of Human Resources Development, was introducing some Employment Insurance reforms, which were being opposed by Brian Tobin, then Fisheries Minister, who was claiming that they would greatly reduce the benefits received by fisheries workers in Atlantic Canada.

It fell to Chrétien, in the time-honoured practice of cabinet government to call the consensus – in other words, to give voice to the will of cabinet, which did not vote formally.

The fate of Axworthy's reform plan rested on the prime minister's reading of the room. The other ministers could tell he had been impressed by [Tobin's arguments] ... But Mitchell Sharp [a minister in the Pearson and Trudeau governments and Chrétien's mentor] had taught him that a prime minister must never rule outright against the responsible minister, which could be construed as a sign of non-confidence and possibly lead to a resignation. Instead, he should simply send a matter back for further study. Which is precisely the course Chrétien took. Axworthy's proposal was good, he pronounced, but it needed some more work. They would look at it again [in three months].[2]

A key player in cabinet is the cabinet secretary – the non-politician present in the cabinet room to record what happened.[3] Can you describe the role of a cabinet secretary, and the traits he or she must have to be effective?

Blakeney: I had some outstanding cabinet secretaries. I think particularly of Grant Mitchell and Wes Bolstad, but there were others. Their formal role is to see that the cabinet's agenda is prepared, that all supporting material is assembled, that cabinet minutes are prepared, and that everybody who needs to be informed of cabinet decisions, *is* informed. The cabinet secretary has to have sufficient stature with the premier that he or she can reject an item for the agenda forwarded by a minister and suggest that it first be reviewed by Treasury Board, or by a couple of deputies who can iron out co-ordination questions. Also, the cabinet secretary must be able to sense when a minister is determined to get something to cabinet that should not go there. (In such a case, the cabinet secretary will probably put the item on the agenda but advise the premier, as chair of the meeting, to refer it to the appropriate place.)

Cabinet minutes are a minor art form. They must be written so that if they become public they will cause the minimum of embarrassment; but they must also convey to insiders with some precision what was decided. Our minutes did not attempt to summarize the discussion; they sought only to record the decisions to be acted upon. The names of movers and seconders were not used, and only on rare occasions were ministers identified, except as presenters of proposals.

I would add that a cabinet secretary usually performs some informal duties for the premier relating to dealings with ministers and deputies, and also helps with shuffles of ministers and deputies. We'll have an opportunity later on to touch on these things.

The most valuable skills a cabinet secretary can have are ones that help a premier keep a team of ministers and deputies feeling that they are connected with the decision-making centre. Not all deputies, and not all ministers, know how to get decisions from a system that by nature is structured and bureaucratic, and in which some undisclosed agendas are perhaps being pursued. Both deputies and ministers often seek the advice of the cabinet secretary on the best way to get a decision.

A deputy might ask the secretary, 'If my minister sends this forward for cabinet, will it simply get referred to Treasury Board?' or, more delicately, 'The proposal that I prepared for my minister and that went to cabinet got shot down. Can you tell me why?' Answering the first question requires only an assessment of how rigorously cabinet is refusing to deal with things that could go elsewhere. Answering the second requires an appreciation of the rules of cabinet confidentiality so that, without revealing the position of any minister, the deputy gets a general idea of just what happened to the proposal. The minister may not have fully understood the dynamics of why cabinet rejected the proposal. The secretary can sometimes convey some of these dynamics and, while doing so, indicate whether the proposal is truly dead or whether a reshaped proposal might be acceptable. This requires great sensitivity on the part of the secretary. It is a necessary service to deputies, since it ensures that those serving ministers who are not fully aware of the dynamics of a group decision do not watch their proposals simply disappear into the cabinet void. The job satisfaction of deputies is important to any government; they must have some confidence in the decision-making processes in order to maintain that satisfaction.

Similarly, ministers need someone to talk to about processes. They can usually talk to their deputies, but not always. They often hesitate to talk to the premier or other ministers about something they feel they are supposed to know already. The good cabinet secretary is the person best able to assure a minister that, for example, failure to get cabinet's approval was not the deputy's fault; or if it was, to deal with the problem by discussing it discreetly with the deputy. Or the minister may reveal to the cabinet secretary a circumstance that the premier should deal with. If a minister and a deputy are not getting along, a switch of one or the other may be indicated. This informal intelligence, which a sensitive cabinet secretary will know how to gather effectively, is important to the work of maintaining morale, both of ministers and of deputies.

Borins: Were any other public servants or political staff generally or occasionally present at cabinet meetings?

Blakeney: The cabinet secretary was the only non-cabinet person at most meetings. On occasion, the assistant cabinet secretary was present, especially at the beginning of the meeting to deal with orders-in-council and other routine matters. I felt that the greater the number of public servants present, the more total frankness by cabinet ministers was inhibited. For cabinet planning conferences, which were longer, public servants attended; but for regular meetings and for decision-crunching sessions, we had no nonelected people except the secretary and, occasionally, the assistant secretary.

Borins: Your cabinet had an annual retreat. Was this simply a two-day state-of-the-nation session, or were other things going on? Also, did any public servants or political staff attend? And if so, what were their roles?

Blakeney: Fundamentally, the annual cabinet retreat was a long state-of-the-nation session. We operated with an absolute minimum of paper. We had an agenda of a general nature. It might have been the following:

1. Review of election promises and what remains to be done.
2. How we are doing with the public, generally.
3. How we are doing with interest groups such as farmers, farm organizations, organized labour, other working people, teachers, people of aboriginal origin, and women.
4. Opposition parties – How are they doing?

I tried to indicate the subject area and then let the discussion evolve. The cabinet secretary was present and made notes. My principal secretary – in effect, my political deputy – was often present, but it was not usual that other public servants were present. The public servants who did attend did not ordinarily participate. They made notes and occasionally provided information.

At these retreats we would often lay out a strategy for dealing with an upcoming provincial party convention and assign duties to particular ministers. Ways of monitoring moves by the opposition parties and replying to lines of attack were considered.

Advice to the premier on how to conduct cabinet meetings, and to ministers on how to put fewer things on the cabinet agenda, was freely offered.

Borins: I'd like your views about an issue that seems to bedevil all prime ministers and premiers, namely, the internal structure of cabinet. I see that you didn't have any rigid stratification within cabinet, such as an inner and an outer cabinet, which makes good sense given that your full cabinet was relatively small. Also, dividing cabinet into an inner group and an outer group would have made it hard to keep the latter fully informed and committed. However, you have mentioned a number of cabinet committees. What principles and practices did you follow in establishing committees?

Blakeney: We had some standing committees but we tried to keep them to a minimum.[4]

The Treasury Board, which had a strong staff from the Finance Department, was a major committee. It performed two distinct but related functions. First, and most important, it prepared the original budget recommendations to cabinet. Working within a fiscal policy framework set by cabinet, it considered the revenue estimates and the spending estimates from all agencies and provided detailed tax and spending recommendations to cabinet, setting dollar and staff limits for all agencies. It identified and sent to cabinet along with its recommendations perhaps as many as twenty real alternatives to its recommendations. Questioning, and frequently challenging, departmental revenue and expenditure estimates, and making the necessary decisions on priorities in order to match spending with revenue, as Treasury Board did, is a long and tedious job. This is particularly true if all agencies and their responsible ministers are to feel that they had a fair hearing.

Second, the Treasury Board dealt with requests for spending or staffing that were not covered by the annual budget – the interbudget requests. In other governments, this function is sometimes performed by management boards.

The cabinet's Planning Committee was important, though in fact it made few decisions that were not referred to cabinet. It acted more as staff to cabinet than as a decision-making body in substitution for cabinet.[5]

The Crown Investments Corporation was a Crown corporation whose board of directors was composed largely of cabinet ministers. It acted as a holding company for the Crown corporations and made a good number of decisions that otherwise might have come to cabinet. Most of its work was on major policy matters, since the corporations acted independently with respect to most operational matters. The Crown Investments Corporation had a strong staff and kept in close touch with the officials at the Department of Finance.[6]

We had a cabinet committee that reviewed proposed legislation, regulations, and orders-in-council. It performed a pure staff function: it decided which decisions were worth cabinet's time. It used seconded staff from the cabinet secretary's office and from the Department of the Attorney General.

We had some ad hoc committees dealing with collective bargaining in all government agencies, with political matters, and from time to time with some other current topic – for example, uranium issues. These committees operated with seconded staff when required.

I opposed the idea of creating, say, a social services committee of cabinet that had its own staff. Competing bureaucracies are an ever-present danger in any government. Competition among line departments can usually be kept to a minimum because the overlap of areas is usually small. Central agencies have a greater tendency to overlap and, hence, to engage in bureaucratic competition. The way to reduce that danger is to keep down the number of central agencies. Cabinet committees with strong staffs have great potential for generating intense competition both with the staff of the Treasury Board and the staff of line departments.

There were further aspects to this question. If the general approach was that deputies of line departments had the clear duty to co-ordinate their activities with those of other, related line departments, this in itself reduced the need for standing committees of cabinet with permanent staffs. And I felt that our government was small enough that cabinet or Treasury Board could deal directly with the major issues that, in other provincial governments, might have been dealt with by program area committees. Finally, I felt that ministers spent too much time in committees already and that what we did not need was more committees.

Borins: Returning to the notion of cabinet as a team, what particular skills were you looking for when you chose ministers for each of those committees?

Blakeney: For service on Treasury Board, I wanted ministers who had patience, a capacity for detail, a willingness to attend lengthy meetings, and an ability to make tough decisions on a 'best we can do' basis. The ability to say no without sounding arrogant was perhaps the most important skill.

The best ministers for the Planning Committee were those who liked to speculate about what the province should be ten or twenty years hence, and who had some sense of the 'art of the possible.'

Members of the Crown Investments Corporation needed to appreciate entrepreneurship, to ride with a light rein on entrepreneurial managers, and to have a sense of how the commercial public sector fitted into the overall government objectives.

Members of the ad hoc committee dealing with legislation, regulation, and orders-in-council needed, most of all, diligence and a capacity to recognize how legal powers could produce results that the framers did not intend. People usually draft laws with the approach, 'This is what we need to do and this law will do it.' The committee had then to say, 'Fine – now what else will it do?' A healthy scepticism and an ability to spot issues cabinet should consider were the chief qualities required for service on this committee.

The political committee of cabinet was made up of people who knew the craft of politics – conducting polls, using networks to gather information, using MLAs as sounding boards – and who could sense changes in the public mood and the unquantifiable trends that are so important to electoral success.

Borins: It is instructive to contrast your approach to structuring cabinet with that of two much larger governments – the federal government and the British government.

The federal cabinet has evolved a great deal in the last fifteen years – ultimately in a direction that is consistent with your approach to governing, Allan. Under Pierre Trudeau, the cabinet increased in size and the cabinet committee system became more elaborate. When he left office, Trudeau's cabinet had thirty-seven ministers, and there were many subject-area committees, with the chair of each major subject-area committee on the cabinet's executive committee, which was called the Committee on Priorities and Planning. This group had between fifteen and twenty members, so it was about the size of an average cabinet in Saskatchewan. As you did with your cabinets, prime ministers have chosen this committee's membership to ensure regional representation. Priorities and Planning was responsible for establishing the government's overall priorities, for making major policy and spending decisions, and for co-ordinating the work of the subject-area committees.[7] Thus, Trudeau's cabinet was a two-tier body, with Priorities and Planning as the upper tier. The subject-area committees included Treasury Board, Economic Policy, Environment, Foreign and Defence Policy, Human Resources, and Cultural Affairs and National Identity. Except for Treasury Board, which since the mid-1960s has had its own secretariat, all the others were staffed by the Privy Council Office.[8]

The Mulroney cabinet was of comparable size, with thirty-five ministers. Mulroney increased the complexity of cabinet's co-ordinating machinery still further by establishing two new committees. The Operations Committee was responsible for short-term political planning and functioned as gatekeeper to Priorities and Planning. The Expenditure Review Committee was responsible for the ongoing review of government expenditures. In effect, it supplemented the Treasury Board. This brought the total number of cabinet committees to fourteen.

The role of the full cabinet in the Mulroney government became even less significant than it had been in the Trudeau government. Katherine Graham wrote that under Mulroney, 'Cabinet as a whole [had] no real role as a decision-making body. Indeed, it [was] at the bottom of the decision-making hierarchy, filling the role instead of a forum for general political discussion. Cabinet [had] become like an inner caucus.'[9]

A very clear example of this approach was the Mulroney government's creation of an ad hoc committee of nineteen ministers to draft constitutional proposals during the summer of 1991. The full cabinet, like the Conservative caucus, saw the proposals only a day or two before they were made public.

Blakeney: Let me contrast this with the cabinet of a small provincial government. With us, representation was important, but it was not a dominant consideration. At the federal level, representation was considered to be so important, and there were so many diverse interests to be represented, that cabinets were very large – sometimes over forty ministers. In such circumstances it was not possible to operate a collegial cabinet in which every minister participates in all major cabinet decisions. When a cabinet had forty or more ministers, the need arose for an 'inner cabinet' or a Priorities and Planning Committee to make the real decisions. But because of the representational role that ministers play, they all had to be seen to belong to cabinet, and to appear to be of equal status. Fortunately, small provincial governments don't have this problem.[10]

Borins: Ultimately, large cabinets fell out of favour in Ottawa, because the benefits of representativeness were outweighed by the costs of cumbersome decision-making. Also, the public perception is that a large cabinet means a government that is fiscally out of control. Toward the end of his time in office, Mulroney commissioned a high-level study of cabinet and departmental organization.[11] Its recommendations – a smaller cabinet, fewer cabinet committees, and the merging of many ministries – were accepted by Prime Minister Kim Campbell in June 1993, and retained by Jean Chrétien when he took office several months later. Chrétien reduced the number of cabinet committees to four. The first Chrétien government had twenty-three ministers and nine ministers of state; the second Chrétien government has grown slightly to twenty-eight ministers and eight ministers of state.[12]

Permit me a slight digression on ministers of state. They are responsible for part of a larger ministry and are, at least nominally, accountable to the minister. These ministers of state often have responsibilities for areas of concern to specific interest groups, such as multiculturalism and Western economic diversification. They are not members of cabinet. Gordon Osbaldeston, a former Clerk of the Privy Council,[13] in his study of deputy ministers, found that these appointments have created difficulty for both ministers and deputy ministers.[14] Ministers of state find their subordinate status frustrating, and push for increased autonomy; deputy ministers find it difficult to work for more than one minister.

It is interesting to compare the federal government's experience with that of the British government, which has also experimented with various ways of organizing the ministry. Beginning with the Attlee government, which took office in 1945, the British divided their ministry between approximately twenty ministers who were members of cabinet and another twenty who, while responsible for departments, were not members of cabinet.[15] This is similar to the two-tier Canadian system of Trudeau and Mulroney, if you equate the Committee on Priorities and Planning with the British cabinet. The politicians found that ministers who were not in cabinet were less integrated into policy-making. The departments certainly preferred to have ministers who had a seat in cabinet.[16]

In more recent years, the British system has also undergone a transition. The number of departments has been reduced by merging smaller departments into larger 'super-departments.' Each super-department has a number of ministers, but only the most senior minister, referred to as the Secretary of State, is a member of cabinet. For example, the Department of Trade and Industry has a Secretary of State, who is a member of cabinet, and six junior ministers, who are not. Cabinet has approximately twenty ministers, and there are usually thirty junior ministers.[17] The rationale for this approach is to have a cabinet that is small enough to function cohesively. Each super-department contains a number of related functions and programs, which means that meetings of the Secretary of State and the junior ministers of a super-department take the place of many cabinet committee meetings in Canada. In addition, the British ministry has a hierarchical structure, in which promising young MPs are appointed as junior ministers; after a time the better ones are promoted to the cabinet. Thus, junior ministers may become rivals; on the other hand, a Secretary of State who is an effective manager will develop a spirit of teamwork among his or her junior ministers.[18]

The key question for large governments is whether it is possible to foster the degree of involvement of all ministers that characterizes a small provincial government. The conclusion seems to have been that the best way to do this is to keep cabinet to a size not a great deal larger than that of a small provincial government.

4

Setting Priorities

This chapter deals with cabinet's role in setting a government's priorities. We review the priorities of the Blakeney governments from 1971 to 1982, differentiating between priorities that were developed as part of a political planning process and priorities that had to be developed quickly in response to external events. We look at priority setting in terms of both process (the cabinet planning conference, the Throne Speech, and so on) and influences (the party, the bureaucracy, and public opinion polls). We conclude by discussing the use of temporary structures such as special-purpose secretariats to implement major priorities, with examples drawn from the experience of the Saskatchewan and federal governments.

Borins: Tom Axworthy, who was Pierre Trudeau's Principal Secretary for much of his last mandate, has strongly advocated a strategic prime ministership, in which a prime minister (or premier) focuses his or her own attention and that of the cabinet on a small number of key priorities.[1] Other matters would be handled by ministers acting on their own, presumably consulting colleagues where necessary, but not taking up much of the prime minister's (or premier's) time.

On the other extreme, you may have government by a workaholic prime minister or premier who knows about almost everything going on in the government and who becomes involved in many issues. By inclination, where did you fit on this continuum?

Blakeney: In principle I think I agree with Tom Axworthy but I suspect that I was closer to the workaholic model. I would regard my successor as NDP leader, Roy Romanow, who has served as Premier of Saskatchewan since 1991, as closer to the model recommended by Axworthy.

I believe I was able to delegate, and there were certainly many powerful ministers in our government who ran their own shows. I still felt a need to know about major decisions even when I had no intention of intervening, and this intention was known. Looking back, I don't think many ministers would complain about my having interfered in their departments. There is clearly a distinction between wanting a flow of information so as to maintain an overall view and wanting the information in order to inject yourself into the decision-making process. Possibly, some ministers were unhappy that I wanted a flow of information because it meant that when they made recommendations to cabinet, they were not the only source of information.

There is also a co-ordinating role for a premier to play. Occasionally, information from one agency suggested that it was working at cross-purposes with another agency. In such instances, I would ask my deputy to check to see if everybody was on side. This reduced the tendency of some agencies to regard themselves as empires isolated from the rest of the government. But this type of trip-wire organization, where a flow of information is used to construct an overall government picture, to spot future problems, and to reduce agency isolation, is perhaps possible only in a small government.

Borins: Though we are generally not talking about policy in this book, I think it would be useful for you to outline, in a very cursory way, the major priorities of your three terms as Premier.

Blakeney: In our first legislative term we were consumed with launching the very detailed program outlined in our 1971 election handbook, *A New Deal for People*. In our first full legislative session in 1972, we started hares running in all directions.[2] We enacted over 150 pieces of legislation, including the following:

- Establishing an Independent Constituency Boundaries Commission.
- Expanding the Bill of Rights Act.
- Setting up a Human Rights Commission.
- Creating the Office of the Ombudsman.
- Enacting a new Trade Union Act.
- Enacting a new and very innovative Occupational Health and Safety Act.
- Establishing new departments of Consumer Affairs, Culture and Youth, Environment, and Continuing Education.
- Setting up a new Department of Northern Saskatchewan incorporating the idea of a single agency for this sparsely populated northern half of our province.
- Creating the legal framework for a universal prescription drug plan and children's dental program.

- Setting up a new and innovative but ultimately unsuccessful agency to use community development approaches with disadvantaged people.
- Putting in place farm protection legislation and an agricultural land bank program.

Borins: This hyperactive government reminds me very much of Tommy Douglas's first year or two in office.[3] Bob Rae also described his government as hyperactive, but he recounts that his government's problem was an inability to focus:

As a government we were doing too much. Ministers had an activist agenda, and together with their political staffs were especially eager to push ahead on every front. Sometimes we would read of each other's well-meaning intervention in the morning newspaper. Some would cheer. I would usually wince, for while I knew this would bring solace to the hearts of some, for many others it would only indicate that government was heading off in all directions at once ... Halfway through the life of the government in the winter of 1993, we were still doing far too much. Every minister had a pet project, which she or he wouldn't or couldn't abandon. In addition, every ministry had its own policy shop determined to solve every conceivable problem with legislation, legislation, legislation. There was an unfortunate synergy between the advocacy and Fabian tendencies of many ministers and their political staffs and an irrepressible policy fixation of the middle-level civil service. The result was an agenda that was huge and almost impossible to manage ... Successful governments have a simple agenda, relatively few items of legislation, and a communications and advertising budget to beat the band. Unsuccessful governments try to do too much, get immersed in the details of legislation, and think that advertising is a sin. David Agnew [Rae's chief of staff and later cabinet secretary] and I agreed thoroughly on these verities, but we were not always successful in persuading others.[4]

Perhaps Rae's problem was that he was elected by a public that was fundamentally sceptical of activist government and at a time when the fiscal situation wasn't supportive.

Blakeney: Our circumstances were different from Rae's; even so, from an organizational point of view I don't recommend the hyperactive approach. At the same time, governments are not elected to run tidy organizations but to pursue appropriate policies and to introduce new ones if they are needed. One of the real satisfactions of public life is that you get the opportunity to change government policy in key areas, and we used the opportunity to the full.

In broader terms, we sought in our first term to stabilize agricultural incomes and the industry generally, to make changes in school grants and teacher bargaining so as to equalize education opportunities for all Saskatchewan students, and to modernize municipal infrastructures in the same way that education and health facilities had been modernized in the two previous decades. In the latter years of the first term, we turned our attention to resource development.

In our second term we continued to expand the health and education systems, particularly by getting the universal prescription drug and children's dentistry plans firmly in place. We also set up major grant programs to raise the standards of municipal facilities and services. Finally, we turned our attention to getting a much larger return for Saskatchewan's people from natural resources – particularly oil, potash, and uranium. Newly established Crown corporations operating in each of these areas became major players in the Saskatchewan economy.

During our third term, agriculture was prospering and resource prices were good. We sought ways to ensure that everybody benefited from the increasing prosperity. We found that it was not true that when the tide came in, all boats were raised, or at least raised by the same amount. Many Saskatchewan people – people of aboriginal origin, single-parent families, and other disadvantaged groups – were not sharing fully in the prosperity. So we gave less attention to universal programs – like the prescription drug and children's dentistry plans, and parks and recreation projects – and tried to target help to those who were missing out. And, not of our choosing, constitutional discussions consumed a great deal of time and ministerial effort.

Borins: How were these priorities chosen? Can you make any generalizations about the process of discussing and formulating priorities?

Blakeney: During our first term, as it turned out, we did not have many hard priority decisions to make. Our election platform had been worked out in some detail. We proceeded to act on it, launching a large number of new programs at once. Many were not costly – for example, providing for a Human Rights Commission, and an Ombudsman, and setting up an occupational health and safety program. Others, such as the prescription drug and children's dentistry programs, would build up costs only gradually. While we had steeply increasing money requirements, by 1974 revenues were rising even faster. In order not to show large surpluses – which would have generated demands for costly services that we knew could not be sustained – we resorted to some unorthodox financing methods. As an example, we announced a five-year municipal capital works grant program, budgeted in one year for the total amount needed for the full five years, and deposited the money in a dedicated community capital fund. The federal government similarly prepaid the cost of the millenium scholarships by setting up the Millenium Scholarship Fund in the 1998 budget.

Expectations of both the public and the party were not high, and modest increases in existing programs as well as some new steps to deal with trouble spots – for example, levelling up grants to the poorer school boards – seemed to satisfy most demands. We were able to set our own agenda based on what we had promised and what we could organize and spend with prudence.

That happy state could not last, and did not last. For one thing, costs were rising sharply. When the election was called in 1971, the wage paid in hospitals and nursing homes was often under $1.50 per hour. Four years later, the lowest wage paid in hospitals was on the order of $3.00 per hour – roughly double. Here are some specific examples. On 1 June 1971, the starting monthly rate for nursing assistants was $242. On 1 June 1975 the figure was $478. The comparable figures for laundry and kitchen employees were $213 and $463. We steadily increased the general statutory minimum wage. When the election was called in 1971, it was $1.25 per hour; by March 1975, it was $2.50 per hour. In social policy terms, we welcomed the changes, but we also knew that they made for massive increases in the costs of government – directly for general hospitals, psychiatric hospitals, and other institutions, and indirectly for general costs.

Not all our major decisions were proactive. We had to react to at least one world event. Late 1973 brought the OPEC oil crisis, which created a need for our government to formulate very quickly a range of new resource policies. Our general policy had always been to get the greatest possible return for Saskatchewan's people from our resources. Until then, this had been done through conventional royalty methods.

Governments can approach resource issues in two ways. One way is to put the stress on encouraging economic activity rather than royalty return, with the government looking to get its revenues from income and consumption taxes paid by the industry and by people directly or indirectly employed by the new enterprise. The other is to maximize royalty returns at the risk of having less employment and economic activity. We favoured the latter approach. We felt that the spinoff from resource activity in Saskatchewan was enjoyed to a large extent outside Saskatchewan, and that we could generate more activity in Saskatchewan by collecting larger royalties and spending them within the province than by taking the high-activity/low-royalty approach.

In 1973 we had to react to the sharp increases in international oil prices. In a very brief time we made the decision to introduce Bill 42 of the 1973–74 session, which tried to secure for the province the major share of the windfall revenues that would accrue to oil producers because of the steep rise in international oil prices resulting from the OPEC crisis.[5] This decision set us on a collision course with the oil industry and, as it turned out, with the federal government.

The federal government felt it was somehow illegitimate for provinces like Alberta and Saskatchewan to take the lion's share of the windfall profits and leave little for the federal government to tax. It reacted by declaring in the 1974 federal budget that royalties paid to provincial governments were not a deductible expense for federal corporate income tax purposes, although royalties paid to private resource owners were still deductible. We regarded royalties as the purchase price of the mineral in the ground, regardless of who owned it. Thus, we thought that it was outrageous for a federal government to take the position that a company could not charge as an expense the purchase price paid to provinces for minerals in the ground but *could* charge as an expense the purchase price paid to private resource owners.

These events, and their impact on the oil-and-gas, potash, and uranium industries, set the stage for a running battle between our government and the government of Canada during the 1970s and early 1980s. It exacerbated disputes between our government and the resource companies, who were caught in the middle of this intergovernmental conflict, and it led to some landmark Supreme Court decisions in cases such as *Canadian Industrial Gas and Oil (CIGOL) v. the Government of Saskatchewan* and *Central Canada Potash v. the Government of Saskatchewan.*[6] The issues were not fully resolved until the constitutional changes respecting resource management and taxation were adopted in 1982. (These will be discussed in Chapter 13.)

So to a considerable extent, priorities in the sense of what issues we addressed were dictated by outside forces – by the OPEC oil crisis, the federal government's tax moves, the resource companies' court actions, and the like. Our response to these external forces was very much a matter of priority setting – not to mention the focus of lively controversy.

Borins: What specific techniques did you and the cabinet employ to arrive at priorities? And was there a difference between priority setting under normal circumstances and under the pressure of unanticipated external circumstances, such as those you have just described?

Blakeney: Under normal circumstances our main forum for setting priorities was the cabinet's annual planning conference. Each summer we asked departments and agencies to submit their budget requests for the fiscal year commencing the next April. After the budget requests were in, but before they had been reviewed in detail by Treasury Board, and after rough revenue estimates were completed, cabinet had a two-or three-day session to review what our spending program would look like and what legislation would be needed.[7] At the same time, the planning committee and the political committee offered their views on where the government should be going. We talked in terms of one-, five-, and ten-year time horizons. At the conference, we decided which things we wanted to push, which things we wanted to slow-walk, and which things we wanted to cut back.

The mindset we brought to this conference would be shaped by party resolutions, by the urgings of public servants who had projects they wished to push, by the discussions in caucus, and by our own discussions at cabinet retreats, as well as by our regular state-of-the-nation discussions and discussions of planning committee reports. This process was a reasonably orderly way to integrate and massage the information we had coming to us.

When our priority decisions were externally driven, our priority-setting process was less leisurely. For example, our decision to acquire about half of the province's potash industry was taken more rapidly. In this case we had, early in 1975, a sharp and ongoing controversy with the potash industry over taxes and royalties. (I will discuss this in more depth in Chapter 14.) My assumption was that after the June 1975 election, if the NDP was re-elected, serious negotiations would start and the difficult issues would be bargained out. Instead, within a few weeks of the election, almost all the companies joined to commence a major legal action.

We felt we could not tolerate the continued nonpayment of royalties and taxes. We had already decided to construct a publicly owned potash mine and to this purpose had organized the Potash Corporation of Saskatchewan. In July of 1975, we looked at the situation and considered our options. One was to acquire some or all of the industry. Public ownership would resolve the question of payment of taxes by the industry; it would also put beyond the reach of the federal tax gatherers all revenue we received from the provincial Crown corporation. In August we began to seriously consider this option along with several others, such as royalty increases or taxation.

We had many cabinet meetings, some with our senior staff and some without. I note in reading some old files that the senior public servants, on leaving one meeting, speculated on what cabinet would do and thought it would not come out for public ownership. We worked out a detailed plan without committing ourselves either formally or informally. We then decided, as a cabinet, on a tentative yes.

The next step was to consult as widely as possible without going public. We took the matter to caucus. Caucus supported the public ownership option, though not unanimously. We then took the matter to the Provincial Council of the New Democratic Party, a body of about 150 people. There was a lively discussion that ended with an agreement to proceed. I think there was an appreciation that acquiring privately owned potash mines, possibly by expropriation, was going to be a major initiative and a major political risk. These consultations, and many private ones, took place without the matter reaching the media. Cabinet confirmed its decision, and the policy was announced in the Speech from the Throne of November 1975.[8]

I don't think we would have proceeded with acquiring potash mines had the controversy with the industry and the federal government not arisen. But given those circumstances, and my own belief that public ownership could work, this option *was* considered. I believe we recognized that if we took this course we would be committing a good deal of our government's time, energy, and political capital for years to come. We would be using quite a bit of our borrowing capacity and possibly impairing our ability to borrow outside Canada. We would be defining our relationship with all the major resource companies and, to some extent, with the business community in general. Accordingly, it was an important priority decision in the larger sense.

Borins: What role did opinion polls play in the determination of priorities?

Blakeney: In assessing priorities, we used some polling. We considered the results but frequently disregarded the message received. In the case of potash, we were under no illusions that our policy would be initially popular, and we did not poll in advance of the decision. Shortly after we announced it, polls indicated about 20 per cent approval, which was worse than I had expected. Three years later the approval figure had risen to 60 per cent, so potash was not a political liability in the 1978 election, although it may have been in 1982, not as a distinct issue, but as part of a 'big government' perception.

Saskatchewan was a rural, conservative, and somewhat racist province in the 1970s. Polling showed that programs aimed at assisting people of aboriginal origin and single-parent families were not popular. We tried to shape these programs so as to attract the least public opposition. I'm not sure we succeeded. In general, we used polling to tell us when we had a problem in marketing our programs. We generally knew what we wanted to do. We were not as sure how best to do it.

Borins: I find it interesting that you haven't said much about the role the bureaucracy played in determining priorities.

Blakeney: I would never underestimate the influence of the bureaucracy in determining priorities. In the first term, our priorities were clearly determined by the way cabinet and caucus decided to carry out the party program. But as time went on, the party program became less of a guide and the senior public servants became more influential. Quite properly, they had developed agendas of their own. The best civil servants were those who had developed some objectives of their own, some things they wanted to see done, but who still appreciated that priority setting is what politicians are elected for.

Borins: I'll respond from two different perspectives. On the one hand, this story of declining party influence and growing bureaucratic influence brings to mind the history of the Douglas government.[9] There is a natural tendency for populist political movements to become institutionalized over time. On the other hand, whatever the nature of the government in power, public servants have ideas and at least some of their ideas become policy. The ideas most likely to be implemented are those which are consistent with the broad outlines of government policy or that are in areas where the government doesn't have strong policy ideas. In my recent research about public sector innovation, I have found that innovations come from a variety of sources. For example, in a sample of 217 of the best applications to the Ford Foundation–Kennedy School of Government state and local government innovations awards, 48 per cent were initiated by public servants below the agency head (i.e., deputy minister) level, 23 per cent by agency heads, 18 per cent by politicians, and 13 per cent by interest groups or nonprofit organizations.[10] The distribution for a sample of thirty-five of the best applications to the Institute of Public Administration of Canada's innovative management award is also similar: 55 per cent initiated by public servants below the rank of deputy minister, 27 per cent initiated by deputy ministers, 30 per cent by politicians, and 6 per cent by interest groups or nonprofit organizations (for both the American and Canadian samples, the totals add to more than 100 per cent).[11]

Blakeney: Any government needs a constant flow of policy options. We got these from our own personal agendas, from caucus members who had agendas, from the party resolutions, from the public servants, and from other key interest groups. The latter included university academics, teachers, trade unions, the professional organizations, and farm groups and co-operatives. The flow from some of these groups was sporadic. Often it was interrupted by a dispute that one of these groups was having with the government or one of its agencies – for example, a strike by Liquor Board employees or a dispute over university funding.

A government must keep its idea channels open. We did not always succeed in doing so, and it got harder rather than easier as time went on. I think that this was partly owing to our shift in emphasis away from universal social programs and broad-group assistance plans. Increasingly, our social initiatives were targeting disadvantaged groups rather than mainstream ones such as farmers and municipal governments. As well, we had begun to focus on issues that did not involve immediate and widely distributed largesse – for example, on broader economic issues such as getting the maximum return from resources and expanding public ownership. Each shift left behind a bit of our broad base of support. This was vividly brought home to me at a trade union demonstration at the time of the potash mine purchases, when I saw some placards that read PEOPLE, NOT POTASH. If trade unionists saw our potash policy as a diverting of the government's money and attention away from labour's concerns, many others must have felt the same way even more strongly.

Borins: When in the political cycle should priorities be determined?

Blakeney: Policy options must be considered on a regular basis. But it is best to set priorities either immediately before an election, when a party may wish to outline a new thrust as part of its campaign, or immediately after an election. Changes take time. They bring disruption. It is impossible to anticipate all problems, and problems have to be solved.

The public does not like change. They very often like the results of change, but rarely do they like the process. So we felt that changes should be introduced as soon after an election as possible so that the results would be apparent by the next election and so that there would be time to deal with a glitch or two. I will say more about this in Chapter 16, which deals with the management of change.

In the same way, we felt that our government should be 'put through the wringer' after each election. A post-election budget should be an austerity budget that cuts marginal programs and marginal staff. I'll say more about this in Chapter 10, where we talk about the expenditure budgeting process.

Almost any government becomes cautious as it approaches an election. It wants enough happening to dominate the political agenda, but it does not want to cope with the problems that arise when new programs are launched. This is not just a matter of avoiding administrative problems; it has more to do with gaining public acceptance for new programs. A premier wants the public feeling comfortable when an election is called.

On a different note, it is easier for a premier to deal with cabinet and caucus if priorities are chosen early in a term so that a clear course can be set. Some in the cabinet, the caucus, and the party will be disappointed by the choices made, but it is best to make them early so that uncertainty is removed. As an election nears, no premier wants to deal with recently disappointed colleagues or uncertainty about priorities.

Borins: Some governments have found that the Throne Speech provides a useful focus for the priority-setting exercise. Was this your experience?

Blakeney: Yes, writing a Throne Speech can focus a government's attention. Some speeches are so vacuous and full of platitudes that they focus nothing. But we had a practice of having each major agency submit a paragraph. The process of sorting through these proposals did allow us to compile lists of items to be included and excluded. Once the content was finalized, we brought in a writer who, in consultation with the Premier and perhaps a couple of ministers, attempted to add some vision and coherence to the laundry list of proposed legislation that a Throne Speech traditionally contains.

Borins: Once you had made a major decision, such as to participate in the potash industry, how did you implement it? Did you simply call on the normal machinery of government?

Blakeney: Only sometimes. When we launched a major policy initiative, we usually shuffled the cabinet and perhaps the deputies. A minister who is well qualified to oversee an existing program of, say, a Department of Health may not be the person to carry out a major hospital reorganization that will be resisted by several interest groups. If that minister is the wrong person for the task, a premier can change the minister. In our case, we set our priorities as best we could after each election. We also had a cabinet shuffle after each election. That allowed us to match ministers with the jobs to be done. Incidentally, this underlines a point I earlier: in order to determine which ministers are the most influential at any given time, you have to understand what the government's priorities are and then determine which ministers are at the cutting edge. Department labels are of only modest help in gauging which ministers are most influential.

A second approach is to give the new job to another agency, usually one created for the purpose. We usually called these special agencies secretariats.[12] We used that approach to deal with key priority areas: early on, with constitutional research and research in grain handling and transportation; later with resource issues; and still later, in a slightly different way, with relations between people of aboriginal origin and the rest of society.

After the OPEC crisis of 1973, we launched a major effort to get a larger share of the increase in value of resources. With this goal in mind, we organized an energy secretariat that pulled together people from the Department of Mineral Resources, the Budget Bureau, the planning staff of cabinet, and other agencies. Its mandate was to arrive at a strategy for increasing oil and gas royalties, and for establishing a new Crown corporation, and to investigate the potential of heavy oil and the viability of constructing a heavy-oil upgrader.

Similarly, when a confrontation loomed with the potash companies and the federal government, we organized a potash secretariat to explore the options, again drawing people from several agencies of government. We used the same approach with uranium.

Borins: It would seem to me that these secretariats can be thought of as temporary special-purpose central agencies, in that they have a mandate to implement the government's approach to a key priority, which will involve co-ordinating the activities of other departments and agencies. A number of questions arise about their relations with the rest of the government, at both the political and bureaucratic levels. First, what was the relationship in your government between these secretariats and the cabinet?

Blakeney: Secretariats are how a premier or an ad hoc cabinet committee can oversee, and perhaps even direct on a day-to-day basis, key government initiatives without a minister feeling that his competence is being questioned and his jurisdiction invaded. With respect to key decisions, premiers and cabinet ministers are apprehensive. They need a way to participate, and this is usually through an ad hoc committee of which the Premier is a member. The committee reports regularly to cabinet, and all cabinet members feel free to talk to committee members in a way that is hardly possible when one minister has charge of the new initiative within his or her department. State-of-the-nation discussions usually accomplish this for smaller matters, but when it comes to key initiatives, cabinet usually feels that it needs not only a chance to talk but also access to important information from more than one ministerial source.[13]

Also, the personality dynamics of cabinet sometimes led me to establish secretariats. Suppose our government had some involvement with a growing cable television industry, largely through our telephone utility, SaskTel. And suppose these developments entered a new phase involving high-level negotiations with the federal government over constitutional jurisdiction relating to cable television. And suppose that I felt that the Attorney General was better able to carry on these negotiations than the minister dealing with communications and telephones. In such a situation I might form the cable television unit into a secretariat and assign responsibility for it to the Attorney General, Roy Romanow. This would be a temporary measure with a life of perhaps a year or two, for the purpose of dealing with a specific situation.

Borins: The public servants who would want to work for such agencies would probably be very ambitious and somewhat risk-oriented. They would have a chance to be in the spotlight, to work on the hot topics, and to be noticed by key cabinet ministers and the Premier.[14] The downside is that their jobs would last only as long as the secretariat itself.

Blakeney: Yes. When the job was done, the secretariats were disbanded. The talent needed to analyse a problem, devise options, examine those options, and recommend one are different and more varied than those needed to oversee a program once it has been established. A secretariat's heavy hitters should not be kept on just to keep the wheels turning. Not only is this wasteful, but it also runs the risk of losing some key people because of lack of challenge.

I make another small point regarding the secretariat's support staff. When a secretariat in my government was disbanded, these people were retrieved and redeployed. In a regular department, when a new program was mounted, new staff were added, quite properly: but by the time the program was running as a normal government operation, those new staff, who would otherwise have been surplus, were often gone, having been gradually absorbed by the department in other operations. This presented a problem for Treasury Board, in that somehow it had to get back the resources that were either surplus or being used in a non-optimal way.

Redeploying the key public servants in a secretariat was not difficult: it was clear to everybody that we would find important roles for them. Any deputy minister who failed to recognize this was neither sharp nor prudent. At other times, we assured the people involved that there would be an appropriate place for them, that we were frequently organizing Crown corporations and launching new programs. Even though we often stripped down the regular public service, there were almost always new challenges emerging.

In times of general government staff restraint, staff seconded to secretariats must be guaranteed the right to return. This clearly creates problems for the agencies from which staff are seconded, problems that involve temporary appointments and the like. But even in those situations, I doubt, for example, that many of the people who worked with Brian Mulroney's free trade unit had any difficulty returning to the regular public service advantageously. And in this case, the team leader, Simon Reisman, did not return to a regular government position. The team leaders of our secretariats almost invariably did return to the public service and were able to help staff in the secretariat find appropriate positions by the informal methods well known to well-placed senior public servants.

Borins: Were secretariats particularly useful as a way of consulting the public?

Blakeney: In the 1970s we were not as outward-looking as a government might be in the 1990s. Our secretariats then did not consult widely with people outside the government. In today's consultative environment, they might well do so or recommend ways that the government might gather ideas. A secretariat might have advantages over a line department if the necessary consultation involved a broad spectrum of the community.

Our secretariats on issues relating to people of aboriginal origin did consult intensively with these groups. But these secretariats were different in that they did not deal with immediate, externally created crises and opportunities, but with important ongoing problems that we were simply not dealing with successfully using regular departmental structures. I will say a little more about consulting with the public in Chapter 15.

The secretariats for people of aboriginal origin were established to deal with a specific kind of organizational problem. I'll explain it this way. The potash secretariat, for example, was an ad hoc agency dealing with a specific problem that was limited in time, and that required skills drawn from many government agencies. The key point is that such an agency was seen as temporary. The aboriginal secretariats dealt with the problems created by organizing government on the basis of function. Ontario has a provincial government with a Ministry of Education, a Ministry of Health, a Ministry of Transportation, and so on. It does not have a Ministry of Women that delivers all government programs for women, or a Ministry of Windsor and Southwest Ontario that delivers government programs in a specific geographic area. The reason is simple: the problems of delivering educational services to men are sufficiently similar to the problems of delivering these services to women that it does not make sense to have two ministries dealing with schooling. Similarly, the problems of delivering these services in Cornwall are sufficiently similar to the problems of delivering these services in Windsor that it does not make sense to have different ministries delivering these services based on geography.

But in some circumstances it does make sense to depart from the functional organization and organize on the basis of geography or client characteristics. Perhaps the problems of delivering school services in Moose Factory, Ontario, are so different from delivering school services in Cornwall and Windsor that they are more like the problems of delivering health services in Moose Factory. In these circumstances it may make more sense to have a Ministry of the Far North that delivers both education and health services in Moose Factory. If this seems to be going too far, it still may make sense to have an agency whose role is to see that the special needs in education, health, and so on of the people of Moose Factory do not get lost in the provincewide organizations devoted to delivering 'regular' school and health services throughout the province. This kind of special problem analysis, co-ordination, and advocacy for a group clearly outside the mainstream was the task of our aboriginal secretariats. They did not deliver programs so much as ensure the adequacy and appropriateness of the programs delivered by the 'regular' ministries.

Borins: Your mention of Mulroney's free trade unit is interesting, because it raises the question of how other governments that had clear priorities organized themselves to deal with them. In this context, the experiences of the Trudeau government from 1980 and 1984, which had as its priorities the Constitution and the National Energy Program, of the Mulroney government from 1984 to 1988, which had as its priorities the Free Trade Agreement and the Meech Lake Accord, and the first Chrétien government, which had as its priority reducing the deficit, are instructive.[15]

At the bureaucratic level, priorities were sometimes assigned to existing departments or central agencies, with a new deputy minister chosen especially to work on the priority. For example, Trudeau chose Michael Kirby, who had previously been in the Prime Minister's Office, to head the Federal–Provincial Relations Office during the 1980–81 constitutional negotiations; and Mulroney chose Norman Spector for that position to prepare, negotiate and implement the Meech Lake Accord. In the case of the National Energy Program, the key bureaucratic players were a group of senior officials in the Privy Council Office and the Departments of Finance and Energy, Mines, and Resources.[16]

In the Chrétien government's deficit reduction exercise (Program Review) and Mulroney's free-trade initiative, leadership was brought in from outside, and also, new organizational units were established. The Chrétien government created a Program Review Secretariat within the Privy Council Office. It was headed by David Zussman, an academic who is a confidant of Chrétien, and who led his transition team in 1993, and staffed by a half-dozen civil servants who had been working on special projects in other departments.[17] The secretariat reviewed all departmental strategic plans. However, given the extent of the cuts to all departmental budgets, plans were then reviewed by a committee of the most senior deputy ministers, chaired by Jocelyne Bourgon, the Clerk of the Privy Council.[18] When the secretariat's work was complete, Zussman returned to academe and his staff went on to other projects.

The Free Trade Agreement was handled in a similar way. The government established a Trade Negotiation Office, headed by Simon Reisman, a former deputy minister of finance, with Gordon Ritchie, a former senior associate deputy minister of Regional Industrial Expansion, as his second-in-command. Ritchie's recent memoir recounts that they had soon built a staff of one hundred, using their political capital in Ottawa to borrow the most able people from other government departments.[19] In their study of the free trade negotiations, Doern and Tomlin wrote: 'TNO was soon the place to be in Ottawa, and recruitment became a mark of status. The chief negotiator created TNO in his own image, choosing bright and aggressive people who were convinced of their ability to take on the Americans and best them with superior organization and skills.'[20]

At the political level, the responsibility for managing a key priority usually went to a strong minister who was a trusted ally of the Prime Minister; for example, Trudeau gave Jean Chrétien responsibility for the Constitution and Marc Lalonde responsibility for the National Energy Program, and Mulroney assigned the Meech Lake Accord to Lowell Murray. It was easier for these ministers to focus on their priority if their other departmental responsibilities were not particularly onerous – for example, Lowell Murray's role as Government Leader in the Senate, or Chrétien's Justice portfolio. This was comparable to your moving Elwood Cowley from Finance to the low-profile position of Provincial Secretary – with added responsibility for potash – or to your assigning a host of different priorities to Roy Romanow in his eleven years as Attorney General.

In addition, both Trudeau and Mulroney watched their key issues closely, and became actively involved at the most critical stages, as did their key advisers and ministers. In the constitutional negotiations, though it was Chrétien who cut the final deal, Trudeau was deeply involved. Mulroney himself handled the final negotiations on the Meech Lake Accord. The key negotiations on the Free Trade Agreement were led by Mulroney's principal secretary and long-time free-trade advocate, Derek Burney, and by the Finance Minister, Michael Wilson.[21]

In the case of the Chrétien government's program review, the political organization was somewhat different. In consideration of the political fallout that would result from cutting spending to eliminate the deficit, Chrétien established an ad hoc Program Review Committee of cabinet to consider departmental plans after they had been through the bureaucratic review. This committee, dubbed the Star Chamber, included the major financial ministers (Finance Minister Paul Martin, Treasury Board President Art Eggleton, and Minister for Intergovernmental Affairs and Public Service Renewal Marcel Masse), as well as a group of politically savvy and regionally representative ministers (Fisheries Minister Brian Tobin, Heritage Minister Sheila Copps, Foreign Affairs Minister André Ouellet, Immigration Minister Sergio Marchi, and Natural Resources Minister Anne McLellan). Deputy Prime Minister Herb Gray was there to represent the traditional viewpoint of the Liberal Party.[22]

Our favourite historical antecedent, the Douglas government in Saskatchewan, also provides an example of this approach. In 1944, Douglas did not want to entrust the responsibility of designing a system of hospital insurance to the Department of Health. Instead, he established the Health Services Planning Commission. The commission was staffed with the sharpest minds in the health policy field, some from Saskatchewan and some from outside the province. In addition, he made himself Health Minister as a way to maintain involvement. This case is somewhat different from the others, because after the hospital insurance program was established, the commission was given the mandate of administering it for two or three years until its work was merged with that of the Department of Health. The program implemented, Douglas gave up the health portfolio in 1948.[23]

One can look at these cases as illustrations of a general tendency that has long been studied by people in the field of business policy.[24] An organization's strategic choices – that is, its priorities – influence its structure. Businesses organize special project teams, task forces, and the like for major new projects – and so do governments.

5

The Responsibilities of Ministers

This chapter deals with the responsibilities of individual ministers. Blakeney discusses the various methods he used to ensure that his ministers assumed collective responsibility for policy-making. Then we look at the minister's departmental role, in particular as it relates to the linkage between the department's programs and the public. Blakeney reminisces about his summer tours of the province. We then make several arguments against ministerial involvement in departmental policy analysis. We discuss briefly how a minister's exempt staff should behave so as to work effectively with the department. Borins concludes the chapter by presenting an interpretation of Blakeney's approach to organizing his cabinet in terms of the cybernetic model of organizations.

Borins: Now that we have discussed cabinet as a group, let's look at individual ministers. In Chapter 1 you presented *the speech* in a very general way. But what are the implications of *the speech* for ministers? If you were giving it to the cabinet as a whole, what spin would you put on it for them?

Blakeney: The speech deals with the role of each individual minister as a member of cabinet. If there is no general manager or CEO in government, which is what I suggest, then my role as Premier is similar to that of a chairman of the board. The cabinet ministers are members of the board, and it is their responsibility as members of the board to set the overall direction of government.

As I mentioned when I spoke about my criteria for choosing cabinet ministers, I tried to choose people who could wear two hats at once. While they were advocates for their individual departments, they also had to see the big picture and assume responsibility for the collective policy-making of the government.[1]

Borins: Beside giving *the speech*, did you have any other ways of making this point?

Blakeney: Oh, yes, I had several. During cabinet meetings a minister might persist in expounding the point of view of his own department again and again. I would say forcefully that this would not do and that if everyone did that, the only people left to balance the competing views would be me and perhaps the Finance Minister. My response was, 'No way. I'm the *chairman* of the cabinet, not the *whole* cabinet. I'm not the only referee.' I was known to tell them, 'There are too many advocates here, and too few judges.' But this was not a pressing problem, except for a few ministers. I recall on a couple of occasions discussing a major issue – I'll call it university funding – and having to exclude from the discussion the Minister of Continuing Education because he felt it necessary to reply to each intervention by another minister. On perhaps one or two occasions, when I must have been feeling bloody-minded, I remarked that we did not need to hear further from the minister because we could hear the same message from the deputy. It's difficult to build a consensus in an atmosphere of adversarial advocacy. Ministers had to check their ministerial hats at the door so that we could make reasonable decisions on a consensus basis and without too much acrimony.

Most of this departmental possessiveness came out at budget time. And it was not all bad. Ministers should feel that their departments are important and that they can prove that the department spends money wisely. But this cannot be their principal focus at the cabinet table or among the public. Otherwise, they lose their capacity to pick up nuances of criticism that caucus members or the public are expressing.

In order not to sound too pedantic too often – and some of the ministers kidded me about this – I occasionally asked another minister to lead the counterattack against a minister who was being too protective of his department. This reduced the danger of a minister developing a 'the Premier is always picking on me' mentality.

I had a few more ways to keep making the point. At cabinet planning meetings, when deputies or other senior officials referred to the policy of the Department of Agriculture, I sometimes interrupted and remarked that the Department of Agriculture didn't have a policy; rather the Government of Saskatchewan had a policy of which the Department of Agriculture's program was a part. This was a matter of semantics, as I and the listeners were well aware, but it reminded departments that we expected ministers and deputies to view the government's program as a whole. Occasionally I used the same verbal formula in cabinet.

As an aside, we didn't let departments create their own departmental logos; instead, we developed a universal logo that all agencies were required to use on stationery, pamphlets, public signs, and the like. This was not dissimilar to the Government of Canada approach.

Borins: In his book about public management, Tim Plumptre at one point recalls a conversation he had with his father Wynne, who had been an assistant deputy minister in the federal Department of Finance in the 1950s and early 1960s. His father was shocked when late in his career, officials at interdepartmental meetings began referring to their departments' positions. To quote Plumptre senior: 'The arrival of that kind of vocabulary, which soon became common, signalled to me an important – and very regrettable – change in officials' conceptions of their role as public servants. It turned the meetings into sessions where departments negotiated with each other and jockeyed for position, rather than trying collectively to solve a problem of government policy.'[2]

Plumptre felt that the collective problem-solving approach was a key characteristic of the era of the civil service mandarins – an era when the senior public servants truly were the best, the brightest, and the most committed to the culture of public service. As a consequence, the federal public service was very highly regarded, both at home and abroad.[3]

Blakeney: We were determined to maintain the collective problem-solving approach in Saskatchewan, both within the public service and within the cabinet. The message that there was a need for it came from me, and it also came – sometimes by precept but more often by example – from some of the other ministers, notably the Deputy Premier, Roy Romanow and several other key ministers. It was clear to all that an ability to take the broader view was a requirement for being considered one of the informal inner group. Positions on Treasury Board and important ad hoc committees tended to go to the people with the broader vision. Conversely, I sometimes put a minister who had potential, but who was too focused on his department, on Treasury Board for at least one budget round so that he could be exposed to public servants – and sometimes ministers – who believed as strongly in the overriding importance of their programs as he did in his. If travel is broadening, so is service on the Treasury Board during a budget round.

This problem of departmental people becoming too focused on their own department and missing the bigger picture is not confined to cabinets and governments. I remember the CEO of a major company telling me that he noticed the same problem among his senior managerial staff. His approach was to announce before the annual planning meeting, at which the management team selected priorities and allocated funds, that several of those present would have new jobs heading different departments in a week's time. The message was clear: 'Don't worry about your department – it may not be yours for long. Worry about what is best for the whole company.'

Borins: I find it fascinating that you repeated your discussion of collective responsibility so often that it was called *the speech*, and that ministers kidded you about sounding pedantic in cabinet meetings, either by reiterating the need for them to be judges rather than advocates, or by taking them carefully through the reasons for decisions.

It is very clear to me that you were performing a key leadership role, tirelessly communicating your government's values about how ministers and public servants should behave and how decisions should be made. Peters and Waterman write about how important it is for corporate CEOs to be not charismatic, but persistent, in creating a 'value-driven' organization.[4] Gareth Morgan discusses how CEOs, in particular the founders of companies, create corporate cultures.[5] The fact that your ministers kidded you for being pedantic signals to me that the message had been communicated.

You've said quite a bit about a minister's responsibility as a member of cabinet. What about the minister's responsibility for his or her individual department? What is involved there?

Blakeney: Several things. First, a minister should be able to provide good political intelligence about how the electorate will react to the policies and programs proposed by the department. This doesn't absolve the department from having political intelligence, as I'll make clear when we discuss the public service. However, the ultimate responsibility for political intelligence rests with the minister. After all, his or her job depends on it, and so does the success of the entire cabinet. If you're looking for a private sector analogy, the minister's job is to provide intelligence about how the market will react.

The other side of this coin is that the minister must be out there explaining the department's programs and policies to the public. So, it's not just a matter of passively gathering market intelligence – the job involves marketing the department as well.[6]

In essence, the minister must act as a bridge between the public and the public service. This provides an effective limit to a minister's span of control: if the portfolio becomes too complex, so that it deals with too many problems and constituencies, that minister loses effectiveness.

Borins: Earlier we talked about the 'strategic prime minister,' who concentrates on a small number of key issues. In the same vein, we can suggest that ministers ought to be strategic as well, concentrating on a small number of priorities that are consistent with those of the cabinet as a whole.[7] Crossman was very emphatic about this point in the context of a British Labour government: 'Select a very few causes and fight for them. The greatest danger of a radical minister is to get too much going in his department. Because, you see, departments are resistant ... There's a limit to the quantity of change they can digest. Select a few, very few issues, and on those issues be bloody and blunt, because, of course, you get no change except by fighting.'[8]

Your point about politicians as gatherers of market intelligence brings us to how you spent at least part of each of your summers as Premier. I understand that you did bus tours of your province's rural areas.[9] How long were these tours, who went with you, and how was the information plugged into the political process?

Blakeney: The Blakeney Bus was an effort to put a human face on the office of the Premier and to get a sense of how people were feeling. As a device for gaining such impressions, it's an interesting study. It worked well at first and less well later on, and the reasons for the change are instructive.

I went for about ten days to two weeks. I travelled by bus, a regular Saskatchewan Transportation Company bus of the kind that traversed the province every day. My wife, Anne, and the two younger children – in the summer of 1974 they would have been ten and five – sometimes came along for portions of the trip. I went to smaller places that I did not ordinarily visit in the course of my regular work. A couple of tour organizers and a couple of assistants went along. Some reporters were there as well. We structured very informal gatherings in a park or a hall, where I would say a few words and then move among the crowd. People would come and shake hands and talk. I would chat and listen for, 'You're doing a great job but I was wondering ...' and out would come the person's concern. One of the assistants was always at my shoulder, and if it was a matter I couldn't dispose of with a few words, I asked the assistant to take notes. Then I would extricate myself, sometimes with the help of an aide, and move on. People in small centres were very polite but we would pick up many dozens of individual problems. When we got back to Regina, each one of these would be researched and a substantial answer prepared, which I would sign and send. If the individual problems fell into a pattern, we knew we had a political problem.

I have some pleasant memories. In one small town of perhaps one hundred people, we had a good turnout. I remember asking some ranchers why they came in the middle of probably a busy day to visit (to use the Saskatchewan term). They said they were curious; this was the first time a premier had ever visited their town. On another occasion the local mayor had asked when the trip was being planned why we were visiting his town, and my staff had replied that I simply wanted to meet the people of the town. When we arrived on a sunny morning, there were chairs around in a large circle on Main Street with some coffee and lemonade at the side and people sitting and standing in a rough circle. The mayor took me around to meet all the people present. Having done that, he told me that three people were away in Saskatoon and two were not well enough to come – and would I go to their house to see them? – and that was all the people of his town. He had interpreted our wishes literally and had accounted for the total population of 105. These were warm, informal occasions.

But as time went on, either by accident or by design, people would come forward to raise issues in a belligerent way, and the press would report this in full colour. My staff then became more protective, and events become gradually more structured. I don't know if this problem can be avoided. If the press had reported on all contacts, no issue would have arisen, but when fifty friendly contacts and one belligerent one produced a headline 'PREMIER HAMMERED ON BUS TOUR,' it was not clear what the best thing was for us to do. The tours almost imperceptibly become more media events instead of opportunities for me to meet in a relaxed way with a cross-section of small-town Saskatchewan. Perhaps in today's media environment it is not possible for a premier to discuss government policies in public in an unstructured way, except on an unannounced drop-in basis.

Borins: It seems to me that the Blakeney Bus was an example of your setting an example for your cabinet, or 'walking your talk,' as the term goes. After all, if the Premier can spend two weeks of his summer meeting the voters, then ministers should be able to spend as much time, if not more.

To shift topics, when a department is involved in policy development, what stance should a minister take toward the department?

Blakeney: It is the duty of the cabinet to outline broad policy objectives, and of the ministers to translate those into more specific policy objectives for their department. It is the deputy's job to know the context in which he or she is working. I tried to stress that it was up to us as cabinet and as individual ministers to give the deputies clear signals about the government's direction. The government's objectives should not be a closely guarded secret: they should be the subject of discussion among deputies. Deputies should hear from us where we are going and observe what policy decisions we make across the range of government decision making. From this they should be able to frame recommendations that are reasonably consistent with the government's policy direction. Deputies can be encouraged to suggest other options outside the current range of acceptable policy, but in such instances they should recognize what they are doing and label the option as outside the current policy stream. I never quarrelled with this approach so long as it was understood that the minister's or cabinet's reaction might be a peremptory no. The minister must require the deputy and the department to produce options for programs or approaches that will advance the policy objectives that have been identified. And these options should be real, if in fact there *are* real options. It's not good enough for the deputy to decide on the bureaucracy's preferred course of action and put it forward as a single recommendation or in company with a couple of improbable straw-man options. This doesn't give the minister a chance either to choose or to learn what the real choices are.

There is a further danger, one against which I cautioned ministers ad nauseam – so some of my colleagues assured me – but which you tell me isn't such a bad thing. The point I now make can sometimes be overstated but is still fundamental to a collegial cabinet approach to government. Ministers should give policy direction but should never, while doing so, allow themselves to be drawn into the process of formulating the recommended policy that will later be put forward by the public service for ministerial approval. There are several reasons for this. One is that the minister will necessarily be discussing many issues of administration about which he or she knows little and which sometimes are presented as insuperable obstacles. When policy is framed in terms of what is administratively feasible, as seen by administrators, a blanket of caution is thrown over the process at too early a stage.

A second reason for the minister to stay out of the process of defining options is that he or she will end up spending far too much time being closeted with public servants – time that should be spent doing the job the minister can do best, which is assessing the public acceptability of government programs.

A third reason is that the minister loses effectiveness as a judge of policy proposals in the light of his or her special knowledge. I strongly recommended to ministers that they give their public servants as clear a sense as possible of what policy objectives the government wanted to achieve, and then ask the deputy to come up with some fleshed out program proposals, with some options. The minister could then look at them with a relatively unbiased eye to test their public acceptability.

There is another, more subtle point. If a minister recommends to cabinet a program recommended by the deputy that the minister has accepted, and cabinet rejects the idea, the minister will be unhappy. But if the minister recommends to cabinet a program that the minister, the deputy, and the departmental staff have lovingly crafted together, and cabinet rejects it, the minister will, in all likelihood, be more unhappy.

I should make a further point. One of the ways that a minister can judge the quality of the advice he or she is receiving is to assess the deputy's recommendations when the deputy is asked to put forward program options based on a policy direction provided by the minister. If the minister has been co-opted to the extent that the deputy never has to make a recommendation that the minister is not already at least partly committed to, then the minister loses an important means of judging the program design capabilities of the deputy. Suppose a program is suggested by a department, and cabinet wants to move in the indicated direction but thinks the proposal has serious administrative flaws. Then suppose, as is likely, that cabinet asks Treasury Board staff to review the proposal and report to Treasury Board. The board will then consider the proposal, after hearing out both the deputy and the Treasury Board staff. In these circumstances, useful information about the deputy's competence is acquired if the details of the proposal were recommended by the deputy. But if the minister was involved in crafting the proposal, less is learned about the deputy's competence and more problems of ministerial ego are involved.

For this complex of reasons, I strongly advised ministers not to get involved in a program design before the deputy and his or her staff outlined the options and gave their firm recommendation.[10]

Borins: This reminds me of discussions in the private sector of upward delegation. Upward delegation happens when subordinates bring problems to their superiors in order to get them actively involved in solving the problems – and, of course, to make them responsible for the solution. Upward delegation is generally poor management practice for all concerned. Superiors have enough problems of their own: they are looking for subordinates who can bring them solutions, not problems. A good manager expects that when he or she has delegated authority, the subordinates to whom it has been delegated will exercise it and be accountable for it.

Blakeney: As I have suggested, the most serious instances of upward delegation happen when ministers and public servants fail to preserve the line between policy and administration.

Ministers are not experts at administration and they are not chosen for those skills. Also, they have a great deal of work that only they can do. At every caucus retreat, when caucus members aired their complaints about how things were going, the chorus was the same – cabinet ministers should get out of their offices. I've turned up the rough notes from a cabinet-caucus retreat in 1976. On the issue of use of cabinet's time, every one of the eight recorded comments by caucus members were to same effect:

- 'We have to get more cabinet ministers, particularly the Premier, into more constituencies. Constituency people want to see new faces.'
- 'Cabinet ministers work hard. But should they be doing work in their

offices? Cabinet has to spend more time on political issues and with people, including MLAs.'
- 'We [cabinet ministers] need to free ourselves, talk to MLAs, remove ourselves from obligations of day-to-day work.'

I was personally torn. I like administration in the broad sense of arriving at policy direction for the government as a whole. I liked to think that our government had policy objectives and that we could do more with less because we usually knew where we were going. But I was aware that we might not be explaining as well as we could why we were pursuing our policies, and that we were not always putting a human face on important policies.

Ministers are, in fact, very busy people with more calls on their time than can possibly be met. They must constantly choose what to do less of. I urged them to err on the side of leaving policy with the deputies and their own ministerial staff. The alternative was to try to deal with all policy issues and thereby risk becoming too involved in departmental administration.

Borins: All this is fine, and makes sense. However, the image you present of a cabinet minister sitting in judgment of her department's proposals is pretty stern and cold. The management literature talks about the importance of senior managers as cheerleaders, raising morale, rallying the troops, and so on. Where does this fit with your picture?

Blakeney: Some of that is the work of the deputy minister, who, after all, is the department's most senior manager. However, the minister can help by visiting departmental facilities and by a bit of what the private sector calls 'management by walking around.' Staff are looking to see the person they are working for. Also, listening to them is a good way for a minister to both raise morale and take the pulse of the organization. They too are a public to be listened to.

Finally, a minister can win the respect of the department by representing it forcefully and by winning cabinet's approval and funding for its program. Of course, a balance must be struck between the department's particular interests and the government's overall interests.

Borins: Crossman identified the effective minister as the one 'who wins the support of [the] department without becoming its cherished mascot.'[11]

We haven't said anything yet about ministers' political staff, executive assistants, and the like. Have you any words of advice for ministers in managing their political staff?

Blakeney: First of all, they should have good political antennae so that they can help the minister with political functions. Second, they should not misunderstand their own function. They are not the minister and should not act as if they are. A few political staff people, especially when they get together, tend to overemphasize the importance of the role they play.

In particular, ministerial staff must use great tact in dealing with the departmental people. They should build a solid working relationship with the deputy. To do their job and not waste everybody's time, they often need to secure information from the department at several levels below the deputy. This must be done in a way that cannot be construed as giving instructions and that in no way undermines the deputy's chain of command. If a staffer feels that he or she might be doing this, the request should go through the deputy's office. All of this requires some sensitivity on both sides. A deputy will not want to be bothered with every request for information that a minister's office may need; but neither will that deputy want the division or branch heads to be receiving communications that can be construed as instructions on departmental matters from people outside the chain of command.[12] The minister's office staff must recognize that not only ministers but also deputies may sometimes act like prima donnas.

Borins: The political staff of a minister deal with other people besides departmental officials. Let's discuss them now.

Blakeney: Every minister's office has a system for dealing with mail and telephone calls. First, a rough sort is done to separate the departmental mail and calls from the political.

Some of the departmental letters and calls are referred to the deputy's office, and some are answered by the minister using information retrieved from the department by the political staff.

The political mail is answered or prepared for the minister's signature by the political staff. The political calls are usually answered by the staff, who will find out what the caller wants and what the issue is. They then organize this information for the minister, who decides whether he should return the call personally or write. Some people will take an answer from the political staff. These are judgment calls.

The political staff ordinarily deal with the minister's constituency offices and key people in the constituency, and also with the minister's constituents on run-of-the-mill MLA business, such as how to apply for a grant or how to get some action from the Department of Labour.

Sometimes a particular political aide builds a special relationship with an interest group that the minister deals with. For example, an aide of the Education Minister may make a point of attending regional meetings of teachers and school trustees and then convey the mood of those meetings to the minister. This is a legitimate function of the department but is sometimes done by someone from the minister's office.

Borins: I would like to conclude our discussion of cabinet and ministers by analysing cabinet in terms of the cybernetic approach to organization theory. I'd better explain. In this approach, organizations are viewed as brains. This may well be a fruitful metaphor for analysing the cabinet, which after all is the government's supreme decision-making body: at the highest level, it does the government's thinking.

Research into mental functioning has shown that the brain has a number of characteristics that support the use of this metaphor. First it has an astonishing ability to organize and reorganize itself to deal with various challenges. For example, people who have had head injuries or brain surgery can often relearn skills they initially lost. This is because brain cells are holographic – that is, they have similar structures so that they can be organized and reorganized to handle different functions.

Second, the brain uses feedback. This includes 'single-loop' learning, whereby performance is compared against operating norms, and 'double-loop' learning, whereby the brain questions the appropriateness of the norms themselves. In other words, we can both learn and 'learn to learn.' A third characteristic of the brain is that it has 'requisite variety,' which means that it can develop internal diversity sufficient to match the variety and complexity of its environment.

By analogy, organization theorists have described holographic organizations as those in which each part incorporates within itself the ability to perform any of the entire organization's functions and to respond to any challenge in the organization's environment. Such an organization has a great capacity to learn, as well as great flexibility. The example of holographic organization most frequently discussed in the literature is the autonomous work group, in which each member acquires multiple skills and is able to substitute for other members as the need arises.[13]

This analogy can be taken much further if applied to your own cabinets. Your ministers were generalists and had not been chosen for their specialized knowledge of particular departments. By participating in collective decision making, they learned how to apply your government's philosophy to any department. This meant that you could reorganize your cabinets by giving ministers either different portfolios or temporary assignments, and still operate effectively.

By appointing ministers with a variety of ethnic, occupational, geographic, and ideological backgrounds, you assembled a cabinet that reflected the requisite variety of its environment – that is, the electorate. By requiring that your ministers devote their time to meeting the public rather than departmental administration, you impelled them to act as information gatherers, collecting feedback from the environment about how successfully your government was performing. Through state-of-the-nation discussions and cabinet retreats, your cabinet engaged in double-loop learning – it both monitored its performance on the basis of the feedback received and examined its underlying assumptions about the environment. Finally, your frequent exhortations to ministers to act as judges, not advocates, were a way to encourage all ministers to think about the government in a holistic way.

I sense a convergence here between the 'good management principles' you used to organize and manage a cabinet and the cybernetic principles an organization theorist would apply if called upon to design a cabinet. It would be fascinating, though well beyond the scope of this book, to use cybernetic principles to evaluate both cabinet institutions – such as different committee structures – and the ways that various premiers or prime ministers organized and managed their cabinets.

Blakeney: As I listen to you now, I find these ideas interesting. Had I heard them when I was in office, I would have been perplexed, to say the least.

Borins: Fine, but what I want to show is that what you might regard as common sense really isn't so common after all.

6

Managing the Caucus, the Legislature, and the Party

We begin this chapter by describing caucus meetings and committees and by showing how caucus can influence the cabinet. We then look at the Blakeney government's practices concerning the appointment and use of legislative secretaries. A number of topics concerning the Legislature are then discussed, including the rationale for introducing a fall session and both government and opposition strategies for handling Question Period. The chapter concludes with an exploration of the relationship between the party and the government – in particular, the participation of ministers at party conventions – and an analysis of why the party tends to be less active when it is in power than when it is not.

Borins: Caucus is a topic we've touched on only fleetingly to this point. This group of people is important to you in terms of both political intelligence-gathering and consultation in the process of setting priorities. More than a few people in caucus believe that *they* should be in cabinet rather than one or another of the present ministers. Also, if you undertook every program or project that your caucus members wanted you to undertake, your government would quickly be terribly overspent. Clearly, caucus poses some management challenges.

To begin with, when did caucus meet and for how long? Who chaired caucus?

Blakeney: In the first weeks of our government, the caucus met frequently. After we settled into a routine, caucus met approximately once a month for one or two days when the Legislature was not in session. When the Legislature *was* in session, we met daily for half an hour before the sitting of the House, with a longer caucus once a week.

The caucus chose its own officers. In fact, I proposed the first caucus chair and secretary. The chair was an older, experienced member who had declined my invitation to join the cabinet. He was a farmer representing a rural/small-city constituency and was respected by all caucus members. The secretary was a new, younger member, a teacher from Saskatoon. There was also a caucus treasurer.

Borins: What did the agenda for a caucus meeting look like, and how did it compare to the agenda for a cabinet meeting? What role did you and the other ministers play in caucus meetings?

Blakeney: A caucus agenda would cover business arising from previous minutes, and reports from the Premier and House Leader and from caucus committees. In addition, any caucus member could put an item on the agenda.

The chairman did a good bit of organizing to see that material was prepared for caucus meetings. The paper flow was much more informal than for cabinet. There was not the same need for precision. The secretary prepared minutes, which were not ordinarily circulated to caucus members. The chair and secretary got copies, as did I. They were available to any caucus member.

I tried very hard to get across to caucus that its officers were its executive, the people who acted on their instructions. The cabinet was not its executive. In the beginning, some caucus members felt that if caucus passed a motion, cabinet should be required to act upon it. That simply cannot work.

Borins: How did you go about getting caucus on what you considered the right track?

Blakeney: For one thing, I attempted, with only partial success, to get caucus minutes to reflect not only the bare decisions made but also the organizational realities. When I was secretary to numerous Crown corporation boards, I had used the technique of having the minutes reflect not only the decision made but also who should do what next. Thus, a decision by a board that we look into buying three D-8 tractors would be recorded: 'It was agreed that the general manager look into the purchase of three D-8 Caterpillar tractors or equivalent units from other suppliers, obtain quotes, and report on the information gathered, together with his recommendation for further action, if any, at the next meeting of the board.' This had the effect of identifying what the follow-up and report-back mechanisms were to be. Occasionally, a general manager would suggest to me that I had called it wrong: that the board had intended for somebody else – perhaps the secretary – to follow up and report back on the decision. I had no quarrel with such a suggestion. We simply sorted it out. Both of us agreed that it was useful to include in the minutes the mechanics of follow-up and report, even though the board did not (and should not) concern itself with these details of administration.

I hoped to get caucus to set out its minutes in the same form, so as to emphasize the mechanics of who was to do what as a result of a caucus minute. The form of the minutes was a minor matter; the mechanics of how decisions were followed up was more important. It took some time to establish that if caucus wanted to pass a motion that 'Highway #20 be rebuilt,' that motion meant that the caucus chair was instructed to discuss with the Minister of Highways the rebuilding of Highway #20 and report back to caucus. If caucus was dissatisfied with the chair's report, there might be a motion to ask the minister to meet with the highways committee of caucus, or the full caucus. At this point, the minister would be armed with the needed information – and with the necessary cabinet support if it appeared that there was likely to be a challenge to the minister's policy. If it looked like caucus was serious, the likely result was the minister offering to have another look at the matter. There then developed some compromise whereby the Highway #20 project was moved up on the priority list and another project moved down.

Borins: How did cabinet handle this upsetting of the spending priorities?

Blakeney: This was not a frequent problem. Caucus had accepted the budget and its priorities, and two caucus members had sat in on the days-long budget finalization process. And cabinet was sensitive to the fact that caucus had to feel it could influence government decisions – and that besides, it might well be right. It would have been a mistake to casually ignore the positions of caucus on issues with political content. What we needed to guard against was some individual caucus member pushing a pet project and other caucus members going along with it – or even worse, going along with it in return for support for their own pet projects in the best logrolling tradition of the U.S. Congress. This never became a serious problem. Undoubtedly, caucus often felt that cabinet did not listen well enough, but I don't think they felt totally shut out of the action.

Borins: You have referred to caucus committees. What were their main functions?

Blakeney: These committees were subject-area committees. Each committee was assigned to deal with several agencies. When cabinet proposed that a significant existing policy in, say, agriculture be changed, or that existing legislation be replaced or amended, the policy or legislation was referred to the appropriate caucus committee. The committee considered the issue and made a recommendation to caucus. Approval was the norm, but sometimes issues were raised for debate. Some ministers raised ideas with the caucus committees at an early stage before a recommendation was made to cabinet. More typically, proposals were referred to the committees after cabinet approval. If a proposal for legislation was forwarded to cabinet for approval, it was not uncommon for cabinet to suggest that it go to the caucus committee before cabinet approved it in principle, there being no point in going to the trouble of getting a bill drafted in legal form if it was likely to die in caucus.

Caucus committees also considered suggestions for program changes that caucus members had raised. Sometimes suggestions for program changes came from the caucus committees directly. Neither event was particularly common.

Borins: What other functions did caucus perform?

Blakeney: Caucus played an important part in finalizing our budget. I think that subject is better dealt with in our chapter on financial management.

Another obvious function was political. I, as Premier, regularly raised issues relating to the state of party organization. Sheets showing membership and financial contributions by constituency were frequently circulated in order to exert pressure on some caucus members to be more diligent in working with their constituency organizations. Party officials often attended caucus meetings to discuss party and electoral matters. I urged caucus members to attend the meetings of the Provincial Council of the Saskatchewan NDP. This was a group of about 150 people that met three or four times a year and that was the governing body of the party between our annual conventions. Only a couple of official caucus representatives could actually vote at these councils, but all could speak and circulate among council members and test the mood of our constituency stalwarts.

In my leader's reports to caucus, I regularly raised issues of how we were doing with the electorate, either generally or with respect to a particular issue. Discussion of the report produced debate and a sense of how caucus thought we were doing.

Borins: You've touched on some of the interaction between cabinet and caucus. What types of problems arose in the relationship?

Blakeney: Cabinet had some firm and well-understood rules about confidentiality and solidarity. Once a decision was made in cabinet, and a policy adopted, all ministers defended it, whether or not everyone had supported it in cabinet. And we did not talk about who had or had not supported the decision. In dealing with caucus, we adopted a somewhat different rule. When we made a decision that was going to be referred to caucus, we decided also whether it was a decision for which we badly needed caucus support or one where we were prepared to accept a different result from caucus. The former we labelled 'class A' decisions, and all cabinet members were obligated to support the decision in caucus. The latter were 'class B' decisions that individual ministers were free to speak against and vote against in caucus. In other words, class B decisions were decisions that cabinet would be prepared to change if the majority of caucus wanted a change. Caucus respected our position and did not try to overturn majority cabinet decisions capriciously. We found this classification system to be a good compromise between cabinet domination of caucus and caucus decision-making based on a weaker understanding of the issues than could be found in cabinet.

Caucus members were obligated to support caucus decisions in the Legislature, except in a few well-defined cases. At all times, members were required to advise the Whip well in advance that they intended either to abstain from voting or to vote against a government measure. If the measure was a key part of the government's program, the House Leader or I would talk to the member. This almost never happened. If the issue was a matter of conscience, as it is termed – for example, if it involved liquor legislation, Sunday observance, abortion, or the like – members were free to vote as they felt they should. During our time in office, we had one member leave and sit as an independent on the ground that we were not sufficiently radical. Another member voted against a provincial wage-restraint program at the time of the federal wage-and-price-control program of 1975, and members voted against the government on a few other occasions. On numerous occasions we had votes on issues of conscience, which were always understood to be free votes. On one occasion the member who was my legislative secretary introduced a private member's bill dealing with Sunday observance. He voted for it, and I voted against. As I recall, I lost.

But on key issues, party discipline was strictly enforced. At one point I toyed with the idea of introducing a system where there would be many more free votes, but also a formalized system of confidence votes so that every vote would not be construed by the press or others as requiring or even suggesting that the government should resign. Such a system would have enhanced the role of MLAs and at the same time put much more pressure on them; it would also have complicated legislative planning for the cabinet. We did not pursue the idea.

Borins: As I understand it, the British Parliament uses this sort of system. I think it would also appeal to any minority government. You have referred to cabinet committees and caucus committees. Were there joint committees?

Blakeney: Not as such. Cabinet members who were members of caucus were members of caucus committees, and two caucus members chosen by caucus sat in on cabinet's budget finalization process, but there was no system of joint committees.

Borins: Caucus members could also serve as legislative secretaries to ministers. How did you chose legislative secretaries? And how did you evaluate their performance?

Blakeney: We operated with a statutory limit of six legislative secretaries at any one time. I agree with a limit. I don't like a system where virtually every government member has some additional formal duties and accordingly some perquisites, such as extra pay, that very few opposition members have.

I selected the legislative secretaries. I consulted with some cabinet colleagues, but not widely. The legislative secretaries served in the major program departments as well as in the Premier's Office. The appointments lasted a year and there was some rotation. To judge performance, I relied on reports from the ministers and on my own observations. Some secretaries undertook major tasks. During our first term, the legislative secretary to the Minister of Health undertook the job of sorting out the many policy issues associated with designing the prescription drug and children's dentistry programs.[1] It was a major job, and he did a first-class piece of work. Others confined themselves to meeting delegations, speaking at official openings, and otherwise helping the minister with his external relations.

Borins: You've said that the caucus was involved with legislation and with budget finalization. Was it involved at an earlier stage in setting priorities?

Blakeney: At day-long or two-day caucus meetings when the Legislature was not in session, we had many discussions on priorities. Sometimes a meeting would be structured as a cabinet–caucus retreat, where caucus members could offer extensive advice and opinions on what our government should be doing.

Borins: Any other thoughts about how a premier deals with caucus?

Blakeney: I tended to deal with caucus somewhat formally. Naturally, I tried to be friendly. My wife Anne and I had caucus members to dinner a few times during the legislative session, and we had some parties at our house. But I never developed the legendary charm of someone like Brian Mulroney, who used the aura of his office and his personal charm so successfully in dealing with his caucus. What he did was great – it is just that not everybody can do it successfully.[2]

Borins: Now we turn to the Legislature. I'm not sure which is the more appropriate term: managing the Legislature, or surviving the Legislature.

Blakeney: What you imply is correct. The legislative session is the best opportunity the opposition has to expose the incompetence of the government, attack its policies, and put forward alternative policies of its own. Every government breathes a small sigh of relief when the Legislature adjourns and the government regains control of the agenda in dealing with the media.

This does not mean, however, that governments do not attempt to manage the Legislature. We certainly did.

Borins: In what ways did you attempt this job of management?

Blakeney: Our government was under its most sustained attack during the lengthy general debates on the Speech from the Throne and the budget. I'm not sure that the media pays as much attention to these debates now as they once did, but certainly media coverage of these debates was extensive in the 1970s. All the debates were broadcast live over radio, and rebroadcast in the evenings, and widely followed. (Television coverage did not come until our last year of office.)

We introduced the idea of opening the session in November, having our Throne Speech debate at that time, and tabling some of our major pieces of legislation. This gave the public a chance to study a particular piece of legislation before we picked it up again for consideration in February or March. This gave opponents of the legislation time to rally; but we still benefited in the longer run because the interval helped us avoid pushing through legislation in a form that would anger some of the public.

Perhaps the chief advantage to tabling legislation in the fall was that it forced cabinet and caucus to finalize most major pieces of legislation by about October 1. We set deadlines. These were always broken for emergency items and for minor items that were overlooked. But we did enforce the deadlines with respect to major pieces of legislation, for which the different agencies had plenty of notice.

During this period the budget process was moving forward; however, cabinet and caucus, except for members of Treasury Board, did not need to make the final tough decisions until January or February. I felt that if caucus and cabinet had to deal with major pieces of legislation and finalize a budget at the same time, tempers would become frayed, people would feel that they were being excluded from the process, and mistakes would be more likely.

The fall portion of the legislative session had to last long enough for us to complete the Throne Speech debate; it could then be adjourned or continued into the pre-Christmas period, at our option. We didn't like to go too far into December, because MLAs wanted to be in their constituencies so that they could circulate at the many social gatherings around that convivial time. But if we had an urgent and controversial matter, we could deal with a filibuster by keeping the session going through the holiday season. It was not a popular move with caucus members. At the same time, it usually reduced press coverage, which was not always a bad development from the government's perspective, since no opposition was going to filibuster through the holiday season unless it had a cause that it felt had widespread public support. We had two such marathon Yuletide debates, one in 1973 dealing with oil royalty legislation, the other in 1975 about potash legislation. Each was an important issue with a strong ideological content.

Borins: I guess the quintessence of the competition for power is Question Period. As Premier, how did you prepare for it? What tactics did you use to survive it?

Blakeney: We tried to deal with Question Period seriously. Almost unbelievably, there was no formal Question Period when we came to office in 1971. Instead, on sufferance, the opposition was allowed three questions before Orders of the Day. Later we changed the rules to institute a regular Question Period of twenty-five minutes. Our general tactic in Question Period was to be responsive and non-argumentative. We did not always succeed at this, but I felt that whenever Question Period was raucous, we lost even if we had the better of the verbal exchange. Our approach was that we were not trying to convince the public that we were good debaters; rather, we were trying to convince them that we were in charge and that all was well. Some of the ministers were crisp in their replies, some verbose. We had one minister who used to finger the button on his suit coat when answering a question. Sometimes, if the answer was long, he would finger two buttons in succession. One day, he wore a three-button jacket, and opposition members jokingly complained about his three-button answer, which took up, so they felt, too much of the Question Period.

We did not do the elaborate preparation for Question Period that appears to be the norm in Ottawa. If some issue was reasonably likely to inspire a question, ministers would prepare, and during our daily noontime cabinet meeting, the House Leader would point out the topics of likely questions. Our rule was that when a minister did not know the answer, it was better to take notice of the question and answer it the next day than to wing it with a rhetorical answer. That had hazards, because the opposition would immediately go to the press and give its version of the facts; when the minister answered the next day with a different version of the facts, the answer was frequently lost. But that was a risk that sometimes had to be taken.

I think the current practices in Ottawa respecting Question Period are fundamentally bad. I think it is nonsense to have twenty or thirty ministers spending an hour or so each day boning up on obscure facts that have been dug up by a hundred staff members about some minor matter in the news, on the off-chance that a question will be asked about it. Surely Canadians do not believe that this is the best use of ministerial time, or the time of some hundreds of able and highly paid staff.

I favour the written notice of questions. Ministers should be told ahead of time that a question is coming and what the subject will be. The probing would come in the supplementary questions, of which there would be no notice except as to the general subject already indicated. It is difficult to conceive of any real scandal to be exposed that would be a scandal on Monday but not on Tuesday. The rules should allow oral questions without notice to deal with any genuinely new issue concerning which the government should give an account to Parliament or the Legislature. But the Speaker would have to see that this was not abused.

Borins: How was the House managed, from the government's point of view?

Blakeney: The House Leader, Roy Romanow, managed the House. He kept the legislation moving. We tried to table the bulk of our legislation early so that there would be many bills on the order paper. This allowed the House Leader the flexibility to call business as he wished, fitting it around ministerial absences and other hazards to scheduling. By maintaining reasonable relations between the government and the other side's House Leader and Whips, we were able to keep business moving along. When the opposition pulled the odd surprise, we reminded ourselves that retaliation was not a requirement. In a provincial legislature, a government should keep in mind that the session is the opposition's forum and that the object should not be to score debating coups but to get the business done and the session over.

Getting the estimates approved was a grind, since the opposition had the right to debate any one subvote – that is, one allocation of money for one branch of one department – for weeks if it chose. In such a debate, any member could speak many times on the same matter and each time as long as he or she wished. This almost never happened to us, but it was always a risk if one agency was in major trouble with the public and a protracted debate would bring more attention to its shortcomings.

Borins: You have been in government and in the opposition. How does the opposition approach a legislative session?

Blakeney: The opposition usually decides on two or three themes that it wishes to stress during a session. Every issue cannot be raised, every battle cannot be joined. In committees, both government and opposition members beaver away trying to improve this or that piece of legislation or make a point on a particular spending priority. But in the high-profile debates, and on opposition days when the opposition can set the agenda, a small number of themes should be stressed. This strategy is based on the assumption that the public does not usually accept an argument that is put once: some repetition is required to make a point. People who sell soap and beer understand this.

The opposition leaves itself enough flexibility that it can exploit new developments as they arise, particularly if the new developments can be related to one of the themes that is being stressed. If a government has committed an egregious error, the opposition can be expected to concentrate on the error almost exclusively for days.

Another aim of the opposition is to introduce to the public its own program. In short election campaigns, complicated ideas cannot be introduced with the expectation that they will be understood and accepted by the voters. These ideas are best introduced before the campaign starts. They can be reiterated and reinforced during the campaign, but the groundwork must be laid before the election is called. In ideal circumstances, the public will have complete program options to choose from, advanced by the competing parties. In practice, it usually has only some policies and some broader themes from which to choose.

Borins: So far we've talked about caucus and the Legislature. Now let's turn to the party. In particular, I'd be interested in knowing what the Saskatchewan NDP did between elections. Were there party conventions, policy conferences, fund raisers, and so on? Some leaders treat a political party as a machine to be conveniently rolled out for elections, and then forgotten the rest of the time. What was your approach?

Blakeney: There was no way that I could have adopted that approach toward the Saskatchewan NDP had I been so inclined, which I was not. I had great respect for the party. When it was the Opposition between 1964 and 1971, it did a great deal of work. The party held a convention each year where hundreds of resolutions were submitted, with many dozens being thoroughly debated.

Our conventions were very serious business. Between seven hundred and eight hundred delegates met for two-and-a-half days to listen to speeches and attend one or perhaps two social events, usually with speeches. They spent the rest of their time in panels debating resolutions submitted by individual constituencies and then debating the panel reports in plenary session. Out of this process came policy trends and often very specific proposals. These were worked into a party program, which was approved by the party's Provincial Council. In the late 1960s we also had a vigorous program committee that commissioned policies on automobile insurance, occupational health, the environment, industrial development, and farm size. The result was that when we assumed office in 1971, we had a pretty good idea of what we wanted to do.

The party was less active in policy formulation when we were in government. There were several reasons for this. First, the government had a ready source of ideas from the public service. Second, a good number of party policy activists had joined the government, particularly as staff to ministers, and were contributing in that way. Third, the government and the party became constrained by the art of the possible. Fourth, the press misconstrued party proposals as government policy, which inhibited the party from adopting unconventional ideas, their fear being that this might embarrass the government or interfere with its timing. Fifth and finally, the party people became overly concerned with shorter-term government actions, since these were what the public wanted to talk to them about, and as a consequence focused less on the larger policy issues.[3]

I attended all provincial conventions in their entirety, and attended virtually all meetings of the Provincial Council and most meetings of the Provincial Executive as well as innumerable constituency functions. The party resolutions were taken seriously by the government. At each convention we reported, resolution by resolution, on what we had done or not done as a result of the previous convention's resolutions. As a cabinet, we reviewed the resolutions that were going before the convention and decided on our approach to them. We did not try to engineer the outcomes of all or most of them. We did note the ones we felt we couldn't live with and attempted to convince the convention to see things our way.

Ministers spoke at the floor microphones, as did I. Delegates frequently resented this ministerial intervention. My position was that if the convention expected the cabinet to take the resolutions seriously, we had to have an opportunity to put forward our point of view. I felt it was better to be accused of plugging the microphones than of totally ignoring the convention resolutions. This tension within the party was not all bad – far from it. It made for real debate and a more realistic assessment of policy options.

The party usually exhibited a good deal of common sense, so when I was at odds with the mainstream of the party, I always asked myself how I came to hold my position.

Borins: Was it true, then, that the party's thinking influenced the government's thinking?

Blakeney: Very definitely. This was true throughout our tenure. The 1971 program the party drafted while in opposition dominated the first term. The royalty and public ownership moves relating to mineral resources, which dominated the second term, were totally in keeping with the party's thinking. The party was perhaps more divided on issues related to empowering disadvantaged groups, and had less pronounced views on constitutional change – these two issues dominated our third term – but I never felt we were out of step with the party.

7

The Election Trail

In this chapter we contrast the traditional specific platforms of the Saskatchewan NDP in the Douglas and Blakeney eras with the vague promises heard more frequently today. Then we discuss the strategies and themes of Blakeney's election campaigns, both winning and losing. Finally, we talk about why the NDP should become a more broadly based party, and how it can.

Borins: The ultimate test for a politician is winning elections. You won three pretty decisively and lost a fourth equally decisively. In your last election, you got more votes than the Conservatives but they won more seats. Shall we call it a draw, or at least a moral victory?

I'd like to get your views about electioneering, and the link between election-eering and governing.

Blakeney: Stop right there. Who says there is much of a link between election-eering and governing? In the last twenty years there has been a trend, which I consider most regrettable, toward running election campaigns like marketing campaigns. The winner seems to be the politician who is most marketable, who has the best image. Television accentuates this tendency to concentrate on im-ages rather than policies.

By *image* I don't of course only mean pictures of politicians. I also mean slo-gans that create a vision of a desirable state of affairs – 'Jobs, Jobs, Jobs,' 'A Fresh Start,' 'Fair Taxation' – but offer no details as to how these desirable states of affairs are to be achieved or even what they consist of. Specifics serve to identify winners and losers; visions identify only winners.

The federal election of 1997 did feature party platforms with some specifics, but I doubt whether many people cast their votes based on a consideration of the specific items in the platforms. It was a marketing-driven campaign with some of the attributes of an American campaign, particularly in its attempts to paint some candidates as being 'soft' on notorious criminals.

Borins: Were your campaigns based on images rather than issues?

Blakeney: I would like to think not. In some sense politics was different in Saskatchewan in the 1970s. We are a small province, and I think a lot more of our citizens had met either me or other party leaders than is possible in most other provinces. Image counts for less in such a setting, and issues for more.

In addition, I think that the public often sees through and resents politicians who attempt to run on image alone, without defending their record or raising serious issues. That's how I would read the 1990 campaign in Ontario. Premier David Peterson had substantial personal popularity, which eroded quickly when he ran what pretty obviously was a campaign without strong issues or clear positions.[1]

In contrast, Saskatchewan voters had had over twenty-five years of elections where parties had set out specific ten-point (or whatever) programs of the 'electrify 20,000 farms in the next term of office' variety. They had seen the government during the next campaign say, 'We promised to electrify 20,000 farms, we got 18,700 done, and we'll pick up that shortfall in a couple of months.' This breeds a different approach to election campaigns. For example, a major plank in our 1971 campaign was that we would lower property taxes levied for school purposes on homes, farms, and small businesses to not more than 25 mills. When I look at that now, I am surprised at just how specific it was. Incidentally, we did just that, and so reported during the 1975 campaign.

Borins: A look at the record of the Douglas government makes it clear that the Saskatchewan CCF and NDP had a long tradition of detailed and explicit electoral platforms.[2] The 1988 federal election campaign was just the opposite of the 1990 Ontario campaign in that it was very issue-oriented, revolving around one key issue – the Free Trade Agreement.

In Chicago, a city that has long been ruled by a strong and successful Democratic Party, they have a saying: 'Good government is good politics and good politics is good government.' Let's interpret the second half of that remark to mean that government should be responsive to voters' interests. As to the first half of the remark, I find it interesting that in each of your five election campaigns as leader, you argued that you had provided or would provide good government. What were the key issues in each campaign, and how did they play with the voters? And looking at the three campaigns where you were the incumbent, did you call elections at the right time on the right issues?

Blakeney: In 1971, Ross Thatcher and his government were tired. Although we didn't know it, he was ill. He died one month after polling day. He had a forceful, not to say abrasive, style that had upset a good number of people. His deputy, Davey Steuart (later Senator Steuart) used to say of that period that if there were any groups in the province the government had not offended, it was because they hadn't met them. In addition, Thatcher had the bad luck to be in office during a serious farm recession.

The NDP were well prepared for the 1971 election both in policy terms and electorally. As I mentioned earlier, we had a detailed policy package titled *A New Deal for People*, which we were distributing several months before the election. We expected to win and in fact garnered a massive 55 per cent of the vote against 43 per cent for the Liberals. The 1971 campaign started slowly but it gradually gained momentum. The big events were the rallies every evening at different centres around the province. The final rallies were huge – for example, 5,000 people in Regina. Television and radio covered the rallies, and that was the campaign. There were many events during the day, but they were not designed as media events or photo opportunities. The campaign was directed at the electorate rather than the media. Each successive campaign became more media-oriented.[3]

In 1975, our campaign was essentially a promise to carry on with our program. We had a platform – *New Deal for People II* (and this before the days of *The Godfather* and *Rocky*). The Liberal Party was in disarray and the Conservatives had revived. By 1975 the federal Liberals were making things difficult for their provincial counterparts. The Liberals ran a very negative campaign against the New Democrats, which hurt us a good deal but hurt them every bit as much. The result was a sharp drop in our vote and in the Liberal vote and a rise in the PC vote. With the opposition parties divided, we won a comfortable majority – 39 seats to 22 for the combined opposition. The election was called in June 1975 because it had been tradition since 1944 for the CCF to call elections every four years, in June. We chose to follow that tradition.[4]

Borins: I notice a tendency in politics for the theme in an election where a party first wins power to be 'A New Deal,' with the implicit message being, 'Throw the Bums Out.' In the next election campaign the theme is some variant on 'Stay the Course.' This would apply to your first two election campaigns and, more recently, to Roy Romanow's and Jean Chrétien's. However, 'Stay the Course' would have sounded a bit unexciting as a theme for your third election campaign. What theme did you use then?

Blakeney: Events had changed, so that by the 1978 campaign we had a new theme and a clear opponent and were riding a wave of increasing prosperity. Our

new theme was that the people of Saskatchewan should be getting a greater return from the resources that were contributing to this prosperity. With a greater
return we would be able to improve our own economic position – as we put it,
'We Can Do It Ourselves.' The clear opponent was the federal government, which
had by then made many moves to keep Saskatchewan from benefiting fully from
the rising value of mineral resources – oil and gas, potash and uranium – and
which had taken some adversarial stances of unprecedented severity in the ongoing federal–provincial disputes about resources.

The timing was out of the ordinary. I knew that the Conservatives' fortunes
were rising and the Liberals' fortunes falling, both federally and provincially. If
I had followed the normal four-year pattern, the election would have been held in
June 1979. Pierre Trudeau had been elected prime minister in 1974, and I felt that
he would probably call an election for the fall of 1978. This would separate the
Conservative victory federally, which I anticipated, from the provincial election
by eight or nine months and allow time for the Conservative momentum to sub-
side. I did not want a provincial election in which the Conservatives would certainly be the chief opponent to be just before or (worse still) just after the
anticipated federal Conservative win. So when Trudeau announced in September that he did not propose to hold an election in 1978, I cut short a holiday,
consulted with colleagues and party officials, and called an election in September for October 1978. That proved to be the right time. If the election had been
held in June 1979, after Joe Clark's Conservative victory of May 1979, it would
have been much tougher.[5]

The election of April 1982 was another story. My cabinet colleagues and I felt
that we could not long avoid the effects of the recession, which was already
biting deep in Ontario and elsewhere. Interest rates were skyrocketing. Things
would get worse. We felt that the economic issues were getting out of our control
and that we could not offer the electorate expensive programs or tax cuts that the
province could not afford. We put together a modest program of improvements
that included protection against the worst ravages of high interest rates. Polling
showed that we had a comfortable lead of 10 percentage points. We decided on a
spring election in 1982, hoping that we could ride out the coming storm – which
we felt would not be of long duration – and then resume provincial growth based
on reasonable grain prices and continued good prices for resources.

We would have to battle still more with the federal government over the federal taxes imposed in 1980 – the Petroleum and Gas Revenue Tax and the Gas
and Gas Liquids Tax (both part of the National Energy Program) – and over grain
freight rates, especially the proposed dismantling of the Crowsnest Pass freight
rates. Our campaign sputtered from the outset. Farmers were not as concerned
with the Crow Rate as we supposed. We may have suffered from appearing to be

not sufficiently anti-Trudeau during the constitutional debates. In retrospect, it appears that the voters perceived us as a government that was well off and yet unwilling to do anything to help them at a time when they were suffering from high interest rates. We, of course, felt that we would need all our resources to weather the coming storm without incurring large deficits. The Conservatives, sensing the public mood, offered mortgage interest subsidies and promised to eliminate provincial taxes on gasoline.[6]

Looking back, I can say that the election was definitely called at the wrong time. The date was wrong: people in Saskatchewan are often grumpy in April, because winter in our province always feels too long and because people's spirits haven't yet been raised by the sight of crops emerging from the ground in the spring or the satisfaction of harvesting them in the fall. As for issues, in hindsight perhaps we should have stated more clearly that hard times were coming and that the government should be cautious. We would still have lost to an upbeat campaign whose theme was 'There Is So Much More We Can Be' – their version of 'Throw the Bums Out' – but we would have been in a stronger position in the 1986 election. But I'm still not sure why we were so badly beaten in 1982.

In 1986 I was proud of the way we recruited an excellent group of candidates. We ran a good campaign, but we suffered from not having clearly in our collective mind whether we were going to emphasize the financial mess left by four huge budget deficits in succession, and the resulting dire financial straits the province was in, or the new programs we proposed, which involved some spending. We tried to do some of both, with a predictable lack of focus. We might have been better off if we had had a new leader before 1986. That is something I have pondered. The polls showed my standing to be high, but I think that polls fail to reflect the enthusiasm which might have built around a new leader. These are the imponderables of politics. On election day we got more votes than our opposition; even so, the Conservatives were returned, albeit with a greatly reduced though comfortable majority.[7]

Borins: The technology of campaigning has become tremendously sophisticated. Some parties conduct public opinion polls each evening to determine voters' sentiments about various issues, and then modify their messages, including the leader's speeches and television commercials, on the basis of this virtually instant feedback. What did the Saskatchewan NDP do in terms of feedback?

Blakeney: We certainly didn't use these high-tech methods in the 1970s and early 1980s. Even if they had been available, I don't think we could have afforded them. We had a rudimentary system along the same lines. In the cities and towns we operated a three-canvass system. We tried to call at each residence three times. This was sometimes supplemented with telephone canvassing.

The canvasser, in addition to identifying the party and the candidate's name, attempted to find out what issues the voter was interested in. The canvasser then reported the names, addresses, and issues to the constituency headquarters. Form letters and special-issue pamphlets were mailed. The better-organized campaigns sent out personalized letters that included a few general paragraphs and then a special section dealing with the issue the voter had raised. This was only possible in the 1980s, and we rarely attained the level of organization to make it work well. We depended much more on our canvassers' ability to deal with issues. When I refer to canvassers I include our candidates, who regularly met a surprisingly large percentage of the 10,000 voters in a typical urban riding.

We used very little polling during the campaigns in the 1970s. Changes in emphasis during a campaign were made on the basis of public reaction as assessed by our party officials. We used polling more in the later campaigns, including some overnight polling. We conducted these overnight polls mainly so that we could know where to make the extra effort by moving workers from one constituency to another, and so that we could judge which issues should be referred to in speeches, press releases, and radio and television commercials. Television spots are not easy to change on short notice, so the decision was largely one of which spots already 'in the can' should be used. Newspaper ads and radio spots can be changed on short notice, and polling information was used to make these decisions.

Borins: One question that any discussion of opinion polling raises concerns which voters you are trying to target. In your case, was the NDP emphasizing certain groups and writing off others? Or did you see yourself as a broadly based populist party, or as a middle-of-the-road party?

Blakeney: The Saskatchewan NDP regards itself as a broadly based mainstream party. Since 1934 it has always elected members to the Legislature, and since 1944 its share of the popular vote in each provincial election has been over 35 per cent. We have some appeal for all groups and a reasonable prospect of winning any constituency. Recently we have done better in urban seats, but we have always had a strong rural base.

Borins: How does this contrast with the federal NDP?

Blakeney: The federal party has areas where it is weak: rural Alberta, rural Ontario, and Quebec. But that is slowly changing. It is becoming more and more difficult to write off particular constituencies. The Ontario provincial elections of 1990 and 1995 reminded us never to rely upon previous voting patterns in many area. They also reminded us how unpredictable the results can be when several parties are contesting the election.

Borins: The NDP has been the government in four provinces. Does a strategy of broad-based appeal work for all four provinces?

Blakeney: In Saskatchewan and British Columbia, the party has a long history of vote totals of well over 40 per cent, so the appeal should be broad-based. In Ontario, and to a lesser extent Manitoba, the party will undoubtedly do some targeting, but less than one would think. Voting behaviour is becoming less and less predictable. Therefore, unless all three tests – namely, past voting patterns, current opinion-polling results, and internal party intelligence – suggest there is no real prospect of success, no riding should be ignored. If at all possible, every riding should be contested.

Indeed, there are strong reasons for running a good campaign in a constituency you feel you will lose. First, you are building support for the next election. Second, it is useful in any election campaign to convey the impression that the party can win. To do this you must have credible campaigns almost everywhere. Third, every visible campaign has a spillover effect in adjoining constituencies. In Saskatchewan I always stressed the need for high-profile sign campaigns in both the safe and the near-hopeless seats, as well as in the hotly contested seats, because the overall provincewide effect was important.

In any case, it isn't that expensive to run a highly visible campaign. You have the provincewide television and radio spots run a trailer giving the local candidate's name: 'In Wellington Centre, vote Susan Sparrow.' You wage a vigorous lawn and pole sign campaign, and have a pamphlet introducing the candidate dropped into mailboxes by volunteers or young people. You also place a few advertisements in local or community newspapers. All of this can be done quite cheaply, and is well worth the effort for its effect on party supporters in the constituency and for its spillover effect on voters in neighbouring constituencies and across the province.

Part Two

The Public Service

8

The Responsibilities of Deputy Ministers

This chapter deals with the implications of *the speech* for deputy ministers. We discuss why co-ordination by deputy ministers themselves is preferable to central agency co-ordination, and how recent developments in management theory and practice support this. We look at ways to encourage deputy ministers to resolve co-ordination problems on their own. Another corporate responsibility of a deputy minister is to ensure that the minister's actions are consistent with the government's overall program, and we suggest ways to go about this diplomatically. We then discuss the expectations a minister should have of his or her deputy – especially the issue of political sensitivity. When a new government takes office, it may be necessary to reassign deputies, and we discuss how this may be done. Finally, we consider how long a deputy should serve in a given ministry, making reference to the experience of the federal government.

Borins: In previous chapters about the cabinet, we occasionally mentioned the public service, because the political and administrative realms often intersect. We will start this section of the book with a discussion of deputy ministers, who must manage the intersection between the two realms. The authors of *Yes Minister* talk about the clash between the 'political will and the administrative won't.'[1] I'm sure your objective was to prevent such open conflict from taking place by getting the political and administrative arms of government to work together.

A good way to begin discussing common values would be with the version of *the speech* that you would deliver to deputy ministers. For them, what are the implications of collective responsibility?

Blakeney: Ministers have to wear two different hats – they are advocates for their ministry, and they are also judges within the cabinet as a whole. Deputy ministers have to wear the same two hats. The difference is that ministers do this at the policy-making level, while deputy ministers do this at the administrative level. As I said in *the speech*, government doesn't have a general manager. As a consequence, deputy ministers have to work together to be the government's collective general manager.

Borins: The implication is that deputy ministers should be doing a lot of the co-ordinating of government among themselves. What happens if they can't or won't?

Blakeney: Then you've got real problems. If they can't do it, then the cabinet ministers and ultimately the premier may have to get involved in sorting out their conflicts, and this is a total waste of our time. It's important for them to recognize how busy we are and how limited our time is. It is vital that we not be involved in administration – if we were, we wouldn't have enough time for our job, which is the political task of linking the public with the government.

Consider the position of a cabinet if one department makes a recommendation that probably affects other departments and other budgets. I'll give a very simple example. I can recall a recommendation that the province declare a day in February as a provincial holiday – Heritage Day, I believe it was to be called. The recommendation suggested that there would be few financial implications. I think the first question at cabinet related to the potential cost to hospitals if this involved paying overtime. This point was not covered in the memo and apparently had not been thought through and costed. I believe we suggested that the proposal be reviewed with other agencies. The initiating department could co-ordinate this review, or the staff to the Treasury Board, the Budget Bureau, could do so on their behalf. In any case, the initiating department understood that it was responsible for the initial co-ordination processes before the matter came back to cabinet.

The alternative to deputies doing much of the co-ordinating is to create central agencies to sort out interdepartmental conflict. In most cases this is the wrong approach, for a number of reasons. First, people in central agencies can never have as much knowledge in specific subject areas as deputy ministers. Second, central agencies tend to be control-oriented rather than service-oriented. Controls are necessary but not a government's main mission. Third, referring matters to central agencies almost always builds in delays and frequently fails to respond to reasonable program deadlines. Fourth, involving central agencies subtly reduces the deputy's responsibility for the success of a program design. Fifth and finally, extensive use of central agencies puts a premium on deputies' understanding the techniques of dealing with control-oriented central agencies rather than those dealing with other deputies who can be expected to have service goals. Anything that puts a premium on managing the system rather than managing a program should be discouraged.

I felt that a small provincial government should have as few permanent central agencies as possible, and should insist that deputies assume as much responsibility as possible for sorting out conflicts and overlapping jurisdictions among agencies.

In the next chapter, I'll say much more about the central agencies that are clearly essential.

Borins: I would reply in one word to your sermon about central agencies: 'Amen!' When you look at trends in management, in both the public and the private sector, over the last decade or so, it becomes clear that central controls have fallen out of favour. In the private sector, Peters and Waterman, in *In Search of Excellence*, argued that excellent firms kept their central corporate staff lean and relied heavily on strong corporate values as a means for co-ordinating of their various business units.[2] Studies of public and private management in Japan have found that co-ordination in that country is achieved through the instilling of corporate values rather than through the specific efforts of central agency staff.[3]

Improved information technology has facilitated this trend. Much more information is now available to all workers in any organization – a phenomenon Zuboff called informating (in contrast to automating).[4] This makes it possible for everyone in the organization to be aware of the big picture and to understand how their activities are part of that big picture. Thus, shared values, rather than central control, can become the factor that brings about co-ordinated action. A second result of improved information technology is delayering, or reducing the number of managers (whether staff or line) between the CEO and the front-line worker.[5]

The same trend toward informal co-ordination is apparent in governments all over the world. The Trudeau era was the high-water mark of strong central agencies in Canada.[6] John Turner's decision to disband the Ministries of State for Social and Economic Development marked the turning point. Public Service 2000, the federal government's exercise in renewal, had as one of its main elements the reduction of central agency controls, particularly those of the Treasury Board Secretariat.[7] In the United States, Osborne and Gaebler have also emphasized decentralization and reduction of central controls as one of the key elements of 'reinventing government,' and this has also become a major theme of the American federal government's reinvention initiatives.[8] Finally, the Organization for Economic Cooperation and Development, which watches trends in administrative reform in the economically advanced countries, also observes that the relationship between central agencies and operating departments is being characterized increasingly by consultation and co-operation, rather than command and control.[9] So I think you should have the satisfaction of knowing that your government was in the vanguard of this trend.

At the provincial government level, the Ontario government led by Premier William Davis experimented with 'policy fields' in the early 1970s. Davis created three policy fields – that is, subject-area committees of cabinet. Each was chaired by a senior minister, who was given no departmental responsibilities, and each was served by a secretariat. Edward Stewart, in his book about the Ontario government, described how the departments became disenchanted with this structure because of the delays it created and because too much effort was channelled into managing the system rather than programs. Gradually, this system was dismantled, and a simpler cabinet and central agency structure evolved that was much more like the one in Saskatchewan.[10]

The argument against central agency co-ordination was made on a theoretical level some years ago by the American political scientist Charles Lindblom, who expounded the virtues of what he called 'parametric mutual adjustment.' This is a system of decentralized decision-making in which actors (such as government departments) take into account the consequences of their actions on other actors. Lindblom considered this a much more efficient practice than co-ordination through an omniscient central decision maker.[11] I'm sure you would find his theory compatible with your practice.

Given that you wanted to avoid central agency co-ordination, what techniques did you use to encourage deputy ministers to co-ordinate their activities on their own?

Blakeney: One technique was to have my deputy who looked after government operations issues (as opposed to long-term planning or political issues) arrange for the deputies whose agencies were in apparent conflict to meet, along with a junior staffer from a central agency who would take minutes and record the points of agreement and disagreement. This put some subtle pressure on all parties to define the problem and to separate the problem from the egos of the protagonists. Sometimes, if the problem appeared intractable, my deputy filled the third-party role. The reputation of being a stubborn turf defender was not one that led to favour with the cabinet, and the deputies knew this. So problems tended to be solved.

Another technique was to ask the deputies whose agencies were in conflict to discuss their problems together and then write to me or to my deputy a joint memo telling me their areas of agreement and disagreement. Then each was asked to outline his or her side of the disagreement and the reasons why this position was the best course of action for the government. Usually the deputies could sort out their disagreements. It is interesting how often deputies' disputes can be resolved when the inability to find a solution must be defended before the premier or his deputy.

As I have often said, in a small government the problems of organization cannot be totally separated from the problems of personalities and skills of the administrators. Sometimes the unofficial comment from the deputy was along these lines: 'I want my agency to do this job. I know that in theoretical terms it makes more sense for agency X to do the job. But if it is given to agency X they will assign it to Jones, and from experience I know that Jones could not organize a two-car parade. So, if the job is to be done, our agency is going to have to do it.' This outlined the problem for my deputy, whose task in the short term was to get the job done but whose task in the longer term was to see if the assessment of Jones' organizing ability was accurate and, if it was, to deal with that problem.

Sometimes interagency disputes take on a life of their own. I can remember one case that was something of a classic when I was Minister of Health.[12] We had a problem with the delivery of health services to welfare recipients where the general welfare program was delivered municipally. The health services were budgeted for by the Department of Health, and rendered to recipients who qualified according to Department of Welfare regulations, but actually delivered by municipal government as part of a package of welfare services. The problems seemed endless and intractable. I finally got someone from the planning central agency to get the three deputies into one room and insist that they come up with a workable solution for the government as a whole. This case displayed as many turf protectors and people who had backed themselves into a corner as any case I ever encountered later. The departmental representatives seemed to want a central agency to impose a solution so that they could each have a glorious defeat rather than a grubby compromise. When this occurs, it indicates that the larger interest has been lost. I learned some lessons from this incident that I carried with me when I was Premier.

Borins: This isn't very different from the practice of effective private-sector managers, who encourage their subordinates to resolve their disputes internally. For example, IBM constructs some of its budgets by negotiation among interested divisions and departments. Disputes are resolved by a central management committee only when divisions cannot agree among themselves. The costs of escalating conflict readily become apparent to the divisions, especially if their positions are inconsistent with corporate objectives and policies.[13]

Did your government have any formal or informal mechanism for getting deputy ministers together? Was your organizational culture strong enough to make it happen?

Blakeney: Yes, we had formal meetings of deputy ministers. These tended to be in the late afternoon and concluded with a social hour. They were used to explain such things as broad budget strategy, for example, 'Cabinet's budget planning will be based on an austerity model with no growth in staff,' or 'Our emphasis will be on broadening our economic base with few new social programs.' I gave my standard speech, complete with charts, on more than one occasion preaching the gospels of co-ordination at the deputy level and of deputies not involving their ministers in administrative and management matters. Of course, I also said that I was proud of our public service, and grateful to them for what they were doing for the people of Saskatchewan and for making Saskatchewan's public service as good as any in the country.

Borins: Once again, just as in cabinet, you were communicating the core values of the organization.

It's interesting that the larger governments, in particular the federal government and Ontario, have in recent years created formal Deputy Ministers' Councils. These are weekly meetings at which the cabinet secretary keeps all deputy ministers up to date about the government's major priorities. Those meetings are also opportunities for deputy ministers to co-ordinate issues of overlapping jurisdiction. It is indicative of the new thinking in Ottawa that the Public Service 2000 was spearheaded by task forces of deputy ministers and assistant deputy ministers rather than by central agencies.

This form of co-ordination is an alternative to central agency co-ordination and suggests that there is less reliance on central agencies now than in the Trudeau era. For example, when Prime Minister John Turner shut down the Ministries of State for Social Development and Economic Development, he also shut down the committees of deputy ministers that mirrored the cabinet committees in these areas. The Mulroney government took this a step further by requiring all departments to ensure that their proposals received adequate and appropriate interdepartmental consultation before being sent to cabinet, and the Chrétien government continues to follow this approach.[14]

Let's now shift to the deputy ministers' responsibilities in managing their own departments. In this context, what should a minister expect from an effective deputy minister?

Blakeney: Effective and sensitive management in the context of the public service has many aspects. But in general terms, as a minister, I would expect the deputy to run the department well in an administrative sense, to take full part in collegial management with his or her fellow deputy ministers and other senior public servants, to consult me on policy matters, and to give me ample warning of impending problems.

I would also expect my deputy to consult me on any step that represented a new or changed direction; or had substantial public impact; or required the department to change its mission, organization, or financing or to consult with external groups in a significant way. Policy matters, in this context, also include steps that, while minor in administrative and broad policy terms, can be expected to generate public or media controversy.

There is a closely related function I would expect the deputy to perform, which is to keep me informed of decisions being made by the department that are important but that do not fall into the category of policy as I've already defined it. A minister has a need to *know* that is much broader than any need to *be consulted*. The distinction is important. As I've said before, the minister should not allow the information flow to be accompanied by a request for comments. This blurs the line between consultation and providing information and is just another technique for co-opting the minister.

The minister's need to know stems from the fact that a surprising number of people who have never been involved in a large-scale organization expect the minister to be aware of almost everything that is happening in the department. It adds to the minister's comfort level if he or she has enough knowledge of what is happening to respond reasonably intelligently when a microphone is stuck in his or her face and a question is asked about a subject of some considerable local interest.

Drawing the line between policy issues requiring prior consultation and other issues requiring ex post information is not easy. The minister and the deputy work out a relationship. I advised ministers that any erring should be on the side of the deputy deciding and informing – in other words, that the deputy can and should make the decision on the close calls. Ministers' time is a resource that needs to be husbanded. A minister should be able to feel that, because the deputy has a good understanding of the political realities of the minister's world, this approach can be used at only modest political risk.

Borins: In one of your speeches some years ago, you very vividly pointed out how a minister could benefit from having a deputy who was sensitive to the impact on the public of changes in departmental policy. Let me quote from it:

Let me contrast my experience as a minister of two departments. In one case, the senior public servants appeared to consider that it was not a part of their function to be tuned in on how the public was reacting to the department's programs. As minister of this department, I frequently found delegations on my doorstep raising problems – sometimes raising hell – with respect to matters on which the officials could give me no prior knowledge, information, or advice.

In the second department, the officials, and particularly the permanent head, had an intelligence system that was marvellous to behold. Here it was a rare day when a delegation met me as minister where the deputy had been unable to brief me in advance on what position the delegation was likely to take, and not infrequently what position individual members of the delegation would assume.

I remember well one of those rare occasions. I had received a telegram from a community called Rama, a small Saskatchewan village of some 260 souls. The occasion for the telegram was one which made my deputy scratch his head. We discovered that a public meeting had been held at which there was strong opposition to some action the department was preparing to take which affected that community, and a resolution had been passed opposing it. The comment of my deputy following the meeting was, 'How in blazes could that organization pass a resolution in opposition to our program without my fieldman knowing about it and letting me know?'[15]

Edward Stewart, former Cabinet Secretary to the Ontario government, made the same point:

To me, the notion that you can keep administrative responsibilities and political considerations in distinct compartments at the highest levels of decision-making, including many of the responsibilities which involve the deputy, is naïve and non-productive ... a deputy who claims that political considerations never influence his or her thinking, or the advice he or she is giving to the government, is either trying to deceive the public or is of limited value to the Premier and Ministers whom he or she serves.[16]

You have told us what a minister should expect of the deputy. Did you as Premier have any expectations of deputies?

Blakeney: We have spoken of the collegial management function. I have noted that deputies in our government were not appointed directly by ministers, and this underlines what the deputies' obligations were to the Premier and cabinet. A deputy who felt that a minister was pursuing a policy at odds with government policy was expected to raise this matter discreetly with the Cabinet Secretary or the Deputy Minister to the Premier. This didn't happen often, but as Premier I needed some protection against a minister who was becoming too entrepreneurial.

When it did happen, I would see if I could get the issue before Treasury Board, or some other cabinet committee where the minister's colleagues could question the course of action. This dealt with the situation without requiring that I become involved and 'pull rank.' Occasionally I would have to ask the minister for a report and then refer the matter to cabinet or a cabinet committee for some collegial guidance. I tried to avoid dealing directly with the deputies, because this put them and the minister in an awkward position. But my senior people regularly monitored what was occurring in those departments where a minister was showing more drive than judgment.

Borins: Deputy ministers are order-in-council appointments, and serve at the pleasure of cabinet. It was you who ultimately appointed and dismissed them. One of the key issues that any new government faces is whether to keep the deputy ministers who served the previous government. How did you handle that?

Blakeney: An immediate point needs to be made. There is a major distinction between retaining a deputy in the position he or she had when the government changed, and retaining the deputy in the public service in a position of comparable rank. In 1971 we dispensed with the services of two or three people of deputy rank. They had been politically active and had expected to fall with the government. The tradition of political activity or political neutrality among deputies varies from province to province, and in Saskatchewan, from deputy to deputy. Of the deputies who had not been politically active, we felt that several would not be able to assist us fully in the policy directions we wished to take, either because they had lost the drive a new activist government needs or because they had too many doubts about our policy directions. After some changes of government, some deputies may feel that their job is to save the province from the policy errors the new government is about to make. Frequently, deputies who do not fit the new government's plans in their present posts cannot and should not be fired. A witch hunt by a new government can create an unfavourable reaction with the public and may well damage morale in the public service. If a deputy has been a faithful and competent public servant, there will be a general feeling that he or she should not be fired simply because he or she doesn't fit in with the plans of the new government. Furthermore, if firing deputies upon a change of government becomes the norm, any new government will have more difficulty recruiting good people as deputies.

Our approach was to reassign deputies.[17] As an example, when we assumed office we had extensive plans for changes in the area of justice. These included establishing a Human Rights Commission, a Human Rights Code, an Ombudsman, and an independent Constituency Boundaries commission. The Deputy Attorney General was a fine public servant, but he was nearing retirement, and we felt he was probably not the person to organize these changes as rapidly as we wanted them made. And we anticipated that constitutional issues were going to become more important on the public agenda during the 1970s because of Prime Minister Trudeau's keen interest in them. So we organized a constitutional secretariat and named the Deputy Attorney General to head it. He was a fine constitutional lawyer. He set about organizing our research in this area, which stood us in very good stead as we moved into a series of major constitutional cases and some extensive federal–provincial negotiations. In fact, the deputy stayed on for several years past normal retirement age and, so far as I am aware, did not resent being moved from his post. (His replacement was a very able younger lawyer who is now a judge of the Supreme Court of British Columbia.)

As I have suggested, in some cases we established new agencies to undertake special projects, and the deputies we wished to move were fully qualified to run them. In other cases, departmental reorganizations created positions to which it was reasonable to appoint the existing deputies. We felt that sensitivity on this matter – including taking a little time to make the appropriate transitions – paid good dividends in staff morale.

Borins: A related issue is that of how long deputy ministers should serve in any one department. What was your preference there?

Blakeney: I found it difficult to establish any hard and fast rules. In a small provincial government, some deputies are really specialists who have learned to manage and some are generalists who have acquired some technical knowledge. Governments are gradually moving away from the specialist model, as are hospitals, nursing homes, and even law firms. But our deputies were not all generalists. The considerations that applied to moving a generalist deputy might not have applied to the specialists.

Here are some observations. There is a learning curve. It usually takes a deputy a couple of years to get to know a department and the publics with which it deals. It may take less time if the deputy previously served as, say, assistant deputy in the same department. In general, deputies should serve at least two years, though I think even that is too short – I would say that a reasonable minimum is three or four years. After that, other considerations should come into play. Does the deputy need a new challenge? Have you had a cabinet shuffle, and are the minister and deputy no longer a good match because of a personality clash, or because together they represent too much talent concentrated in that particular department, or too little, or the wrong mix? Deputies tend to be financial or economic deputies – 'hard side' deputies in bureaucratic parlance – or, say, health or social services deputies, who are 'soft side' deputies. A few quite remarkable people could be deputy of any department and would be as acceptable to the Saskatchewan Licensed Practical Nurses Association as to the Dominion Bond Rating Service. But such people are rare.

Borins: That thinking is akin to private sector notions that executives are most effective when they stay within one functional area – for example, technology or marketing strategy – when moving from one firm to another.

On average, how long did deputies in your government stay in their positions?

Blakeney: Averages can be a little deceiving. But allowing for that, and commencing with the deputies we appointed or who were in place one year after we assumed office, the average length of service was about three years.

Borins: Your position is certainly consistent with that of Gordon Osbaldeston, who compiled statistics showing that in the past twenty-five years the average tenure of a federal deputy minister in a department has fallen from 4.5 to 2 years. Over the same period, the percentage of federal deputy ministers who have spent three or more years with their current department has fallen from 40 per cent to 6.5 per cent. Osbaldeston was quite scathing in his criticism of this state of affairs, in that it leads to deputy ministers working with incomplete information, prevents ministers and their deputies from forming strong bonds and cohesive teams, reduces departmental accountability, and may result in the department being balkanized into unintegrated fiefdoms managed by assistant deputy ministers. He then contrasted this practice with that of the private sector and found that the typical CEO generally has spent more time with the company before becoming CEO and serves longer as CEO. Indeed, CEOs 'were generally astonished at the turnover rate among federal deputies and could not understand how government could operate under such conditions.'[18]

In my study of the Japanese senior bureaucracy, I found that deputy ministers and ministers served short terms of only a year or two; but the fact that senior bureaucrats spent their entire careers within one department meant that the Japanese bureaucracy still had the advantages of continuity and organizational memory. Again, contrast this with the situation in Ottawa, where not only deputy ministers but other senior officials move rapidly from department to department.[19]

So we end this part of our discussion on a note of criticism of Ottawa – a note you have on occasion played – and move back to the virtues of the Saskatchewan way of doing government, at least in a smaller province.

9

Central Agencies: Only the Minimum

This chapter focuses on the central agencies in the Blakeney government: the Premier's Office, the Executive Council, the Department of Finance, and the Public Service Commission. The work of the planning unit of the Executive Council is described in detail, and its value is assessed. It is then compared with the planning unit in the Douglas-Lloyd government. The Department of Intergovernmental Affairs is also discussed. (The Department of Finance is described in more detail in Chapters 10 and 11, and the Public Service Commission in Chapter 12.)

Borins: Throughout our discussion to this point, you have been arguing the case for informal co-ordination, both within cabinet and among deputy ministers. But the fact is that some functions are best co-ordinated by a central agency rather than informally. Let's go through the central agencies you did have, looking at their rationale and functions. Why don't we start with the Premier's Office and Executive Council?

Blakeney: The Executive Council, along with the Premier's Office, performed several functions. There was the purely administrative function, which had to do with processing orders-in-council and other formal documents. The Cabinet Secretary, as discussed in Chapter 3, provided support and co-ordination for cabinet members individually and collectively.

The Deputy Minister to the Premier was responsible for administering my office. This involved, among other things, dealing with mail, schedules, congratulatory messages, and greetings, and preparations for most governmental speeches (as opposed to political ones). He also acted as my representative in dealings with the public service. This frequently involved considering departmental reorganizations, monitoring preparations for major new programs, and keeping in touch on my behalf with Finance, the Crown Investments Corporation, and other key agencies. He also did general firefighting.

The Principal Secretary to the Premier was my chief political adviser and was responsible for relations with ministers in a political sense, with caucus, and with the party, and for generally assessing the political acceptability of the government's performance. He gave direction to the cabinet press officer and prepared speeches of a political nature.

The Chief Planning Officer headed the economic advisory and planning unit of the government and supervised the staff to the cabinet's Planning Committee.

During the last couple of years, I had a staff development deputy who helped select executive staff and also organized senior staff training and career development. I did not regard this as necessarily a permanent arrangement, but it utilized the skills of a very senior and very wise public servant, who proceeded to get the best out of our senior and junior executive staff.

In 1972 the Executive Council had a staff of fifty, not including constitutional and intergovernmental staff. By 1982 this group had seventy-five staff on board, of whom eighteen were in the planning unit.[1]

When I reviewed the changes in organization over the decade, I noted a phenomenon that often is found in a small unit: an organizational structure tends to change so as to adapt to the special skills of the senior staff. That is not a bad thing; after all, organizations don't get things done – *people* do. The purpose of an organization is to allow people to work more productively. If it can be tailored to the people involved, so much the better.

I'm not sure the principle is confined to small organizations. There must be some reason why some chartered banks are so byzantine in structure. An acquaintance of mine once told me that he wanted to send notes of congratulation to friends of his who had been promoted in the course of a management shuffle at a chartered bank. His problem was that while he knew who had been moved, he couldn't be sure just who had been promoted and whether a move from senior executive vice-president to one of several deputy chairmen was a move up, down, or sideways. He considered heading his congratulations 'To whom it may concern.' In the end, he abandoned the project altogether.

I can't help but feel that such an organization is designed to cluster people around the CEO's office with duties that can be varied depending on the special skills or claims to preferment of the incumbents.

A further point worth making about the Executive Council staff is that for us there appeared to be no right way to organize the planning function of the government. We started with a planning unit headed by a senior person who reported directly to me in my capacity as Premier and as chair of the cabinet's Planning Committee. At another point, we had the planning unit report to the Deputy Minister to the Premier. At still another time we considered having the unit report to the Cabinet Secretary.

The planning unit included the Saskatchewan Bureau of Statistics. At various times we considered moving this unit either to Finance or to Industry and Commerce. The planning unit also included a number of macroeconomists who did the economic forecasting upon which a number of programs were based. There were suggestions that these people be transferred to Finance, which is where they are located in some other governments. I opposed transferring the economic forecasting unit to Finance. Economic forecasting is partly a science, partly an art. I felt that if they were in Finance, the forecasters would be steeped in the caution that does (and perhaps should) shape the thinking of tax gatherers. I wanted caution to be applied near the end of the forecasting process, not earlier, when it would have shaped the inputs at all stages. Some of the public servants felt that my concerns were overdrawn, and that in a small government it made the most sense to have all long-range forecasters in Finance, along with the short-range forecasters who were necessarily there to do the job of budget formulation.

Borins: Could you tell us more about the types of issues the planning unit was involved in? If the departments had their own planning units, what was the relationship between the cabinet planning unit and these units?

Blakeney: The staff of the cabinet planning unit performed a number of functions. As I have noted, they established and maintained a number of statistical bases, largely through our Bureau of Statistics. This supplemented the work that Statistics Canada does at the federal level. They also made the economic forecasts upon which our revenue estimates were based. This was important work and not as simple as it may sound. It involved estimating future personal and corporate income levels to arrive at estimates of yields from income and sales taxes and so on. Estimating wage and salary income is relatively straight going; estimating future farm and resource income is anything but simple. Some other revenue estimates are equally daunting, in that they involve calculating the future level of economic activity in Ontario manufacturing and British Columbia forest production so as to forecast per capita yields from various types of taxation in those provinces, all in order to estimate whether Saskatchewan will be entitled to payments under the federal–provincial equalization program and, if so, how much and when. The federal government regularly supplied estimates, but the program is of such mind-boggling complexity, and there are opportunities for so many judgment calls, that it behooves any province to have the capacity to check, and if necessary challenge, the federal estimates. The staffs of the planning unit and Finance performed this function together.[2]

We also had economists who made themselves expert in agricultural production and farm income, keeping abreast of conditions worldwide that were likely to affect farm production, prices, and income. They were conversant with issues of farm ownership and farm debt, and with other matters likely to present problems in the decade ahead. The unit had demographers who tried to estimate population growth and decline, both rural and urban, by age groups and the like. There were economists who concentrated on resource production and marketing and on manufacturing, as well as 'soft side' people whose fields were education, health and welfare, and so on.

The various departments of government had planning units as well, although some were quite weak. The cabinet planning unit worked in concert with these units. Thus, when our government was attempting to estimate the likely number of students in postsecondary educational institutions five years hence, the Department of Continuing Education and the cabinet planning unit did their own estimates and then tried to reconcile them for presentation to, say, a cabinet planning conference. The fact that economic forecasting is an inexact science is illustrated by the fact that all of the forecasters in the government and the universities substantially underestimated the number of people who would seek to enter our universities in the late 1970s.

As another illustration of its work, the planning unit developed a long-term housing policy based on estimates of demographic shifts, rates of family formation, levels of disposable income, and other components of future housing demand. Based on the model, the planning unit drew conclusions regarding the need for different types of units in different locations. Both social need and effective demand were considered. We were particularly interested in housing for several reasons. One obvious one was that adequate and affordable housing makes a major contribution to social well-being. Another was that residential construction plays a role in generating employment: it is perhaps the easiest lever a provincial government can pull to increase or decrease economic activity.

Another factor that we considered was rent control. We had introduced residential rent control at the time that national wage and price controls were introduced in 1975. We found that when this program was dismantled federally and provincially, we were not able to dismantle residential rent controls. By the same token, I felt strongly that it was not going to be possible to maintain them unless enough new units were brought into the market to virtually eliminate the scarcity component of rent increases. We did not apply controls to any units built after 1975. As to units existing in 1975, we attempted to deal with increased costs that landlords faced by allowing rent increases. We responded to the pressure to circumvent controls that arises in any scarcity situation by encouraging construction, particularly in the low-rental and senior-citizens' housing sectors, where market forces cannot be relied on to create sufficient supply. We also got very heavily into the land assembly business, in partnership with the municipal governments, so that scarcity of land for residential construction would not be a significant factor. I've expanded on this function at some length because our planning people gave a good deal of support to the Saskatchewan Housing Corporation, which was the delivery mechanism of much of our housing policy.

In organizational terms, the planning unit maintained data bases for governmental and nongovernmental use, and pursued major projects for the cabinet's Planning Committee. In co-operation with other departments, it also prepared annual, five-year, and sometimes ten-year projections for a whole range of matters, some of which I referred to earlier. These were available for cabinet to consider at its cabinet planning conferences, which were held so that the cabinet and Treasury Board could arrive at a fiscal and policy framework for drafting the annual budget. (We will discuss budget planning in the next chapter.)

Borins: The literature on planning cites two dangers for such planning offices. On the one hand, they can get immersed in long-run social and demographic trends or various other forms of 'futures' forecasting, producing work that is interesting but politically irrelevant. (This is what happened to the planners in the federal Privy Council Office in 1968–72, and again in 1974–5, after a Trudeau majority government was elected again.)[3] On the other hand, they can get totally involved in firefighting, which is exceedingly relevant but not really planning. Did this office succumb to either problem? Or was it able to produce politically relevant long-range plans? That is, plans relevant to your government's mandate.

Blakeney: Our planning unit was kept relevant in the shorter term by its close involvement in the annual budgeting process. Since this process involved five-year projections by departments as well as annual budget requests, there was some consideration of the longer term. But we politicians did not study the five-year projections with the same care as the annual budget unless they revealed very 'lumpy' increases that differed sharply from normal incremental trend lines.

Some of the longer-range work done in special areas was well done and relevant. What we did *not* manage to develop was a small team of planners who were tuned in to the cabinet's thinking sufficiently well that they could offer an overview of all the major issues the province would likely confront and then recommend ways that cabinet might respond to them. This was largely because after the first five or six years in office, our government's objectives became less clear – or at least the policies we wanted to pursue to reach those objectives became less clear.

The broad general objectives were clear enough – economic diversification, getting the greatest possible financial return from resource development, encouraging greater participation by Saskatchewan firms and people in economic activity ('We Can Do It Ourselves'), and promoting the widest possible distribution of economic well-being and social influence among Saskatchewan's people ('Fair Shares for All in a Free Society'). In the 1960s a well-known Canadian journalist, Jeannine Locke, had written that 'in no place on earth are the good things of life more evenly distributed than they are in Saskatchewan.' I often used this quote, asserting that if it was not true with respect to the world, I felt it was true with respect to North America, and that we wished to strengthen this aspect of our society.

So the broad objectives were clear. But in the early years we knew not only where we wanted to go but how we wanted to get there; in the later years we became less certain about means. I don't know whether we could reasonably have expected a planning unit to formulate broad program options for us, since we could no longer offer them precise direction. In any case, we received a number of discrete program proposals but no comprehensive plan of action.

Borins: I think it would be useful to compare the planning unit in the Douglas government with that of your own. In 1946 the Douglas government established an Economic Advisory and Planning Board, composed of four senior ministers and two cabinet advisers. The first chair was George Cadbury, an economic planner who came to Saskatchewan from Britain. The EAPB had wide-ranging powers to advise the Premier on policy issues, to formulate a long-term economic plan for the province, and to oversee the activities of Crown corporations as well as the government's budget. The EAPB's mandate for economic planning owed much to CCF ideology, which placed great importance on a planned economy, and also to the poor performance of many departments in the first eighteen months of the Douglas government.[4]

In the early years of the Douglas government, the EAPB was 'the most dynamic and forceful agency in the government – its influence was felt in every department and Crown corporation.'[5] It was involved in broad economic development planning and sectoral economic studies, especially in such areas as resource development, agriculture, and industrial diversification. Some studies it undertook on its own; others it conducted jointly with relevant department(s).[6]

Over time, the EAPB's role diminished. Budgeting was handed over to the Treasury; Crown corporations were given to the new Government Finance Office. In the matter of planning, the EAPB saw itself as a standards setter for other departments to emulate; as a consequence, in the late 1940s and early 1950s it began to step back as the various departments expanded their research and planning capabilities.[7]

The pattern here – a once-powerful central agency moving to the sidelines –

seems to foreshadow the role you intended for central agencies. I also notice that your central planning apparatus – cabinet's Planning Committee and the cabinet planning unit – was not as powerful as the EAPB in the Douglas–Lloyd era.

Now, could you briefly introduce the two other major central agencies? These, of course, were the Department of Finance and the Public Service Commission. We will discuss them in more detail in the next two chapters.

Blakeney: The Department of Finance had a wide range of functions. The largest number of staff were engaged in collecting revenue. This function was taken over by the new Department of Revenue, Supply, and Services in 1978. There were also the usual pre-audit and accounts payable functions, and debt management functions dealing with bond issues and redemptions, sinking funds, and money market operations. Functions that might be thought of as belonging more directly to a central agency were those dealing with taxation and fiscal policy, government budgeting, governmentwide organizational procedures and methods, and personnel management. (The latter function was shared with the Public Service Commission.) Finance worked with the cabinet planning unit in developing fiscal forecasts and overall fiscal policy. Those two groups were the government's designated agencies in dealing with federal–provincial fiscal arrangements.

A couple of years ago I did a check on how many federal–provincial agreements there were involving spending–usually federal spending in areas of provincial or shared legislative jurisdiction. The number was well over two hundred. I don't know how many agreements Saskatchewan had with the federal government in the 1970s, but even then it would have been many dozens. Equalization agreements and those relating to sharing the costs of postsecondary education and health and welfare programs involved hundreds of millions of dollars a year for Saskatchewan.

The Budget Bureau was the section of Finance that served as staff to the Treasury Board. The bureau's functions were these: to review and analyse departmental budget submissions; with the cabinet planning unit, to analyse and evaluate programs to see if they were the best way to achieve the government's policy objectives; to work with departments to improve their budget submissions; to develop and improve performance measurements, on both an input and an output basis; and generally to assist Treasury Board in its duties as the government's financial gatekeeper.[8] I'll say more on this in the next chapter.

Finance also had an organization-and-methods unit that did studies for departments on organizational problems, developed and improved organizational systems, and tried to make the organizational ideas developed by one agency available to other agencies. It also began to introduce data processing systems in the government.

Eventually, this data processing activity led to the creation of a systems centre, which was transferred to the new Department of Revenue, Supply, and Services, along with central purchasing, the central vehicle agency (which operated the government's vehicle fleet), and some other common services.

Finally, Finance had some personnel and staff training functions.

Borins: Since the discussion has turned to personnel matters, could you discuss the Public Service Commission and outline how it shared the personnel function with the Department of Finance?

Blakeney: In 1947 the Douglas government introduced legislation that set up an independent Public Service Commission. Job descriptions were developed, and a system of competitions was introduced for positions in the classified public service.[9] This was a huge change for Saskatchewan, which till then had had a patronage-driven public service, common in many governments at that time.[10] Patronage still exists in some provinces. Just a few years ago a senior person in Nova Scotia gave his opinion that when the voters voted out a government, they not only wanted a change of Highways Minister but a change of highway maintenance workers as well.

Borins: I think the operating principle was, 'If it moves, pension it; if it doesn't, pave it.'

Blakeney: The system that Saskatchewan adopted in 1947 – and it was largely unchanged in the 1970s – set up procedures for fair competitions. For a given position, the PSC certified three qualified applicants, from which the employing agency could choose one. When I was pressured to find a job for the relative of an undoubtedly worthy citizen, I asked my political staff to watch out for competitions for which the would-be employee could apply. The potential exercise of patronage was restricted largely to some temporary appointments and some appointments of out-of-scope employees who were not in the classified service.

This meant that most appointments for all agencies were made through the PSC. The commission set the standards and ran examinations and tests for stenographic and clerical employees. It also evaluated the qualifications of applicants for other positions to determine whether the requirements contained in the job description were met.

The Finance Department did not deal with personnel issues in the rank-and-file public service. It confined itself to recruiting, running courses, and doing some career planning for management trainees. I'll say more about this in Chapter 12 in the context of human resource management.

Borins: Where was the line drawn between PSC appointments and order-in-council appointments?

Blakeney: Senior people were order-in-council appointments. This included deputies, assistant and associate deputies, and some other senior people. When we came to office, we found quite a few people outside the classified service – that is, who had been appointed by order-in-council though they did not need to be. We set about to regularize the system, and to a considerable extent we did so.

Then we fell into the practice of using order-in-council appointments in order to speed up appointments and so that a specific offer could be made to someone we wanted to attract to the public service. Sometimes this was followed by a competition, and sometimes it was not. This practice rarely involved employees within the scope of union agreements. The public service unions would have objected, and rightly so.

However, it did happen with out-of-scope employees. The reason for skirting the PSC regulations in this way was rarely one of patronage. The usual problem was that a good person was available but was unwilling to wait until the competition was advertised and all procedures completed. This is not a very good excuse; but I can well understand why a deputy, seeking a good employee, would try to get him or her by whatever means possible, and why the cabinet followed the path of least resistance. Procedures that guarantee impartiality usually guarantee substantial delay. This is a serious and largely unresolved problem in public sector management. By the end of our time in office we had not resolved it.

Borins: It is understandable that public servants would arrange an order-in-council appointment when they thought it necessary in order to attract a certain 'high flier' to Saskatchewan. After all, as we will discuss in Chapter 12, attracting these people was an important part of your government's approach to human resource management, as it was for the Douglas and Lloyd governments before you. On the other hand, your government's use of order-in-council appointments made it easier for Grant Devine, your successor, to purge the public service of these people in 1982.[11]

The PSC should also protect the public service from that close cousin of political patronage, namely, nepotism.

Blakeney: Very much so. Most of the nepotism was with respect to temporary summer jobs. Frequently, summer jobs were not filled through the PSC but directly by departments. My office watched carefully for appointments of relatives of cabinet members and MLAs. There is simply no reason to anger voters by appointing sons and daughters of politicians for summer jobs in, say, the provincial parks. Those voters have sons and daughters who are looking for summer jobs, and who may well be more deserving than relatives of – so many people think – well-paid politicians. The more difficult problem for us was to eliminate nepotism in the public service – the sort of thing where, by the efficient operation of an old-boy network, sons and daughters of senior managers seemed to get summer jobs readily, although not in the agencies where the parents were employed. I felt that public service patronage was more common and harder to spot than political patronage. The public expects and accepts nepotism in the private sector but, rightly, objects to it in government, whether it involves politicians or public servants.

Borins: What other central agencies operated in your government?

Blakeney: The Office of Intergovernmental Affairs – later to become the Department of Intergovernmental Affairs – was similar to a central agency. Early in our term we sought to bring some formality to Saskatchewan's style of intergovernmental relations. (Premier Thatcher, my predecessor, had taken a highly personal approach to them.) The Saskatchewan Federal–Provincial Agreements Act of 1972 provided that our Department of Finance must approve the financial arrangements contained in any federal–provincial agreements. Later, an Office of Intergovernmental Affairs was set up in Executive Council, and still later, in 1979, a full-fledged Department of Intergovernmental Affairs was established. Its primary role was to deal with negotiations among federal and provincial governments respecting proposed changes to the Constitution. But it also monitored and provided general support for other federal, provincial, and interprovincial negotiations – particularly those which might affect constitutional or economic relations among governments. While the department did not actually control all intergovernmental agreements and contacts, it did provide negotiating expertise and co-ordinated the activities of most agencies in the intergovernmental field.

The department could be viewed as another special-purpose secretariat, in that it was created to play the lead role in constitutional negotiations and all related activities. This was clearly an activity of the highest importance to the government – these negotiations dealt not only with legislative issues but also with Saskatchewan's right to regulate and tax resource industries. But we resisted giving the new department actual control over all intergovernmental contacts. We still expected the Department of Finance, the Treasury Board, and the Crown Investments Corporation to act as central agencies in many areas of intergovernmental relations. In 1983 the Department of Intergovernmental Affairs was dismantled by the Devine government.[12]

Soon after the Romanow government assumed office in November 1991, it became embroiled in intensive intergovernmental negotiations – the negotiations that led to the Charlottetown Accord of August 1992 and the referendum of October 1992. These negotiations were carried on by the Department of Justice, which promptly engaged Professor Howard Leeson, a veteran of the 1979–82 federal–provincial negotiations – the 'patriation' negotiations – to head up the negotiating team. A seperate department was established in 1993 and has continued under successive ministers. Dr Leeson returned to university life in 1994, to be succeeded by another academic with impressive credentials in intergovernmental matters, Dr Gregory Marchildon. Given his particular experience and interest, I suspect that Premier Romanow kept in close touch with the new department.

Notwithstanding its name (the Department of Intergovernmental Affairs), I do not believe the department tries to oversee all or most intergovernmental matters. As but one example, intergovernmental fiscal relations are still dealt with by Finance. As in the past, the Department of Intergovernmental Affairs deals primarily with constitutional issues, broadly defined, and accordingly has a limited role as a central agency.

Besides these central agencies, there were service-oriented central agencies that supplied office space, automotive equipment, printing services, and the like, to which I have referred briefly. Some of these exercised control functions. For example, we had a purchasing agency that operated under precise and detailed rules about tendering for goods and services.

But we did try to limit agencies serving as staff to the cabinet to the ones I have mentioned. As discussed in Chapter 4, we did form ad hoc central agencies, which we called secretariats, to deal with special problems. I've mentioned, among others, those which dealt with energy, potash, and uranium. These were a way to organize a group of public servants to help cabinet formulate a specific policy. Once the policy was decided upon and delineated, we made sure the group was disbanded.

We continued to believe that we were better off with the minimum number of central agencies. As I have been heard to say, central agencies can become barnacles on the ship of state.

10

Financial Management 1:
The Budget Process

This chapter, the first of two on financial management, deals with the budget process, namely, decision making about public spending. We outline the major elements of the process: the setting of priorities at the cabinet planning conference, the review of expenditures by the Budget Bureau and Treasury Board, and cabinet's finalization of the budget. We discuss a number of tactical issues, such as the timing of spending over the electoral cycle and how Treasury Board responds to interbudget spending requests. We compare the budget process in times of relative prosperity – most of the period when Blakeney was Premier – and in times of constrained resources, such as the current decade. We also look at the implications of the New Public Management for financial management, in particular how central agency constraints on line departments have been relaxed. We conclude by looking at the work of the Management Improvement Branch in the Department of Finance.

Borins: Financial management is, I imagine, a topic close to your heart. You began your career as a public servant in this area. Clarence Fines, Provincial Treasurer in the Douglas government, was your mentor. You yourself were Provincial Treasurer in the Lloyd government and in the first few months of your government in 1971. And you described yourself as the 'bean counter' of the Blakeney–Romanow duo.

Let's begin by looking at the role of the Department of Finance and Treasury Board in budgeting.[1] Where did your government's budget process start?

Blakeney: Any financial planning starts with the setting of some priorities. A government sets its general priorities in its election program or sometimes by reaching a general understanding in cabinet and caucus as to what its broad objectives are. Each year in the fall we had a cabinet planning conference to set priorities for the next year and, more generally, for the next several years.[2] We started with revenue projections, assuming current tax levels, for the next year and the succeeding four years. We then made spending projections based on the programs presently in place and the additions or cuts already agreed to.

With this rough information, we made tentative but reasonably firm decisions as to what we wanted our surplus or deficit to be in the upcoming budget. For example, we might agree that we would aim for a balanced budget, or for a balanced budget but using only, say, 75 per cent of resource revenues for current expenses, with the rest set aside in a special fund. We did not have that luxury in our first few years and had to fight hard to achieve a balanced budget. We felt it prudent to establish a clear surplus or deficit target before considering proposed spending in detail. The alternative would have been a financial result that was a residual figure derived from the revenue and expenditure review.

Borins: How was the cabinet's fall planning conference related to the cabinet retreat, which was always held a few months earlier? What sorts of issues were discussed at the cabinet planning conference, and what decisions were made? And what role did officials play?

Blakeney: Our conferences moved from large-theme generalities to specific decisions, which were sometimes arrived at acrimoniously. Our cabinet retreats dealt with the overall political health of our government and with the broad objectives we wished to pursue. Our cabinet planning conference in the fall focused on translating the broad themes into the priorities we wanted to pursue – specifically in the next year and more broadly in the next few years. The purpose was to give Treasury Board some reasonably clear guidelines about where our emphasis was to be and where it was not to be, and about what financial target we were aiming at. When Treasury Board reported its recommendations, usually in January, we would have a budget finalization meeting of cabinet, which was also attended by two members of caucus. This meeting was often a real hair pull. At higher levels of abstraction, agreements can usually be reached, or verbal formulas can be found that mask the disagreement. But when the final hard choices of dollars or no dollars, staff or no staff, are to be made, differences are sharply highlighted and nasty decisions must be made.

The cabinet planning conference was midway in the continuum. Cabinet was there. As I recall, a few caucus members were sometimes present. Public servants in good numbers were present for portions of the conference. Senior people from the Budget Bureau and cabinet planning unit were there for the whole conference. It was their opportunity to get a feel for where cabinet was coming from.[3]

When we dealt with a specific agenda item, and I'll use nursing home care as an example, we would have material before us relating to the projected numbers of older people and the different levels of care they might need – which could be none, or special housing, or home care, or nursing home care, or chronic hospital care. The senior people from the agency or agencies involved would outline how they saw the issue, what the options were, and what they felt should be done. They might suggest that we hold back on nursing home construction and press hard on home care and grants to citizens to renovate their homes so that disabled people would be able to stay at home. Cabinet members knew that community pressure for nursing home construction was strong. The general issue of aging and long-term care for the elderly would be canvassed. We would then excuse these officials and go on to another topic.

Some topics were dealt with simply to allow some officials to make a pitch, even though no real issues needed to be resolved. Some public servants get a morale boost from meeting with cabinet and explaining their work.[4] The tougher issues would be identified for us by the staff of the Budget Bureau and the cabinet planning unit.

After reviewing the subject areas, cabinet, with a few officials of the Budget Bureau and cabinet planning unit, would make our decisions on what our priorities should be and what surplus or deficit target we should aim for. After the planning conference, Treasury Board would begin reviewing the budgets in detail with the individual agencies and putting together a package for consideration by cabinet.

Borins: This exercise set the stage for the Budget Bureau and Treasury Board to do their work during the fall and winter. This involved arriving at departmental expenditure estimates for the fiscal year starting the following 1 April. How did you organize this budgetary review?

Blakeney: The technique was to identify those activities the government was certainly going to continue to fund, not necessarily at the full level of the current year but at least very close to the same level. The Budget Bureau staff would start with the previous year's budget for an activity and then factor in an allowance for inflation to arrive at a 'level activity' figure, which was the cost of carrying forward the activity to the next year at the same level as the present year. Then they would calculate, say, 95 per cent of the level activity figure and designate it as 'A' budget. This really meant that everyone acknowledged that Treasury Board had next to no discretion to lower the budget allocation below that figure. Then programs or portions of programs would be identified that could be eliminated. These were designated as 'X' budget items. Desirable new programs, or monies to bring ongoing programs up to last year's level or beyond, were designated as 'B' budget items. If the 'X' budget items were agreed upon, the battles were fought over 'B' budget items.[5]

The staff of the Budget Bureau worked hard to improve the quality of the information that went before Treasury Board. They tried to devise measuring sticks for outputs rather than just inputs. The public is interested in what the system produces for them, not in how much it consumes in resources. Occasionally our government was criticized because our per capita spending on health was sixth or seventh highest among the provinces. That never bothered me very much, so long as the public felt that the health system was good, and so long as we had a system appropriate to a small province, even though it might lack some of the sophisticated modes of treatment available in Toronto.

The Budget Bureau established some standards for the use of office space, cars, and the like, against which various agencies could be measured. If one agency showed up well, the bureau found out why to see whether the successful methods could be passed on to others. The identification and transfer of administrative know-how was an important function of the Budget Bureau. This involved developing measuring tools that would convince some agencies that they still had something to learn.

Borins: This sounds to me like benchmarking, which has become an important practice in the private sector in recent years. Firms discover which firm is the best in some particular function and then try to learn that firm's secret and emulate it. As a consequence, we are seeing more transfer of business know-how than in the past. In some instances, leading-edge firms have made a business out of this and are charging for the benchmarking presentations they are giving. Once again, your government sounds like it was ahead of its time.

Blakeney: I like to think so. As with the study of administrative efficiency, the analysis of budgets must always be comparative. It is never good enough to ask whether program 'Q' is a good one. My reply to an assertion that an activity was a good one and well received by the public was always, 'We are spending a million dollars on program "Q." It must be doing some good. And I'm sure many people are pleased with it. But the question is whether program "Q" is the best use we can make of a million dollars. If it isn't, then program "Q" should go.' On the face of it, this is simple and straight forward. But in practice, the existing program 'Q' will have defenders within the public service and outside, while its replacement may well be just an idea with no stout defenders or advocates either inside or outside the public service. So considerable pressure needs to be applied to strip marginal activities from a budget.

Borins: You've spoken before about the importance of drawing a line between policy and administration. How was this line drawn between the Budget Bureau, who were the staff to Treasury Board, and Treasury Board, which was a cabinet committee? My concern is also with ministerial time, that terribly precious commodity. I suppose that you and the other members of Treasury Board could have spent vast amounts of time overseeing all kinds of administrative matters. How did you avoid this?

Blakeney: You are right in identifying the problem of ministerial time in operating Treasury Board. The board had five ministers. It was chaired by the Finance Minister. As Premier, I never sat on the board. I could not afford the time, and in any case it would not have been wise. Cabinet reviewed the report of Treasury Board, and it was desirable that cabinet ministers feel it was a real review. If I had been on Treasury Board and defending its report, ministers would have been much less likely to feel that they could convince the full cabinet that the board was wrong in one of its cuts.

The board's membership rotated according to which ministers had the time or the inclination, or needed the experience. The ministers were fairly diligent in attending meetings during the budget finalization process. They were far less diligent in dealing with the many interbudget requests for extra money or staff. Indeed, these latter requests were divided by the chair of Treasury Board and the director of the Budget Bureau into three categories, as follows: those which the director would dispose of, those which the chair of Treasury Board would dispose of, and those which would go to the full board. The many submissions that were simply reprises of ones that had already been turned down during budget finalization process, and that did not relate to a real change in circumstances, were rejected summarily. We suspected that some agencies did not include proposed new projects in their annual budget submissions because the knives were then very sharp. They preferred to propose them as new and urgent interbudget proposals. The Budget Bureau tried to be alert to this kind of games-playing.

Borins: Both the Japanese Ministry of Finance and the British Treasury have had the same tradition. In the federal government, with its focus on deficit reduction, the Treasury Board is not at all receptive to requests for supplementary appropriations, and is likely to tell departments that if they want to do something new, they should fund it internally by reducing spending on an existing program.[6]

Blakeney: We were susceptible to interbudget requests in the 1971–5 period because our budgeting procedures were new and untried and because there was a genuine need to launch new programs in the interbudget periods. There was so much to be done that new policies needed to be planned and launched on a continuous basis. But these were the classic start-up problems of an activist government, and we had by and large resolved them by the end of our first term.[7]

Borins: Johnson's history of the Douglas government tells a similar story. There was an extremely rudimentary budget system at the outset – it was little more than a ledger book. In later years it was replaced by a budgeting system that, like yours, involved budgetary analysis and program evaluation.[8]

Blakeney: You also raised the issue of what the Budget Bureau did as opposed to what Treasury Board did. The staff of the bureau did a great deal of analysis – and even more as their skills developed – and also suggested whether a given program met the objectives outlined at the planning conference. Treasury Board made the final judgment. The board also had to assess whether cabinet could live with, say, no increases in school grants in order to free up some more money for home care. And it had to make the judgment whether some political risks could be taken at a particular point in the political cycle. And it had to decide whether an implicit increase of, say, 3 per cent in public service salaries was sustainable. As an aside, each budget factored in an allowance for estimated wage increases, but this was not included in the figures tabled in the Legislature. It was usually deducted from the revenue estimates so that the amount of the allowance would not be disclosed to the union negotiators.

Treasury Board had to make the tough decisions associated with making the budget palatable to the public. It is easier to ensure that a budget provides value for money in an administrative sense than to ensure that it is acceptable to the public as a reasonable way to spend tax dollars.

Treasury Board had to be prudent without being overcautious. Though finance ministries take pride in budget surpluses, it is not surpluses that quicken the pulse of the electorate but new schools, and better roads, and help in looking after aged parents. So it is up to any Finance Minister to avoid being co-opted by the pervasive caution of financial people, and up to the rest of Treasury Board to ensure that the government's program goals and the public's expectations are not forgotten.

Borins: Based on your experience as Provincial Treasurer in the Lloyd government and in 1971–2, could you describe the types of decisions, pace of decision making, and the like when Treasury Board got down to the crunch in finalizing the estimates?

Blakeney: Treasury Board's budget review started with a fairly detailed review of the budgets of the agencies, one after the other. After each agency was reviewed, the board usually made some tentative decisions, often identifying spots where savings could be made, for example, 'We can cut our grant program for rural roads, it's done its job,' or 'We can stretch out the Hanson Lake highway construction by a year.' These were noted. After this, the 'A' budget and 'X' budget items were confirmed and the 'B' budget items were reviewed. Tax increases were considered: the Budget Bureau identified and listed for the board the yield from, say, five cents on a package of cigarettes, or one cent a litre on gasoline, and so on. The options were listed and the hard choices made. The crunching could take anything from a few hours to a couple of days, depending on the extent of the interim decisions made and whether they became unstuck. Clearly, when money was tight the going was tougher. But decisions must be made, and they were. Then the report was assembled, together with ten or twenty real options for change, and the whole package went to cabinet.

When I chaired the cabinet's budget finalization meeting, I usually started with a review of our decision to meet our surplus or deficit target. This decision was almost always affirmed, occasionally with a rider that we would be a little more optimistic on our revenue estimates. This had to be guarded against, especially in a tough year, because we knew there would be many interbudget requests for money. In a tough year, we also knew that some of the budget cuts in the package could not be lived with. At this stage, we did not know which ones – only that there would be some. Similarly, in a tough year we knew there would be less underspending of budgeted amounts because budgets had already been carefully pared. So revenue growth was our best hope for extra money. We felt that this should not be spent at the outset.

I next canvassed the cabinet on cuts versus tax increases. After the nearly universal agreement to increase taxes on alcohol and tobacco, agreement all but vanished. The public mood was the governing factor – our general approach was to raise taxes if we thought those increases would be accepted.

We then moved to the specific cuts. There was a good deal of gnashing of teeth, but eventually we reached a decision, usually with some modest changes in Treasury Board's recommendations. One or two ministers might be very disappointed. When this happened, the old hands in the cabinet usually moved in. They sympathized with the ministers who felt hard done by and complained about the cuts to their own agencies, and then added that while it was rough, it was about the best we could do.

The two caucus members who sat in on our budget finalization session were free to report to caucus about the issues we had dealt with and the options we had considered, but not about who was on which side of an issue. We really had no difficulty convincing them that it simply would not work to personalize the issues and that we had to look at them in the light of what was best for the government, the party, and the province.

Borins: How did your practice of making ministers manage the government collectively play in Treasury Board? What techniques were used to ensure that they behaved liked judges rather than advocates?

Blakeney: Most ministers had no difficulty being judges so long as their own agency was not involved. So when there was full attendance at Treasury Board, there were at least four judges. The rhythm of decision-making that developed encouraged ministers to take a governmentwide perspective even of their own agencies. Usually the problem was not that of a minister defending his turf in an obvious way. Rather, it involved an honest difference of opinion as to what priority ought to be given to a particular department's activities. Ministers can sometimes become firmly convinced of the overriding importance of particular programs of their own departments. Fortunately for a premier, such ministers usually don't want to change portfolios and are amenable to some subtle diplomacy of the carrot-and-stick variety – that is, they respond well to the suggestion that if they can't live with the department's budget, then perhaps a change in departments is in order. This tactic has hazards if a premier feels that a minister might resign over a budget allocation. I never faced such a threat explicitly or implicitly. It would have been deeply resented by cabinet and caucus alike; accordingly, it was unlikely to happen in the atmosphere of a collegial cabinet.

Borins: The literature on budgeting is suspicious of 'X' budgets. It is suggested that departments propose cuts that treasury boards and cabinets can't possibly accept. The Americans refer to such proposals as 'Washington Monument' cuts. I suppose the Canadian equivalent would be 'Musical Ride' cuts.[9]

Blakeney: We certainly saw those. They got the inelegant name of 'silly bugger' cuts. It arose from a comment by a member of Treasury Board when an early example of a proposal for a 'Washington Monument' cut came forward. The testy comment was, 'Who was the silly bugger who suggested that?' As an example, if the Health Department was directed to find some cuts or revenue increases to equal 3 per cent of its budget – a common budget-building technique – and if that department then proposed instituting utilization fees for medical and hospital use, after we had campaigned against them in 1971 and abolished them in our first sixty days of office, this proposal fell into the 'silly bugger' class. Suggestions that were technically possible but clearly politically unacceptable did not endear the public servants who made them to Treasury Board or its staff, because they simply delayed the process of finding cuts that met both of the valid tests, which were administrative feasibility and political acceptability. 'Silly bugger' proposals were either playing games or showing a profound ignorance of the political environment in which the department was operating. We did not discourage proposals that might be marginally unacceptable politically so long as the problem was acknowledged and alternative proposals offered. It was up to Treasury Board – and, on major issues, cabinet – to make the judgment calls. The line between the unacceptable area and the grey area was usually reasonably clear.

Borins: As George Orwell wrote years ago, language has a way of affecting behaviour, and I can see how you were using language here.

Was your approach to spending different at different points in the political cycle?

Blakeney: Yes. We were politicians and so were aware of elections and of the desirability of having as few angry people at election time as possible. We had a practice of 'putting the government through the wringer' after each election. We began this in earnest after the 1975 election. The whole point of comprehensive annual budgets is to balance staffing and funding priorities. The budget process becomes much less effective if spending is approved between budgets by procedures that necessarily do not provide the same opportunity to balance the proposed spending against other possible uses of the funds. We were determined to get more order into the system.

We were well aware that tidiness of administration was not the objective of government activity; rather, the objective was to deliver services to the public. But we were also aware that sloppiness of administration could seriously hinder our ability to achieve our objectives. We were particularly aware of the dangers of unchecked incrementalism. This is the approach which says that since we did something last year, and since it is a 'good program,' and since it needs some modest expansion, the prudent thing to do is carefully control the rate of expansion and carry on. If this approach is used, the increases in expenditure will consume all available extra money and there will be none for new initiatives.

The idea of zero-based budgeting recognizes this. But as a practical matter we did not think it would work if it meant questioning the basis of each program. We knew that most programs were at their core untouchable, and should be untouchable. However, we embraced zero-based budgeting in the sense of reviewing each program to see whether savings could be made in the manner of delivery. We sought to identify activities that could be discontinued or curtailed, and savings that could be made in continuing activities. As I have noted, the fact that an existing program was 'good' and had a vociferous following did not determine the matter. My approach was that any organization should do new things and that in order to do them, it has to stop doing old things. A statement I made almost as often as I gave *the speech* was this: 'I refuse to believe that every single thing we are now doing is more important than any new thing we *could* do.'

The search was therefore to find money and staff that could be cut. Most cuts upset some of the public, public servants, or the public service unions. It is better to leave time for wounds to heal. When we cut an existing program to free up money for a new activity, nobody cheered. Those who benefited from the new activities did not recognize the source of the new funds; and the business press, which might have been expected to welcome cuts, found it very difficult (as it still does) to see around its ideological blinkers and examine the financial performance of governments without regard to party label.

To return to your question, yes, we did do our severe cutting and paring early in the term; and we eased off in the more sensitive areas in election years.

Borins: I'm not the least bit shocked or appalled by your admission, because it's clear that many politicians attempt to time expenditure and taxation decisions pretty carefully over the budget cycle.[10] In Ontario the Harris government made its big spending cuts in 1995 and 1996; as it looks toward an election in 1998 or 1999, it is no longer cutting, and is even restoring budgets in some areas. To repeat what they say in Chicago, 'Good politics is good government.' But how tight was your government's wringer, really? You had the advantage of a rapidly growing economy, concurrent with rising farm and resource prices, that produced a lot of new revenue every year. What were some of the notable programs that, to continue the metaphor, got wrung out of the estimates?

Blakeney: We disbanded the Human Resources Development Agency in 1977. We had established it to help disadvantaged groups organize so that they could make their conditions and grievances known. We seemed unable to find the appropriate means to do this job. Later, we funded the Saskatchewan Association of Non-Government Social Service Agencies, which took over this problem as part of its mandate. This arm's-length approach seemed to work better.

We kept a tight rein on the number of public servants. For example, the budget tabled in the spring of 1976 announced that Saskatchewan's outstanding debt, including all agencies, was the lowest per capita of any province in Canada. Also, that only two provinces enjoyed lower borrowing costs, and that the provincial unemployment rate was 2.9 per cent, and that the province was running a surplus. Despite all this, we announced that the number of provincial employees would not increase at all, and in fact would be reduced. At a time when the provincial economy was booming, the Minister of Finance felt it necessary to deny that the budget was one of retrenchment. He described it as 'Restraint, yes – austerity, no.'

Along the same lines, we announced in 1973 that we would attempt to accumulate surpluses in the good years to deal with any future difficulties. In the next four fiscal years we achieved annual surpluses of about $30 million. On spending of about $700 million a year, this represented about 4 per cent of revenue. This was a significant savings rate when you consider that our accounting system charged as budgetary expenditures all spending except the self-liquidating kind (which is paid back from revenues other than taxes).

Borins: The statistical evidence supports you. The following table shows the level and annual rate of change in provincial government expenditure for the decade your government was in power. Clearly, expenditures rose more quickly just before elections, and more slowly immediately after. This is particularly apparent when the expenditures are expressed in constant 1981 dollars.

TABLE 1
Saskatchewan Provincial Government Expenditures, 1970–82

Calendar year	Expenditure ($ millions)	Annual change current $ (%)	Annual change 1981 $ (%)
1970	559		
1971	610	9.1	–
1972	691	13.3	8.2
1973	754	9.1	2.5
1974	1002	32.9	21.5
1975	1316	31.3	18.5
1976	1469	11.6	2.8
1977	1694	15.3	5.6
1978	1954	15.5	6.6
1979	2193	12.1	3.1
1980	2491	13.6	2.9
1981	2922	17.3	5.0
1982	3449	18.0	8.3

Note: Election years are in italics.

Source: O. Yul Kwon, 'Saskatchewan: Provincial Public Finances,' in Melville McMillan, ed., *Provincial Public Finances: Provincial Surveys*, vol. 1 (Toronto: Canadian Tax Foundation, 1991), 216.

Blakeney: Almost immediately after our election in 1971, we launched some programs whose costs were certain to increase sharply. For example, there was a children's dentistry program, which we planned to introduce over five or six years. There was also a five-year capital spending program for local governments. All of the funds for this were budgeted in one year, 1974. These partly accounted for the 1974 and 1975 lumps. But the electoral cycle undoubtedly affected the level of our spending.

In an ideal world this pattern might not be found. But politics is an endless balancing act between what a government sees as fiscal realities and what it perceives are public expectations. Virtually no member of the public – and that includes business groups and the upscale press – has even a rough idea of government income and expenditures. Accordingly, almost no member of the public has any sense of the tax impact of specific program increases, or of the impact specific tax cuts would have on programs or deficits. Everybody believes, rightly, that existing programs could be cut to generate the funds needed for various pet projects. The problem is that there is no agreement as to which particular program should be cut.

I have tried to explain to groups that they should be reasonably happy if 95 per cent of their tax dollars are spent as they would wish – after all, many families don't achieve that high a level of agreement. Accordingly, if they are advocating a certain project, they ought to single out cuts that add up to at least 5 per cent of the budget before claiming that they have found the means to finance that project. Some groups may agree in theory that not everyone can have 100 per cent of tax money spent in accordance with their priorities, without regard to the priorities of others. But these same groups do not acknowledge that this justifies what they are pleased to label 'waste,' which is the name they give to any spending that is not in accordance with their priorities.

Borins: I would say that completely explains the frequent recitations of government 'waste' published in the business press. Besides such gambits as 'Washington Monument' and 'supplementary budget emergency,' did departments resort to other tactics to maximize their budgets? If they did, how did you deal with them?

Blakeney: I suspect that the general problem of making departments stick to their annual budgets will exist as long as budget gamesmanship is a public service indoor sport.[11]

The problem of how to handle interbudget spending requests has its complexities. In the final slash-and-chop to make budget spending fit the revenue framework, some cuts may be made that turn out to be simply unrealistic. In some cases cuts have been made on a 'Let's try it and see whether it can be lived with' basis. In most cases the staff work during the annual budgeting process has been good enough that the cuts identified are in fact endurable. On a few other occasions, adjustments must be made. So the system must have a small measure of sensitivity as well as an ability to distinguish between serious public pain and simulated public service pain.

There is another type of problem. Some public servants, through either sloth or cunning, fail to include in their annual budget submissions items that should have been there and that may in fact have to be accommodated. Any interbudget request has to be considered outside the process of measuring and weighing options that is the very heart of the annual budget process. This puts Treasury Board and cabinet at a serious disadvantage. Therefore, the board must take a very hard line with such submissions. But it may still find itself outflanked if a genuine public need can be demonstrated. Quite often, the interbudget request would not have been rejected had it been made in the annual budget formulation; rather, some other program would have been cut – very possibly a program of the same agency. But by the time the interbudget request is received, it is too late for Treasury Board to substitute the latecomer for the earlier approved program. Both, perforce, get approved.

Treasury Boards develop an arsenal of weapons to deal with the games players. One, which you referred to as becoming increasingly common in Ottawa, is to require that the new program be financed by virements from other programs of the agency. A virement is a transfer of funds from one subvote of, say, the Department of Highways to another subvote – for example, from urban arterial street maintenance to highway bridge repair.

The situation might develop something like this. The Highways Department suspects that an engineer's report is going to recommend urgent repairs to a major bridge. The department wishes to proceed with some needed work on urban arterial streets and arranges to delay the engineering report until after the budget has been finalized. That budget approves spending for arterial street maintenance. But soon after, the department makes an interbudget subission based on the engineer's report on the bridge. This report may leave Treasury Board little choice; it must now attempt to claw back some money from a subvote like arterial streets; that expenditure would probably have been delayed if the bridge problem had been fully disclosed. If the bridge problem had been disclosed as a contingency, it is likely that provision would have been made for the bridge repair and that arterial street spending would have been struck out. Alternatively, arterial street spending might have been approved but frozen until the bridge situation was clarified, the idea being that if the money was needed for the bridge, the street spending would be delayed until the money for it was transferred from the bridge budget by virement.

There is no complete answer to the problems of interbudget requests, but there are particular partial answers, and we pursued these with vigour. No Treasury Board likes to be boxed in, especially by public servants.

Borins: Before we leave the subject of the budget process, could you comment on the budgeting situations that have faced a number of federal and provincial governments in the 1990s? Because of profligate spending in the 1980s and a significant economic recession in the early 1990s, some governments found themselves having to take draconian measures to deal with their recurring deficits. Have you talked with some of your former colleagues about this situation, which you really did not face in the 1971–82 period?

Blakeney: It is true that in the 1971–82 period we did not face the need to cut spending sharply. In the early years we did not have much money to take on very many new and costly projects, but we also did not have a debt that had been incurred because of continuing annual budget deficits, and we also did not face high debt-servicing charges arising from this level of debt. I have talked to some of the people whose task it was to get the province's finances in shape when the Romanow government was elected in Saskatchewan in 1991. While Saskatchewan's problems were perhaps more acute than those of any other province, several provinces had problems of the same kind, if not to the same degree, and so did the federal government. I think we can now draw some conclusions about how these sorts of situations ought to be dealt with.

Borins: What are some of the steps that governments can take in these circumstances?

Blakeney: One technique that seems to work well is to get a good grasp of the problem right after your election and then explain it to the public – and explain it in sombre terms. In Saskatchewan, the government knew there was a budget deficit. The previous government's budget of April 1991 forecast a budget deficit of $265 million. The new Romanow government knew this figure was probably understated but did not know the extent of the problem. It turned out to be a deficit of not $265 million, but something in the range of *$850 million*. As part of the learning process for the government, and particularly as part of the process of explaining the situation to the public, the government appointed a Royal Commission, which was headed by a widely respected Saskatchewan senior partner of an international firm of chartered accountants. He and his commission painted a dark picture of Saskatchewan's financial status and strongly recommended urgent action. The public reaction was one of shock, but not of total shock. The public knew that things were not in good shape. In Saskatchewan there is still a widely held public belief that debt is bad – a belief resulting from the privations suffered in the 1930s by farmers, particularly by farmers who had unpaid debts. The risks of high debt were underscored in the 1980s when many farmers were unable to pay debts incurred for farm expansion. Many of these farmers lost their farms, notwithstanding elaborate government provisions to help them deal with their creditors. As the government sought to tell its story, financial institutions joined the chorus, and the public became convinced that urgent and drastic action was probably required.

Borins: The Chrétien government, elected in 1993, took a similar approach, though more gradually. Finance Minister Paul Martin was its high-profile spokesman about the perils of massive deficits. His first budget, delivered in February 1994, contained a commitment to reduce the deficit to 3 per cent of GDP within three years, but was not specific about the spending reductions required to achieve that goal. The program review exercise (see Chapter 4) produced the necessary spending cuts, which Martin included in his second budget, delivered in February 1995. During the year between the first and second budgets, Martin's efforts, warnings from the financial press, and Mexico's currency crisis all influenced public opinion, so that the public came to accept that severe measures were necessary.[12]

Blakeney: The Klein government in Alberta took fewer pains to lay the groundwork with the public for sharp spending cuts, but it seems to have been no less successful in gaining general public acceptance.

In Ontario, the Rae government, when it came to office in 1990, did not have a serious debt problem compared with most other governments. But it had a problem of rising annual deficits. In the interest of preserving employment and economic activity, it did not cut spending in its first year but rather incurred a 'Keynesian deficit.' The government found that it could not sustain this level of spending when faced with a drop in revenues because of cuts in transfers from the federal government and a sharp recession in the Ontario economy. The result was that the Rae government did not have enough time to convince the public that significant spending cuts were necessary. It went ahead in any case, but it suffered from a lack of a public understanding of the need for the measures taken.

Borins: Yes, and in his memoir Rae recounted the great difficulty he had trying to convince some of his government's traditional supporters of the seriousness of the deficit problem, and of the need to take radical measures – the Social Contract, with its limits on public sector wages – to respond to it.[13]

The Harris government began its mandate with a very clear commitment in its platform, the Common Sense Revolution, to balance the budget, concurrent with a substantial tax cut. The Common Sense Revolution also set priorities, in that it indicated many of the cuts in detail – for example, a 20 per cent cut in welfare payments, and a $400 million, or 15 per cent, cut in transfers to postsecondary education. I heard Harris speak two months before the election was called, and asked him what the implications of his policies would be for universities. He responded that I should read about the $400 million cut in the Common Sense Revolution. Before the Conservatives' first budget, planned for November 1995, rumours swept the academic community of a cut far greater than $400 million, and our lobbyists argued that the cut should be no greater than promised. In the past two years the Harris government has been fortunate to enjoy a strong economy producing increased tax revenues and low interest rates. On the other hand, it has faced determined opposition to some of its proposed cuts – for example, reductions in transfers for primary and secondary education, which were part of the impetus for the teachers' strike of 1997. As the government approaches the second half of its mandate, it is not clear whether it will be able to deliver a balanced budget by the next election.

What do you think we can conclude from these stories about how these governments have faced the need for sharp fiscal restraint?

Blakeney: My conclusion would be that in most circumstances governments need to take particular pains to lay out the nature of the problem and to get influential sectors of the public, including the 'natural' constituencies of the party in power, to agree to the need for action. There is a clear need to at least try to carry large segments of the public with you as you make your spending cuts. My Saskatchewan friends tell me that the Minister of Finance and his staff had to work hard to get cabinet and caucus to accept the nature of the crisis and to commit themselves to dealing with it.

Borins: Assume now that a government has the political will and the broad public support to make spending cuts. What techniques should be applied to implement this mandate? I imagine this would involve the public service as well as the particular publics who would be receiving reduced funding for 'their' programs?

Blakeney: The first, and key, decision when the government came to office in November 1991 was to deal with the crisis as quickly and as fully as possible. It turned out to be impossible to pull together a budget to present in March (the usual time for presenting a budget) and deal with the issues in a comprehensive way. So the budget was delayed until May.

The second decision was to set out a multiyear financial plan for eliminating the deficit and putting into place the expenditure cuts and tax increases that would be necessary to make the plan work.

The third key decision was to identify some core programs that would be sheltered or partly sheltered from the spending cuts. A number of welfare programs for the most disadvantaged were exempted.

The fourth decision was to start laying out a communications strategy for explaining the budget arrived at. It is not enough to convince the public of the need for urgent measures to raise taxes and cut spending. It is necessary to convince them, as far as you can, that the particular tax increases and spending cuts proposed are fair in the circumstances.

Tax increases provide quick results. Expenditure cuts work much more slowly. A large proportion of the spending of any provincial government is grants to schools, hospitals, nursing homes, universities, and the like. These institutions must be given time to react. The course chosen was to advise school boards, universities, and municipal governments that their grants would be cut by set percentages for two years. Examples were cuts in years one and two of 2 and 2 per cent for schools, and 1 and 2 per cent for universities. It was felt that this would provide reasonable time for adjustments to the new reality without forcing large increases in local government taxes or tuition fees such as a (say) 10 per cent cut would have done. A good deal of care was taken to work with the people whose grants were being cut.

Borins: This contrasts with Ontario, where the Harris government's politically popular promise of tax cuts required spending cuts of $9 billion, rather than the $6 billion that would have been necessary if taxes had not been cut. Many of our budget cuts, such as the reduction in transfers for postsecondary education, were delivered immediately, instead of being phased in.

Blakeney: In the second budget the technique was adopted of signalling cuts many months in advance. In almost all cases the announced cuts were adhered to.

Health care was a more difficult problem. The government concluded that costs could not be contained, and appropriate levels of care could not be delivered, without a major restructuring. This involved consolidating hundreds of hospital and nursing home and public health boards into about thirty regional health boards and closing or converting to out-patient health centres over fifty small rural hospitals, all with a view to reducing the role of institutions in the health delivery system and increasing home care and community-based services.[14] The changes were made amid much travail, especially in rural communities. As a result, the cuts proved too severe, and to ease the transition, the bare-bones health budget was increased to its previous level.

With respect to staffing, there were no large cuts at any one time, but there was steady attrition. No collective agreements were broken, and there were no legislated cuts. Guidelines for wage increases for three years of 0, 0, and 2.5 per cent were announced, and the government was able to make them stick. They were greatly helped by events beginning to take place in other provinces that made these measures look moderate.

With respect to arriving at the government's own program cuts set out in the 1992 budget, there was continuous dialogue between officials of Finance and the operating departments. The Treasury Board (the cabinet's committee on financial matters) went over the departmental budgets minutely. Sometimes it did so two or three times, if some of the cuts proposed by the public servants were unacceptable. The board had to be able to explain and justify its decisions to the cabinet and to caucus, and to satisfy itself that the cuts were sustainable.

Some fortuitous circumstances made the process easier in the first year. Some of the key public servants had worked with the Minister of Finance, Ed Tchorzewski, when he was Minister of Finance in the 1970s. They knew and trusted one another.

The second budget, in 1993, set out a financial plan for eliminating the deficit in five years, and provided the economic, revenue and spending forecasts on which it was based. So within about sixteen months of its assuming office the government had devised and outlined its plans in detail, along with the third-party grant levels already communicated, and all the players both inside and outside the government knew that rough waters were ahead.

By careful planning and with the help of that great ally of the politician, good luck, the government was able to get the province's financial affairs in order in a commendably short period of time. The budget was balanced in three years and has remained so. The huge debt renders the situation precarious, but the trends are in the right direction.

Borins: From the point of view of the public servant, constructing a budget in times of restraint was done not much differently than in times of more affluence.

Blakeney: That seems true. There were some differences. In the first budget the cabinet ministers making up Treasury Board spent much more time on proposed cuts to assess their level of acceptability. The government was highly aware that many members of the public would be unhappy. Public servants were asked to identify particular pressure points, and efforts were made to head off problems by talking with the groups involved. When a budget represents a sharp change in direction, not only is a special effort needed to explain to the public the measures being taken and the reasons for them, but some fine tuning is likely required.

Borins: It seems that 1970s methods were applied to the new realities.

Blakeney: In meeting the challenges of restraint, there was a consolidation of agencies, and a general, across-the-board downsizing, but no major changes were made in the respective roles of politician and public servants.

Borins: Another recent trend in financial management is giving departments more flexibility. It is a response to the challenge of restraint, but it should also be applicable in more prosperous times. You have already mentioned virements between programs. In addition, more governments are consolidating their departments' administrative expenses into a single budget line, which gives the departments more flexibility in using administrative resources in the most efficient way – for example, by substituting information technology for staff. Often, as in both Australia and the Government of Canada, these consolidated administrative budgets are subject to ongoing annual reductions of 2 or 3 per cent, which puts constant pressure on departments to increase efficiency.

Another common budget game in a world of fixed annual budgets is that departments follow a 'use it or lose it' philosophy, making sure to spend their entire budget before the end of the fiscal year. That practice has kept many consultants very busy in the fourth quarter of the fiscal year. The obvious way for a budget bureau to counteract this is to allow departments to carry forward unspent balances up to a certain limit; in the federal government, carryforwards of up to 5 per cent of budget are now permitted, and the Australian government permits 6 per cent carryforwards.[15]

Another way that governments have begun to deal with constrained budgets is through the imposition of user fees, assessed either directly or by establishing markets for public assets, such as radio frequencies and landing rights at airports. This has been facilitated by modern information technology, which makes monitoring feasible in situations where it previously was not.[16] In the next chapter I will describe an example of this in the area of highway pricing. From a budgeting point of view, the question is how to treat user fees. If they are all to be returned to the Department of Finance (or what governments call the 'consolidated revenue fund'), there is little incentive for departments to develop user fees. The obvious solution is to allow departments to keep some or all of the revenue, or, if budget cuts are being imposed, to count some or all of the revenue against the cuts.

Let me move to a different topic regarding the Saskatchewan government. In addition to its budget and program analysts, the Budget Bureau had an Administrative Management Division, later known as the Management Improvement Branch. What was its mandate, and how was it of help to you as Premier?

Blakeney: After the Second World War the U.S. government and some state governments formed administrative management units. The Canadian federal government set up a small unit in 1948. Saskatchewan added an Administrative Management Division to its newly formed Budget Bureau at about this time. This division played an important role in the Douglas and Lloyd years.

Borins: Johnson described how in the late 1940s and early 1950s the AMD advised on several departmental reorganizations, which were based on the following management principles: structuring the department on the basis of a limited number of major responsibility centres, establishing a planning branch and an administrative services branch, and setting up a unified field staff in which regional or local departmental agents could deliver all departmental programs to clients.[17]

Blakeney: In the 1970s we emphasized management improvement less and policy analysis more. But in our first term the Management Improvement Branch of the Budget Bureau did contribute greatly to the formation of new departments and agencies such as the Departments of the Environment, Northern Saskatchewan, and Consumer Affairs. The MIB also helped with some personnel problems that required administrative reorganization. I do not recommend a departmental reorganization to deal with a senior manager who is unable to do the job you want done, but it may be the best solution available, at least on a short-term basis. The MIB did the early work on introducing computers for general government use. The computer systems it established were later centralized in the new Department of Revenue, Supply, and Services.

The MIB staff were very good at devising organizations to solve management problems. Understandably, they were not as perceptive when it came to political problems. They once proposed that we combine the Department of Highways and our rail transportation planning unit to form a Department of Transportation. I recall asking the senior people who recommended this to me who they thought the minister should be. They made it clear to me that they did not think such a question addressed their field of expertise. Then I asked them whether they thought we needed the same kind of minister to do the grass roots public relations involved in highway construction and maintenance in a rural province as was needed to battle with the railway companies and the federal government on grain freight rates. From that point on, it was clear to them that sometimes it is more important to organize an agency around the skills of a particular minister than to provide the most logical organizational structure.

Borins: This brings us back to your comment in Chapter 8 that a good deputy minister is one who is sensitive to the political realities of the minister's world – indeed, a good principle with which to end this chapter.

11

Financial Management 2:
Government Enterprise

In this chapter we begin by exploring Blakeney's first experience in the public sector as secretary of the Government Finance Office and secretary to the boards of several Crown corporations. Blakeney also mentions some of the things he learned from his first boss, the Provincial Treasurer, Clarence Fines. He then shows how he applied the lessons he learned in the GFO to the monitoring of Crown corporations during his time as Premier.

We then look at instances where Crown corporations departed from strict business principles to advance the government's social or policy objectives. We then present some guidelines a government should consider following if it wants to invest wisely in the economy. These are based on Blakeney's experience and on Borins's research into government investment. We also apply these rules to some investment decisions made by the Devine government in Saskatchewan, the Alberta government, and the Rae government in Ontario. We conclude the chapter with a discussion of why the Blakeney government decided in 1971 to abandon a major pulp mill project that the Thatcher government had supported.

Borins: The Douglas government established the Government Finance Office to oversee the operations of Crown corporations.[1] In large measure, this was a response to some precipitous decisions by Joe Phelps, the Minister of Natural Resources and Industrial Development, to invest public resources in a woollen mill, a tannery, a shoe factory, and a brick plant – none of which was ever profitable.[2]

You worked in the secretariat of the GFO from 1950 to 1955, a few years after the time when the priority was to rein in Phelps. What were your duties in the GFO?

Blakeney: By 1950 the Government Finance Office was well established as the central agency for Crown corporations.[3] The secretary of the GFO served as secretary to the board of directors for each corporation. Its treasurer acted as an adviser on accounting for all Crown corporations to ensure some uniformity of accounting practices. The GFO also provided advisers on industrial relations, who promoted some uniformity of industrial relations practices, which made it harder for the unions to play one corporation against another – a technique known as 'whipsawing.'

I served for five years as the GFO's secretary and as secretary to the board for about ten corporations. My job was the obvious one: to prepare agendas for and minutes of board meetings. Usually the board chairmen were cabinet ministers. A less obvious part of my job was to help the minister ensure that the board focused on issues that should have come before the board. One or two general managers sometimes indulged in the practice of agenda-loading, referring quite minor matters to the board so as to divert attention from the major issues facing the corporation, regarding which management would rather have made unilateral decisions. It was also my job to see that the minutes were phrased as instructions for staff action, in the manner I described during our discussion of caucus minutes in Chapter 6. I also acted as a source of information to boards on how other corporations were tackling specific issues, especially legal and labour issues. Finally, I was a source of information for the board and staff of the GFO about what was going on in the corporations.

The GFO provided the capital funds for all corporations except Saskatchewan Power Corporation and Saskatchewan Government Telephones (as it was then called).[4] Each year, in the course of asking for capital, the corporations outlined their present and future operations. Capital requirements were carefully scrutinized. Profits were transferred annually to the GFO, which served to reduce the availability of self-generated funds for corporations.

Operating decisions were made by the board and management of each separate corporation, except when those decisions were likely to have a major impact on other corporations and agencies. Typically, these exceptions had to do with industrial relations – with, say, the holiday provisions in union contracts, the salaries paid to top management, and so on. The GFO's board approved senior managers' salaries as well as any major departures from the pattern of union contracts. When comparisons were made, they were made with other government departments and agencies in Saskatchewan and with similar corporations in other provinces. Thus, for the Saskatchewan Power Corporation, an effort was made to keep its union contract provisions and its senior staff salaries more or less in line with those of our provincial phone company and, say, with Manitoba Hydro.

The staff of the GFO had little formal power in dealing with individual corporations. The smaller corporations welcomed our help. The larger ones regarded us as either a valuable link with the government, because we understood their operations and would protect them from any needless tendencies toward governmentwide uniformity, or, alternatively, as representatives of their sources of capital who had to be tolerated.[5] I suspect that we were regarded much as agents of the centre are regarded in most conglomerates, public or private. Our basic assumption was that corporation general managers were a valuable resource – very likely to be prima donnas – who should not be needlessly harassed as long as they were playing fair with their boards and the government, particularly when it came to disclosing significant present and future problems and issues.

If, however, the management was weak, we were available to assist the board in either replacing managers or providing support for the existing ones. We offered advice in situations that we had probably seen several times and that most of the board members had not seen at all.[6] Board members were chosen from the public, with a few from government agencies. It is worth noting, however, that in the 1950s, and even in the 1970s, there was no great reservoir of people in Saskatchewan who had worked with large commercial organizations and who therefore knew what could reasonably be expected of management in such organizations. This general lack of knowledge about the workings of large-scale business organizations extended to the cabinet. Among ministers, a notable exception in the 1950s was the Provincial Treasurer, Clarence Fines.

Borins: If you were to compare this management structure with those found in the private sector, you would find that it is most similar to a multidivisional firm composed of many strategic business units (the individual Crown corporations) and overseen by a corporate office (the GFO). This management structure began in the 1920s in corporations such as General Motors, Dupont, and Standard Oil, and has evolved to characterize most large corporations.[7] It is interesting to note that Saskatchewan developed this management structure as early as 1946, but that neither the federal government nor any of the other provinces established anything like it for at least another twenty years.

Let's turn now to Clarence Fines. People who write about that era refer to him as the advocate of fiscal responsibility in the Douglas government – as the Treasurer who argued strongly and successfully for balanced budgets and a reduction of the provincial debt.[8] What were some of the things you learned from Fines?

Blakeney: Clarence Fines was a schoolteacher from Manitoba. As a young man he was an alderman in Regina. While still in his twenties he was active in politics. He convened the Calgary conference of 1932 that commenced work on organizing the CCF – a task that was completed at the Regina Conference of 1933. By the time I met him in 1950 he had developed what I thought were great organizational skills.[9]

I watched him in action as chair of the board of an insurance company, the Saskatchewan Government Insurance Office. SGIO operated the province's compulsory auto insurance plan; it also had about half of the fire and casualty insurance business written on a competitive basis in Saskatchewan. It was one of the ten largest general insurance companies in Canada. He absolutely insisted that management bring problems to the board with recommendations. Unless there was a clear management recommendation, the matter was summarily deferred to the next meeting without discussion.

Borins: I see an influence on your insistence that public servants provide clear recommendations.

Blakeney: Yes. Delegating upward is so common and can so easily enmesh more senior people in matters they ought not to be dealing with in the raw state that I put great stress on ministers insisting on clear recommendations from deputies, and on cabinet insisting on clear recommendations from ministers. Returning to Fines's method of operation, I remember an occasion when a general manager got into difficulties as a result of allegations that he was accepting payments from some agents for referring business to them. Allegations also were made against Fines. There was no substance to them in the case of Fines, but there may have been in the case of the general manager. Nothing was established, and all allegations were denied.[10] About six months later the general manager resigned for personal reasons. I thought it was an 'admit nothing in public, clean house in private' operation. As viewed by some, it was a case of Fines, when improperly accused of wrongdoing, defending his staff as well as himself and not hanging anyone out to dry. But staff changes would be made after a decent interval.

Another time, Fines was being questioned in the Legislature about an obvious error. The questioner asked who had given the advice upon which the error was based. Fines professed a failure of memory and added that it didn't matter: he had accepted the advice so the error was his. His willingness to protect his public servants against public attack built strong loyalty. The other side of the coin was understood to be that since he was accepting responsibility for the performance of his staff, he demanded top-quality staff work. He got it. If the work was less than top quality, and if he had concluded that somebody had to go, he could be pitiless in a small meeting when exposing the shortcomings of the staff member. On one occasion I watched him grill one of his people quietly but relentlessly, each question he asked exposing another layer of shoddy work. I was uncomfortable. The man being questioned must have been extremely so. His resignation quickly followed.

Fines served as chair of the board of the GFO. Most of the cabinet ministers who chaired boards of Crown corporations were on the GFO board. I was secretary of the board. Fines used the information that came from GFO staff to prod ministerial chairmen into addressing problems. He paid particular attention to the capital requirements of the big corporations and to corporations that were losing money.

Borins: Didn't your role as secretary to the board put you in a position of some conflict with general managers and individual cabinet ministers?

Blakeney: Of course, and it was a great job in terms of learning how to manage conflict. It was also a great job for an eager young lawyer just entering the public service. It gave me occasional contact with Premier Douglas and frequent contact with the Deputy Premier, Mr Fines, and with the ministers who chaired corporation boards. I had a great opportunity to learn how the government operated, and to observe the mix of personalities of the people, at once co-operating and competing, who made up a sizable and dynamic organization. I wouldn't have used the words then, but it was a study in constructive conflict resolution.

Borins: When you became Premier and the Crown corporation sector became larger and more complex, and the GFO was renamed the Crown Investments Corporation, did you retain this monitoring structure?

Blakeney: Yes, I thought it was a good one. Size had made the whole operation more complex. Several people served as corporate secretaries, and the focal point was the executive director of the Crown Investments Corporation. I kept in more or less regular touch with him and with the minister in charge. Once again, I wanted and felt I needed information about a range of issues, though at the same time I had no desire to play a decision-making role. Information flowed to the CIC because one or two of the CIC's staff were on the board of each of the operating corporations. I got a condensation of that flow for my purposes. Corporation managers knew this, of course, and some of them seemed to resent it. In their view, my office was looking over their shoulder. We tried hard to get across to each corporation's board and management that I did not want to become involved in management.[11]

The information flow was meant to provide us with early warning of potential major policy issues, and to let us know if a Crown corporation was proceeding at cross-purposes with government policy in other areas. As an example, the province's electrical utility put forward as a power generation option a major dam on the Churchill River in northern Saskatchewan. We warned them early that there might be other considerations besides economics, such as potential opposition from people of aboriginal origin who lived in the area, and from environmental groups. The management therefore did not dig themselves in; instead, they presented the Churchill River project as one option among several, and reported on the comparative economics of each. Eventually, after public hearings about its environmental impact, we decided not to go ahead with the Churchill River project.

I virtually never involved myself in operational matters with corporation managers, except to discuss our power generation options with the general manager of the electrical utility. The specific issue involved hundreds of millions of dollars, and the decisions made by the boards of Saskatchewan Power and the CIC had to be ratified by cabinet in any case.

Borins: You mentioned that Crown corporations were expected to behave consistently with government policy. Did that hurt their economic performance?

Blakeney: In some cases, probably yes. We had some common personnel and industrial relations policies that may have cost some corporations more than they might otherwise have had to pay. But these were not big factors. In other situations the issues were major – to require the power utility to serve a sparsely settled area *did* cost more. Then there were other less important but interesting issues.

The electrical utility had its peak load in the winter. As a policy, it tried to reduce peak power demand in winter by high demand charges. Some major industries had stand-by power units that they used a few days a year to cut down their peak demand and thereby reduce their demand charges. The classic Saskatchewan issue was whether these high demand charges should apply to curling rinks. These were usually community-operated and short of cash. More to the point, they were almost always the social heart of village life in January, and making their greatest power demand near the very peak of the electrical utility's load cycle. To the extent that pressure was applied to the utility to shave its charges to curling rinks, we have an example, writ small, of a larger issue of government policy that affected the operating results of the utilities. Generally, our Crown corporations followed policies that kept down the cost of living in rural areas.[12]

Most corporations were set up to maximize profits, and few issues arose. As an example, the Potash Corporation of Saskatchewan sold almost all of its product outside Saskatchewan, and most of it outside Canada. The primary objective was to maximize financial return to the Crown. But even this corporation sometimes produced for inventory in order to pace its staff layoffs to better accommodate the needs of employees, many of whom were part-time farmers. Whether this was furthering government policy or just good employee relations was not always clear. The point I make here is that the corporations were subject to almost imperceptible influence from general government positions. This may have cost them something at the margin, but it probably made a positive contribution to the overall provincial economic and social well-being.[13]

Crown corporations are instruments of government policy, so our government saw no problem in asking them to assume costs if the general benefits to the government and the public balanced the costs assumed by the corporation. Even so, measuring the trade-offs is important. Governments should identify the extent of cost transference and cross-subsidization. I will give these examples: there is certainly no agreement on whether long-distance telephone users should subsidize local service or vice versa, or on whether industrial electricity and gas users should subsidize residential users or vice versa. These issues arise particularly in the operation of utilities, whether ownership is public or private. It is useful when setting policy to identify the amounts of the cross-subsidization. But this is a highly controversial area. Even the appropriate method of calculation is disputed.

Borins: There have been movements to privatize Crown corporations in Canada and elsewhere. What are your thoughts on this trend?

Blakeney: My approach to these trends is a very pragmatic one. It is to ask why the activity was organized as a Crown corporation, and whether the reasons are still valid, and who would benefit from their continued operation as a Crown enterprise, and who would benefit from their privatization. In this analysis ideology is of little help. A simple 'who benefits and why' approach is more useful.

It should be noted that there is no set answer as to whether an activity should be organized as a Crown corporation; rather, the answer varies with time and place. This is particularly true for different provinces. In Saskatchewan, privatizing a public enterprise would almost certainly mean that the head office activity and all that flows from it would move outside the province unless special arrangements were made to prevent it. And these special arrangements are consistently opposed by stock exchanges and frequently opposed by private holders of the shares of the privatized enterprises. How long such arrangements would last is a real question.

As long as provincial governments are responsible for financing their own health, education, and welfare services, and particularly as long as federal transfers for such services are declining, any province will make strenuous efforts to maintain an economic base within its borders. In such circumstances arguments based on the merits of an unfettered free market make less economic and political sense.

Conversely, where there is little practical benefit from continued Crown ownership, there is merit in privatization. The matter should be approached on a case-by-case basis with a minimum of ideology and a maximum of financial and economic data.

Governments exist to provide services to citizens. Crown corporations can help with this. They should be considered tools for helping government do its job. When they stop being useful tools, others should be employed.

Borins: I was a director of the Ontario Transportation Capital Corporation, an Ontario Crown corporation responsible for building and operating Highway 407, an electronic toll road running east-to-west through the northern suburbs of Toronto. The highway is technologically leading-edge because drivers are assessed tolls by transponder or, if they don't have a transponder, by video-imaging. So there are no time- and space-consuming toll booths. The highway opened in June 1997, and tolling began four months later.

The Rae government was responsible for establishing the corporation. It was widely recognized that, because of substantial congestion on Highway 401, the major east-west route, a new highway was necessary. However, given the large deficits that Ontario was running in the early 1990s, the government decided that this highway would be self-financing. The Crown corporation was responsible for choosing and then overseeing one private-sector consortium that built the highway and a second private-sector consortium that developed the tolling technology. In addition, the corporation borrowed over a billion dollars, under the authority of the Province of Ontario, to finance the project. After some initial glitches, the technology is working and the road is producing revenues. The Harris government has decided to privatize the highway; the purchaser would be buying the income stream of toll revenue, and the purchase price should at least cover the government's investment. The public interest could be protected by means of some constraints on, or regulation of, the tolls that the purchaser can charge. In this situation, I see no strong public policy purpose for keeping the road in the public sector.

I want to turn now to the role of the government as investor. This goes beyond Crown corporations, since governments have been involved as lenders and guarantors of loans to major privately owned industrial enterprises. Some of these might be ventures in new technology; others might be bailouts of failing firms in the private sector. Some years ago I wrote a book called *Investments in Failure* – not a best-seller – which described what happened in five cases when government invested heavily in spectacularly unsuccessful commercial ventures. The examples I chose were the Canadair Challenger, the Glace Bay heavy water plant, the Bricklin automobile, Churchill Forest Industries, and Consolidated Computer Corporation. None of these happened in Saskatchewan in your era, though your government did do some investing in other firms.

The Devine Government, which placed a high priority on attracting private sector entrepreneurs to diversify Saskatchewan's economy, had some spectacular failures when it acted as investor.[14] The government hastily gave Pioneer Trust $28 million in loan guarantees, which had to be paid when the latter went into receivership.[15] Over $5 million of public money was invested in GigaText, a translation company that was closed down before it ever translated one sentence, though it did temporarily provide a luxurious lifestyle for its owners.[16] Another $2 million of government loans was lost by Supercart International, a company that tried and failed to develop a plastic shopping cart.[17]

The Government of Alberta, using the massive resources of the Heritage Trust Fund, also tried to play the role of investor in order to diversify its economy. Among its investments that went sour were Novatel, a cellular phone company that required the government to pay off a $435 million loan guarantee; General Systems Research Inc. and Myrias Research Corp., two high-technology ventures that cost the government a total of $44 million; and Magnesium Corporation of Canada Ltd., a magnesium smelter that closed down, leaving the government obligated to cover a $103 million loan guarantee. In addition, the government has paid more than $480 million in bailouts for financial institutions, including the Principal Group.[18]

Blakeney: The Government of Saskatchewan has a long history of operating commercial enterprises and of giving financial assistance to private entrepreneurs. Our telephone utility became a public operation before 1910. Other corporations followed: the power utility in 1929 and insurance, interurban bus, and northern airline companies, along with several others, in the 1940s. Our province's first organized loan fund for private entrepreneurs, the Industrial Development Fund, was established in 1947.[19] In 1950 I became the fund's secretary and lawyer, and during the 1950s there was a good deal of activity. Major resource corporations were organized in the 1970s.

We had some clear rules, not always followed. I'll mention this one first: *Be suspicious of bailouts.* If one management group failed to operate the business successfully, there may be excellent reasons why. Don't assume that new managers will be better managers unless the evidence is incontrovertible.

Borins: I agree with you, but the pressures on government to bail out troubled corporations and save jobs can be enormous, especially in the case of high-profile firms like Lavalin in Quebec, or when the firm is the only industry in town, like Algoma Steel in Sault Ste Marie.[20]

Blakeney: Algoma Steel in Sault Ste Marie and Spruce Falls Pulp and Paper in Kapuskasing certainly illustrate that government support for private industry cannot be reduced to a set of rules that apply in all cases. In both these cases the Rae government in Ontario worked with employee groups and with business to restructure troubled firms. These deals appear to have saved the industries for those towns for the present, and provided major benefits for employees; they also seem to offer good prospects for long-term viability. All of this was at little or no cost to the government. In each case the involvement and commitment of the employees seems to have been a very important ingredient.[21]

Borins: What other rules, as you call them, did you try to follow?

Blakeney: Another one was this: *Be sure that the sponsor of the project loses if the project loses.* This issue arises when the government is asked to put up the cash or to guarantee a high percentage of the total capital cost, with the sponsor contributing know-how, plans, patents, and the like, along with a minimum of money. The know-how, plans, patents, and so on are not worth anything unless the project proceeds, so these don't represent real risk capital, even though they may fairly be counted as money's worth if the venture succeeds. It is important that money's worth if the venture succeeds not be confused with risk capital if the venture fails. The sponsors must put up enough true risk capital that their attention is fully engaged while the project is being launched. And they must not be able to get their money out in fees and payments before success is assured.

Borins: Agreed. One of the worst investments in failure I studied was Churchill Forest Industries. The Manitoba government required the entrepreneur to put up only 14 per cent of the cost of the project, and then did not stop him from subcontracting work to companies he controlled. In effect, his equity was coming out of his profits on the project. Of course, this was an incentive to inflate costs.[22]

Bob Rae recounts that one of his government's wise decisions was not to grasp an 'opportunity' to bring Piper Aircraft, an American manufacturer of small aircraft, to Ontario. The firm was in receivership because of frequent lawsuits in the United States when its planes crashed. In this instance the entrepreneur was looking for a government to put up most of the money. Ontario said no, as did the other provinces that were approached.[23]

Blakeney: A third rule is this: *Regard a guarantee and cash as the same thing.* I personally didn't like government guarantees, except of specific loans with specific repayment schedules that could not be varied without the guarantor's express written consent – in short, no chartered bank guarantee forms. Payments are ordinarily made on loans. Guarantees are sometimes drafted so that they are a continuing guarantee. This sounds self-evident, but I felt that there was a danger that guarantees would be undertaken with less detailed consideration of repayment terms, extensions, and the like than would be given to a loan. Along the same lines, when there is a government guarantee of a specific loan, do not rely on the lender to police the loan. Sometimes it doesn't bother. More than one organization has been burned by the totally false belief that a guarantee is somehow a lesser commitment than a cash loan.

Borins: Again, agreed. Banks don't monitor loans guaranteed by the government. Treasury Boards seem to overlook them until they have to be paid. Parliaments and the public are also unaware of them. I suggested bringing them into the budgetary process and requiring government to make annual reports to Parliament or legislatures on the extent of loan guarantees and the performance of the recipients.[24]

Blakeney: Here is a fourth rule: *Assess whether the loan was a mortgage loan or an equity loan.* The way I look at it, a mortgage loan is a loan where there is a reasonable chance to get full recovery, if the project fails, from the breakup value of the assets. The security for the loan is based on the resale or breakup value of the assets, not on the success of the enterprise. To the extent that repayment depends on the commercial success of the enterprise, the loan is an equity loan. These are the realities regardless what name is given to a loan. To call a loan a secured first-mortgage loan doesn't make it one – not unless the facts support it.

If our government was making an equity loan as I have just defined one, we attempted to get some equity – usually some shares that would increase substantially in value if the enterprise succeeded. This was an appropriate reward for the risk assumed. If the amounts involved were high, we insisted on seats on the board of directors. The Douglas government guaranteed or lent money for a cement plant, a steel pipe plant, and a steel mill, and the Thatcher government backed a pulp mill.[25] No money was lost and some handsome profits were made, although the steel mill gave us some anxious months. During the Douglas years and the 1970s, we made many smaller loans to television stations, farm machinery manufacturing plants, high-technology electronics plants, and a range of other enterprises. There were successes and failures, but the losses were modest, partly because of careful lending practices and partly because of good luck – success in financing new entrepreneurial ventures requires both. In this regard, on a depressing number of occasions Canadian governments have enjoyed neither when backing commercial ventures.

We protected ourselves against one of the main hazards of financing new ventures – construction cost overruns – by developing an elaborate system of progress payments. We engaged consulting engineers, who divided the construction project into cost centres and provided us with running calculations of what would be needed to complete the projects. If we were lending or guaranteeing the money that was to pay for the construction, we attempted to retain enough undisbursed funds to finish the job. If overruns were encountered early in the project, the tough questions could then be faced. Should additional construction capital be found? If yes, by whom? If no, should the project be abandoned? These techniques didn't solve the problem, but they did provide early warnings. If the sponsors have their money in first and if not too much of the government's money is in the project when the problem is detected, a government has a little more leverage to insist that the sponsors find some more equity. At that point, the sponsors are the big losers.

Borins: Your government abandoned one major project, the Athabasca Forest Industries pulp mill at Meadow Lake, when you took office in 1971.[26] What led you to make this decision?

Blakeney: We had three basic concerns: finances, the resource base, and the environment. We were not greatly concerned about the sponsoring group, Karl Landagger and his associates. They had built and were operating a mill at Prince Albert and so far as we could tell, it was a good mill, built within budget and operated well.

We *were* concerned about financing. Most of the money for the project was being raised in the form of loan guarantees, or direct investment by the Government of Saskatchewan. The mill was to be built by a Landegger company, which meant that the Landegger group could probably recover its nominal investment during the course of construction and accordingly would have little at risk. They would still, no doubt, do their best to make the venture a success, as they had done at Prince Albert. But we thought that such an arrangement was not good enough.

We were also concerned about the resource base. The mill was designed to use both softwood and hardwood. In our view there was plenty of low-grade hardwood available of the poplar and aspen varieties, but not enough softwood in the area to feed the mill on a sustained yield basis. We also doubted that the mill would be economic using the amount of hardwood planned. We regarded the softwood resource as one that would in the future provide an economic base for people of aboriginal origin who lived in the area. We feared that we would later find ourselves faced with this difficult choice: make the mill confine its use of softwood to the amount planned, thereby risking the government investment of over $100 million; or, allow the mill to use more softwood than could be cut on a sustained yield basis 'temporarily,' thereby risking losing all the merchantable softwood forests in this large area where people of aboriginal origin lived who needed a long-term economic base.

Our third concern was environmental. The effluent was going to be dumped into the Beaver River, which flowed north into the Churchill River system. This is a large river system that provides a livelihood through fishing and tourism to many people of aboriginal origin across northern Saskatchewan. The environmental planning was clearly inadequate. It is possible that this could have been remedied, but when we had to make the decision, what we knew was this: the proposal posed a major danger of badly polluting the Beaver and damaging the Churchill system, and we didn't know whether remedial measures were possible.

For the above reasons we decided against proceeding with the project and negotiated a settlement with the Landegger group in which we paid them $4.4 million to terminate our obligations under the agreement they had signed earlier with the Thatcher government.

It isn't possible to know whether our decision was sound. The project might have worked out well. But I have no doubt that the deal was one of seriously unbalanced risk, and accordingly, if faced with the same decision today, I would do what we did in 1971.

12

Human Resource Management

In this chapter we discuss how it was that Saskatchewan developed a very high-quality public service in a small province. We examine in some detail the career assignment and management education policies that supported this public service, and compare these with the practices of several other public services and major corporations. We then look at the employment equity policies of the Blakeney government. We consider the impact of the 'purge' by the Devine government of many public servants at all levels. We evaluate the level of job satisfaction in the Saskatchewan public service in the 1970s, and compare it with the Zussman–Jabes studies of job satisfaction in the federal public service. Finally, we outline the major components of the 'new public management' paradigm and briefly consider its implications.

Borins: When the CCF and NDP were in power in Saskatchewan, the province had a reputation, surprising for a small province, of having one of the most creative and efficient public services in Canada. What did Saskatchewan do to recruit, develop, and retain high quality public servants?

Blakeney: In the Douglas–Lloyd era from 1944 to 1964, Saskatchewan developed an active system for recruiting people from outside the province. In the early years after 1944, people came from across Canada and the United States to participate in the social experiment of North America's first social democratic government.[1] The social changes involved launching provincewide hospital insurance and transforming mental health care. The economic ones involved organizing or expanding Crown corporations to operate electric power, telephone, interurban bus, and northern airline services; and also to produce timber, bricks and tiles, sodium sulphate, and other products. Compulsory automobile insurance, comprehensive medical care in one region of the province, an air ambulance service, and many other innovations were introduced. This ferment attracted senior people from far and wide.

Borins: Accounts of that period by both Johnson and Brownstone sound exciting. Johnson wrote about how the senior public servants 'tended to move together, socially, and often in company with the ministers, resulting in a cross-fertilization of ideas and arguments and criticisms that knew almost no limit; there was no social occasion attended by ministers or senior civil servants that wasn't seething with shop-talk.' And Brownstone recalls that 'anyone who visited the cafeteria in the legislative building in Regina during this period will understand this clearly. There was invariably a mixing of politicians and civil servants at lunch and conversation was informal and stimulating.'[2]

Blakeney: Two further innovations for Saskatchewan were the setting up of a merit-based public service and the introduction of many new management techniques, some of which I've already noted in Chapter 10.[3] The Douglas government attached great importance to recruiting a corps of young, able public servants. It combed Canada's universities to find people who were interested in designing and administering new government programs. Serving with the newly established Budget Bureau was usually the first assignment. At that time the bureau carried out both program analysis for budgeting purposes and studies in administrative organization and methods. In the 1940s and 1950s the Budget Bureau did administrative surveys of many government agencies to assist these agencies in organizing themselves in the most effective way. New employees would be added to a bureau survey team to watch first-hand how administrative problems were identified and dealt with. They would also serve on a team doing program analysis for budgeting purposes. In addition, they would attend formal lectures on how cabinet government operated and on how the evolving central agencies fitted in with the governmental structures. There were weekend seminars. I attended them as a minister and, in the 1970s, as Premier. These activities were successful in imparting knowledge and building esprit de corps.

The way the system operated during the 1950s, after a couple of years around the Budget Bureau about half the people recruited from the universities would have decided that they liked what they saw. Others would have left to pursue other opportunities. The next step was to second the trainee to a program department in a position such as administrative officer. There the trainee was immersed in more management problems, this time from a departmental perspective. Up to that point the training program had concentrated on management and control. But the purpose of government is not to control itself but to deliver goods and services to the public. So the next move for the trainee was usually to assume the management of some branch of a service department that had extensive dealings with the public.

Once this career circuit had been completed, the employee, no longer a trainee, was in a position to compete for a range of positions as they came open, according to his or her inclinations and skills.

I do not mean to suggest that all managers were drawn from the Budget Bureau trainee alumni. Some joined operating departments, rose in their management structures, and then competed for jobs in other departments. But the existence of the Budget Bureau crop each year, and the winnowing process I have just described, provided a regular source of management talent and served to set standards against which people entering the management ranks from other sources could be measured.[4]

In the 1970s we followed similar though somewhat less formal procedures. People were recruited from the universities in the same way, but many now had masters or doctoral degrees. Some had some specialized knowledge in a particular field, and most had a somewhat better idea of how a provincial government worked. But there were still formal training sessions and weekend seminars, and people were still deployed to service delivery departments for seasoning. Though the annual 'class' was a little less homogenous, the essential principles of our training methods were the same.

Borins: You have mentioned some management education techniques. Were there others?

Blakeney: We tried to get across to trainees not only the principles of government but also some sense of the province and its people. We suggested that they read S.M. Lipset's classic study of the early days of the CCF, *Agrarian Socialism,* and W.O. Mitchell's novel and mood piece, *Who Has Seen the Wind?* If it were being done today, doubtless Tommy and Ian McLeod's biography of T.C. Douglas, *Tommy Douglas: The Road to Jerusalem,* would be on the syllabus.

The seminars I've referred to were often very well done. I've looked through some papers in the archives to answer some of your questions and have run across dozens of papers of good quality on the theory and practice of one or another aspect of government.

Borins: As Sir Humphrey Appleby, the Cabinet Secretary in *Yes, Prime Minister*, would have said, with respect, Premier, wasn't there a problem keeping these people in Regina, with its gentle climate, as their careers advanced? Were there enough opportunities? Didn't they want to go to Ottawa or Toronto to play on a larger stage?

Blakeney: Spoken like a true Torontonian, professor. The answer to your question is a paradox – namely, that we were more likely to keep these people in Saskatchewan the easier we made it for them to leave. We weren't unaware that many people don't consider Regina centre stage, that they think they would prefer the action (if not the housing prices) in Toronto or Ottawa. So we made it easy for them to leave by providing lots of contact with public servants elsewhere – for example, by supporting their active participation in the Institute of Public Administration of Canada and other professional organizations.

We also gave many public servants educational leave and underwrote the cost of their obtaining advanced degrees at places like Harvard.[5] As examples, Dr A.W. Johnson, later president of the CBC – and to whose work we have made many references – obtained his Harvard PhD in Public Administration while on educational leave from the Saskatchewan government. He was certainly not alone: others attended universities like the London School of Economics and Queen's to earn their postgraduate degrees.

This meant that these people could feel that they were neither isolated from the public service mainstream in Canada nor destined to spend their entire careers with our small provincial government. Good experience, good academic credentials, and a knowledge of the senior public service network across Canada gave them readily marketable skills. They could stay in Regina while the challenge was interesting without feeling that, to avoid being 'trapped,' they had to take any opportunity that came their way to work with the federal or Ontario government.

In any event, we were prepared for attrition. I would estimate that we lost half our trainees in their first couple of years. We consciously hired more potential high-fliers than we absolutely needed so that we wouldn't be hurt by attrition. I would also point out that losing strong people to other public services had indirect benefits for us down the road. In a difficult intergovernmental negotiation, it was no bad thing to have on the other side people who were familiar with our arguments and who might, while remaining loyal to their new employer, have some sympathy for them.

Borins: All right, they stayed in Regina. But how did these people move from being high-performing ambitious middle managers to positions at the top of the public service?

Blakeney: Deploying people around a public service in the best way possible gets more difficult as the service grows. To a considerable extent, middle managers make their own career paths by deciding what special skills to acquire and what jobs to bid on. At the same time, governments must seek out people with high potential and move them into key mid-management positions. In a small government the informal networking that centres on the Department of Finance, the cabinet planning unit and the deputies' informal club is an effective way of spreading the word about good people. Some deputies have been known not to advertise the qualities of a good middle manager. This is not a good long-term policy, in that any department that gets the reputation that it does advertise the skills of its good people is likely to attract the cream of the crop. The converse is also true.

In the later years of our term of office, I felt the need for a more organized system of personnel management. This was because my government deputy was spending more and more time trying to deploy senior management to the best possible advantage than either of us should have spent on this activity. To a lesser extent, so was I. So I asked a very senior and very wise public servant who was in his sixties, who had served for some time in the demanding job of Deputy Minister of Health, and who wanted to be relieved of some of the day-to-day stress, to assume a new position of Co-ordinator, Executive Development and Government Organization. This person, Mel Derrick, handled the deployment of senior staff. He advised my deputy and me whether and how deputies should be changed as a result of cabinet shuffles; he found places for unhappy senior people or people whose ministers or deputies were unhappy with them; and he generally sketched out who might succeed moving or retiring deputies.

The position also involved recruiting or identifying high-flying junior and middle managers and working with them and with deputies to lay out career paths that would be in their best interests and those of the government.

Borins: Your government's practices concerning high-fliers are very similar to those followed by the British, Japanese, and Singaporean governments, as well as by many successful private-sector corporations such as IBM and Exxon.[6] Hire high-fliers from élite educational institutions. Use rigorous competitive entry exams as a screen, like the Japanese and British do. In the first few years, move them around the organization and give them a variety of challenging assignments. Provide them with lots of management development, including both technical knowledge and an understanding of the organization, its environment, and its history. Instil in them the organization's core values. Broaden their horizons by providing them with opportunities to study for advanced degrees at the best universities. Have their careers followed closely by personnel development officers, initially at the departmental level and later at the government or corporate level. Have a senior person do succession planning for senior public service positions.[7] A lot of public and private sector experience shows that this formula works.

In 1991 the federal public service initiated a Management Trainee Program based on this model.[8] The program is aimed at recent masters graduates; entry is on the basis of competitive examinations and interviews designed to assess leadership potential. Trainees join participating departments, and the costs of the program are shared between two central agencies – the Treasury Board Secretariat and the Public Service Commission – and the department. Trainees spend five years in the program on a variety of developmental assignments, just as in Saskatchewan and in the private sector programs. It is expected that graduating management trainees will move to middle or senior level positions. It is interesting that the federal government developed this program during a period of downsizing; it is always necessary to develop future leaders.

What intrigues me about the Saskatchewan experience is that you were able to build a model public service in a hinterland location. By comparison, the Japanese and British public services are located in London and Tokyo, cities that are in every way their national 'Big Apples'; and IBM and Exxon – at least in their glory days – were so powerful in their industries that they were, by definition, the centre of the action.

Looked at from the perspective of theories of motivation, the Saskatchewan government in its employment practices was aiming at the top of Maslow's well-known hierarchy of needs. It was providing a sense of belonging to a community; it was providing self-esteem through opportunities for competence and achievement; and it was providing a means for self-actualization. These are powerful means for counteracting the hinterland location.[9]

Let's now move to an area that has been of great concern in public-sector human resource management – namely, employment equity policies. Was the Saskatchewan government ahead of its time in this area? What were your government's achievements in employment equity programs?

Blakeney: We had a number of such programs. The first dealt mainly with women – in particular, with bright women who had been dead-ended in stenographic and clerical jobs in the public service. In 1975 we established an Administrative Development Diploma program. The idea was that people who had worked a minimum of three years in the public service and who were in the higher clerk and stenographic grades could take two afternoons a week from work to take designated courses at the Universities of Saskatchewan and Regina in administration, political science, literature and composition, and similar areas of study. It would take on average three years to complete the courses and get a diploma. For those who wished to continue university work, the diploma was accepted as one year in the arts and commerce areas. The time off was with pay, and the government paid for books and supplies. We had a good response, and while there were problems, there is no doubt that the ADD graduates did better in getting promotions than comparable people who had not taken the courses, and that the graduates attributed their success largely to the ADD program.

When I read over some old material and noted that the committee overseeing the ADD program had 'one person named by the Premier,' I chuckled. The person I named had at one time been my secretary; she had then served as my administrative assistant and, still later, as Clerk of the Executive Council. She knew the public service and had enough confidence to call a deputy 'from the premier's office' to find out why his department was not co-operating fully in helping an employee take advantage of the ADD program. (Such managers, of course, were almost certainly men.) At that time, some of our managers did not give high priority to employment equity, particularly if it meant they might lose the services of their personal secretary two afternoons a week. The message that this reluctance to co-operate was not appreciated needed to be communicated, and my former secretary performed this job effectively.

We had no formal program to increase the number of women in senior management positions. This was a stated objective of the Women's Division of the Department of Labour, which pursued this goal both inside and outside the public service.[10] The methods were largely informal. In 1971 we had no women of deputy minister rank in our government. Ten years later we had four. (This was out of twenty-five or so deputies.) This was modest progress, but respectable in the context of the 1970s.

A quite different problem of employment equity had to do with the small number of people of aboriginal origin in the public service. Our efforts to increase their numbers were not very successful. We did very well in employing people of aboriginal origin in northern Saskatchewan, where they constituted most of the residents. Our programs to get qualified teachers of aboriginal origin were real successes. The Northern Teachers Education Program (NORTEP) and the Southern Urban Teachers Education Program (SUNTEP) provided innovative ways to get people of aboriginal origin trained and employed as teachers in schools in northern and southern Saskatchewan. We were also able to increase the number of aboriginal people in universities – probably by ten times in ten years.[11] We were also able to get jobs for aboriginal people as miners and provincial court judges, but not in any significant numbers as senior managers in the regular public service.

I've formed a theory that when dealing with employment equity, the easiest task is to get reasonably high-status jobs for disadvantaged people in the skilled technical areas. Next easiest is to bring them into the professions as lawyers, accountants, medical doctors, and the like. Hardest is to bring them into the ranks of senior management. I'm not sure that this is true for all organizations, but for us that seemed to be how it worked.

Borins: After your government was defeated, the Devine government initiated one of the most significant 'purges' of public servants in recent memory, removing some 1,500 public servants, including both order-in-council appointments and regular public servants. Many were fired or had their positions abolished; others were offered early retirement.[12] The rationale given was that the Saskatchewan public service had grown too large and powerful, that senior public servants had developed too cosy a relationship with your cabinet, and that it was necessary for the new government to assert control over the bureaucracy.[13] What do you think of the appropriateness of this policy?

Blakeney: The politest term I can give to what happened is that it was grossly inappropriate. There was no reason for the purge. Nobody objects to staff in ministerial offices being released. Indeed, the employment of this group and a few other political employees was concluded by the outgoing government before it left office.[14] But many others were fired. Long-time employees who had not engaged in any political activity were terminated because, to quote the government's counsel in the huge number of wrongful dismissal cases launched, the government had 'lost confidence' in them. No reasons were even offered as to why they were not good employees. As you suggest, the total number fired totalled many hundreds. A single law firm opened four hundred wrongful-dismissal files. One Crown corporation employee, dismissed for incompetence, sued. He got a handsome settlement and went on almost immediately to become vice-president of a major trust company. Within six years he was CEO of a major Canadian company in the private sector.

There were no grounds for believing that more than a small number of public servants had developed 'too close a relationship' with our cabinet. Certainly a new government must assert control over the bureaucracy, and certainly it must put some of its people in key positions; but just as certainly it can depend on the vast bulk of the public service to give loyal service to the government of the day, whatever its political stripe.

Nor was the purge in keeping with Saskatchewan practice. In 1964, when the Liberal government of Ross Thatcher took over, a considerable number of senior people left or were pushed out.[15] Their move to other governments, particularly the federal government, has often been noted. In Ottawa they became known as the Saskatchewan Mafia. Their numbers included A.W. Johnson, later president of the CBC, Tom Shoyama, later Deputy Minister of Finance, Don Tansley, later Deputy Minister of Fisheries and Oceans, and many more. At one federal–provincial conference shortly after 1964, of the eleven governments represented, six had people in their delegations who had worked for the Government of Saskatchewan before the 1964 election. But Thatcher's dismissals did not reach down into the second, third, and fourth ranks of management, as did the Devine firings.

When our government succeeded the Thatcher government in 1971, we fired only a very few senior managers and virtually no one in the classified public service.

Borins: I would add that the Douglas government, when it took over a patronage-ridden public service in 1944, did not purge the public service the way Conservative governments later did.[16]

Blakeney: Mass firings demoralize a public service. Those who remain keep their heads down and await orders. Since the reason for many of the firings is often obscure, public servants do not volunteer new ideas out of fear that they may attract disfavour. In one unusual case, a senior officer of the Department of Health was discharged in 1983, apparently for political activity. He *had* been politically active: he had attended the federal PC leadership convention as a delegate and, reportedly, had supported Brian Mulroney. I believe he was later hired by another agency.

There is a further result of public service purges: it makes it difficult to recruit top-calibre people to fill the vacancies, since tenure no longer appears to depend on performance. And this is bad news for any provincial government, in particular one, like Saskatchewan's, that does substantial recruitment outside the province.

Borins: A very influential book in Ottawa in the last decade has been *The Vertical Solitude* by University of Ottawa professors David Zussman and Jak Jabes.[17] They did surveys of upper and middle level managers in the federal public service and in a number of comparable large private-sector organizations. They found that there was, on average, a higher level of job satisfaction in the private sector than in the federal public service. They also found that the level of satisfaction decreased as you moved down the ranks in the federal public service, while it stayed relatively constant in the private sector. This second finding was what they were referring to in their book's title.

Zussman, Jabes, Jans, and Frazer-Jans replicated the survey for upper and middle level managers in the Australian public service and found that the Australians were more positive about their work and their departments than their Canadian counterparts.[18] While there was some decrease in job satisfaction as one moved down the ranks in Australia, this vertical solitude effect was less pronounced than in Canada. They attributed this difference in part to the creation in Australia in the early 1980s of a servicewide body of 1,600 senior officers, called the Senior Executive Service (SES). This signalled that a greater emphasis would be placed on making their careers more flexible, on developing their management skills, and on freeing them from central agency constraints. The Australian experience makes the point that public management reforms can improve morale.

Suppose that such a study had been done in the Saskatchewan public service when you were Premier. What do you think it would have found?

Blakeney: I believe that job satisfaction in the public service was generally high. But those were times of innovation and change, when it was easier to generate and maintain enthusiasm among public servants. I suspect that job satisfaction in the federal public service was greater in the 1970s than the 1990s. I've no way of comparing job satisfaction in the Saskatchewan public service with that of the private sector during our time in office, but I believe it compared well. We lost few people to the private sector.

I expect that in Saskatchewan then, as in Ottawa now, satisfaction may have been higher in the senior ranks of management, but I don't believe the spread was great. In a small public service it is much easier to make every public servant feel that he or she is part of the action and a valued member of a team that is pursuing a known objective. Some public servants who headed a division dealing with, say, regional parks, or fish and game, or rural roads, became well and favourably known throughout the province, and they and the people who worked in their agencies knew from many public contacts that their efforts were appreciated. I've noticed that at their funerals, years after their retirement, representatives of the public they had dealt with came from across the province to pay their respects. There is job satisfaction in serving when you know your work is appreciated.

Some public servants were able to take their favourite idea and see it become part of the way the province operated, and in some cases how Canada operated. I am thinking of a senior public servant in the Department of Labour, Robert Sass. Bob had ideas about occupational health and safety, partly taken from Sweden, partly developed on his own. The new Minister of Labour was interested. Among other things, Sass was proposing that workplace safety committees be established on which managers and workers would be equally represented, and that employees be given the right to refuse dangerous work and to be informed of workplace hazards. These ideas were clearly ground-breaking in the North American context. Over a period of several years legislation was introduced, employers and unions were consulted in depth, and gradually acceptance was won. I'll say more about this program in Chapter 16. The ideas worked. Parts of the program have been adopted by most other provinces. Sass's efforts resulted in a major change in approaches to occupational health across Canada. The chance to 'make a difference' provides a powerful motive for public servants to work hard and effectively. As an aside, Bob Sass has been teaching for many years at the University of Saskatchewan's College of Commerce. For him, as for many others, working in an innovative public service opened up career paths outside of government.

Borins: I want to conclude this chapter with a discussion of the 'new public management,' a set of trends in public management that some writers, myself included, feel constitute a new paradigm.[19] In earlier chapters we discussed some aspects of the new paradigm, for example, the reduction of central agency controls with respect to both policy-making and financial management. In the latter area, we've discussed how departments, though subject to increasing spending constraints, have been given more internal autonomy to move money between programs, to manage their administrative costs comprehensively, to carry forward unspent balances, and to impose user fees – and keep at least some of the savings on the revenue raised. We've also discussed the trend toward privatization.

I've developed a definition of the new paradigm. Because it has a number of components, the new paradigm cannot be reduced to a sentence, let alone a slogan. It contains the following key elements:

- Providing high-quality services that citizens value.
- Increasing the autonomy of public managers, particularly from central agency controls.
- Measuring and rewarding organizational and individual performance on the basis of whether demanding targets are met.
- Making available the human and technological resources that managers need to perform well.
- Appreciative of the virtues of competition, maintaining an open-minded attitude about which public purposes should be performed by the private rather than the public sector.

The new paradigm came about in response to a number of powerful external forces that governments everywhere have had to face in the last fifteen years.[20] The public sector debt problem has created pressure to cut programs ('Doing less with less') and/or increase efficiency ('Doing more with less'). The rapid development of information technology has given the public sector a major opportunity to increase efficiency. People, whether one calls them citizens, clients, customers, or consumers, are demanding quality and service from both public and private sector organizations, and comparing their performances. Employees, especially knowledge workers, are looking for work in either the public or the private sector that provides opportunities for personal growth and fulfilment, rather than just a paycheque. One measure of the power of these influences is that governments of various ideologies, both conservative and social democratic, have embraced the new paradigm.

The first component of the paradigm is reflected in service quality initiatives, such as surveying the users of public services and then providing improvements they want – for example, service using information technology (electronic kiosks and websites) and collocation of programs (one-stop shopping).[21] The United Kingdom established a Citizen's Charter, which enjoins public sector organizations to publish service standards, to compensate for failures to meet standards, and to strive for improved service.[22]

The second and third components of the paradigm are related, in that the reason for giving managers more autonomy is to enable them to meet demanding performance standards. One example of this is giving managers autonomy over the allocation of their administrative budgets while requiring them to produce annual efficiency gains. The United Kingdom again has carried this principle farthest, with its Next Steps program. Many units of government have been defined as agencies, with clear performance targets and greater managerial autonomy to meet them. At this writing almost three-quarters of British public servants work in agencies. The Government of Canada has adopted this approach to a lesser degree by creating a limited number of special operating agencies.

The fourth component refers on the one hand to the increased investment in information technology in the public sector, and on the other hand to new human resource initiatives. Human resource initiatives include giving individual departments and agencies more autonomy from central agency controls (for example, in staffing and compensation), and making greater investment in training.[23]

The fifth component refers to governments using markets and marketlike mechanisms to achieve efficiency gains. In some cases this may mean privatization; in other cases it may mean inducing competition between the public and private sectors – for example, by giving departments the right to choose between public service agencies (say, a government-owned automobile fleet) and private sector competitors (automobile rental firms). Finally, it could encompass competition among public sector entities, such as permitting parents to choose which public school to send their children to and allocating school budgets on the basis of enrolment.

I wonder what you, as a former politician, think of this new paradigm. Does it make sense to you? Some of the critics of the 'new public management' argue that it would reduce political control over, and accountability for, the public service. For example, when public servants survey citizens about service, the critics would claim that politicians are being short-circuited.

Blakeney: I've certainly seen an increased emphasis on customer service. I believe this is sound. I believe public servants who deal with the public have a higher level of job satisfaction if they have reasonable working conditions and if – and here is the challenge – they know and accept the limitations under which they must work. Everybody knows that there must be rules governing the services that a government delivers to the public. The employee must know what the rules are and why they are in place, and agree in general terms that they make sense. There's a hoary old army joke about the new recruit being asked at a training session why the butt of his rifle is made of walnut. He guesses that walnut is durable, that it looks good, and so on. The sergeant rejects all these speculations and gives him the answer: 'Because it says so in the regulations.' That is supposed to be funny, because we know that there should be a better answer than the silly one that the rules call for it for some totally unknown reason. The point here is that sometimes public servants are asked to administer programs according to rules that can be equally obscure.

I hope that an emphasis on customer service will motivate public service managers to explain to their people the reasons for the rules. This may well call some of the rules into question, which will be no bad thing – the reason for particular rules and activities must be regularly questioned. Regulatory patterns, like spending patterns, must periodically be put through the wringer. My very unscientific sample of federal public servants leads me to believe that the greatest level of dissatisfaction is found among those middle and junior managers in Ottawa (and to a lesser extent in the regions) who don't fully understand why they are doing what they are doing and just how the rules they are asked to follow fit into the larger picture. If serving the public becomes a higher priority – at the possible expense of service to the deputy, or to the minister for Question Period, or at the expense of meeting some quantitatively insignificant complaint of the Auditor General – then the job satisfaction of public servants will rise with the level of service to the public.

I hope that governments in Canada are moving in this direction. I think it is consistent with points I've made earlier about the role of central agencies, and about the way that Question Period is handled. To state the obvious, public servants are there to serve the public first and the system second. That approach makes good sense in serving the public, in saving money, and in improving job satisfaction. Having noted that it is a good idea to give public servants scope to innovate – for example, in improving customer service or within the structure of a special operating agency – setting the basic priorities of a government is still a political decision.

13

Intergovernmental Relations

In this chapter we discuss the rationale for maintaining good relations with other governments. We show how it can be done, giving some examples. We then draw some lessons from the major intergovernmental negotiation of Blakeney's career – the constitutional negotiations of 1980–82. Among the lessons to be learned are how to build support for your position, the value of having an acceptable alternative to an agreement, and the importance of making your draft agreement the focus of discussion. Borins interprets these lessons from the standpoint of the 'getting to yes' theory of negotiation expounded by the Harvard Negotiation Project.

Borins: What are some of the things a provincial government can do to be successful in its intergovernmental relations?

Blakeney: I'll speak first about regular, ongoing intergovernmental relations, then about the crisis atmosphere of constitutional change. I don't intend to give a history of the constitutional negotiations in which I was involved during 1980 and 1981, since the history of that episode is well known.[1] Rather, I will look at some of the lessons that can be drawn from that history.

Many matters of intergovernmental relations are conducted on a day-to-day basis at the officials' level.[2] Here it is important to have good information about what other governments are up to, and to be respected by other governments. I think that our human-resource management practices, and our overall approach to public management, served us well. One area that draws respect is technical competence. We had a high-quality public service, the equal of those in Ontario and Quebec, and generally better than those found in other small provinces. Thus, we were taken seriously by the other governments.[3]

Our policy of hiring high-fliers certainly served us well. Many of these able people later moved to other governments, particularly the federal government. As a consequence, we had great contacts – people in senior positions who would give us candid inside information. Indeed, the exodus of senior people like Al Johnson, Tom Shoyama, Art Wakabayashi, Don Tansley, David Levin, Bob McLarty, and many others after the 1964 election meant that we had an excellent set of contacts in Ottawa and many provincial capitals for years after.[4] This, by the way, is not said to justify the personnel policies of the Thatcher government, some of which I would criticize almost as vigorously as those of the Devine government.

I found it vital to maintain informal contacts even when federal–provincial relations were rocky due to policy disagreements, as was the case in the 1970s when we were battling Ottawa over resource taxation. I was very careful about this. As an example, I asked successive Ministers of External Affairs whether they minded if I dealt directly with the undersecretary (that is, the deputy) on information matters. For quite a time, the undersecretary was Basil Robinson, whom I knew well. We had played hockey on the same Oxford University team.

I recall a time when France was refusing to sign a nuclear nonproliferation treaty. Canada was threatening to prohibit the sale of Canadian uranium to France. I thought the position of the French government was unwise and untenable. At that time, a French consortium owned and was bringing into production the largest known uranium deposit in Canada, part of which was the richest known deposit in the world. I recall advising Basil Robinson privately that if the Canadian government felt that it had to bar shipments of uranium to France, there would be no protest from the Government of Saskatchewan. Our protest would be directed against France for not reaching an agreement on the nuclear nonproliferation treaty.

When I went on overseas trips, I was careful to find out from the Department of External Affairs and from other federal agencies like the Canadian Wheat Board what Ottawa's position was on questions I would likely encounter. When I went to Japan, China, and Southeast Asia in 1976, the Department of External Affairs sent people to Regina to give me and some of our people extensive briefings over a period of several days. Similarly, I arranged for people from the Canadian embassies in foreign capitals to accompany me on my meetings with officials of foreign governments. When I was in Japan, the Canadian ambassador there accompanied me when I went to discuss the availability of Saskatchewan uranium to Japanese power utilities. I felt very strongly that whatever our differences at home, Canada should speak with a single voice when dealing with other countries. Some departure from this rule can be tolerated when dealing with the Americans, who understand the schizophrenic nature (if not multiple personalities) of federal states. But at no other time.[5] It is enough of a challenge to deal with the Japanese or the Germans without weakening our position by showing a divided house.

When we decided to acquire a substantial portion of the potash industry in Saskatchewan, we set out our policy in our Throne Speech of November 1975. I had called Prime Minister Trudeau the day before so that he would not be taken by surprise. We also informed officials of the Department of External Affairs and arranged for a senior official of our government to fully brief them in Ottawa before the speech was read. Our official remained in Ottawa to assist in fielding questions from foreign business and governments. As a consequence, External Affairs was able to explain our position fully and fairly, so that when I went to New York a few weeks later to meet the business community, the mood of disapproval was not compounded by an overtly critical federal government position.[6]

Similarly, I kept Alberta's Premier, Peter Lougheed, with whom I had developed a good working relationship, informed of moves that might affect Alberta.[7] We had an agreement that neither of us would campaign in provincial elections in the province of the other. When he agreed to speak at or near an election time in Saskatchewan – on one occasion at a tribute to John Diefenbaker – he called me first. I had an arrangement with him that I could speak on behalf of my warm friend the late Grant Notley, who was then NDP leader in Alberta, for whom, I suspect, Lougheed had a soft spot. On one occasion I made a speech in Notley's northern Alberta constituency and a press report misinterpreted my position. Lougheed must have expressed his dissatisfaction to one of his staff. This was relayed to one of our staff, who relayed it to me. Next time I saw Lougheed, I raised it with him. He said that yes, he had been unhappy with the report. I gave him a copy of my speech and said that I felt the press had reported it badly. And our good relationship continued without further interruption.

The press generally adopts the stance that conflict is news and co-operation is not; as a result, it can be very difficult to keep open the lines of personal respect and co-operation. But it is important to do so. Prime ministers and premiers are very human. They may pretend to slough off criticism but it often does affect the way they react. That's why premiers' conferences in a social atmosphere are valuable – they allow personal relationships to be rebuilt after a year of press reports of differences and divisions.

I tried to keep my lines open to the Atlantic premiers. We had many mutual friends. At one time in the 1970s, the premiers of Nova Scotia, New Brunswick, Prince Edward Island, and Saskatchewan were all graduates of Dalhousie Law School in Halifax. For a brief period it appeared that John Crosbie might soon become Premier of Newfoundland. He would have been the fifth Dalhousie Law School graduate, bringing our contingent up to five in ten. We joked that this was about the right proportion.

Most of the ministers in our government were careful to keep the lines of communication open to their counterparts in the federal government and in other provinces.[8] Governments are driven largely by policy considerations, but good interpersonal relations do help. I found them very important when working to arrive at the common objectives I felt Canada needed.

As I have mentioned, we asked our senior public servants to make a point of keeping in touch with their counterparts in other provinces and in the federal government. This provided our government and theirs with a steady source of information; it also created a climate in which ideas could be floated and compromises suggested in ways that did not commit the politicians at too early a stage. This adds greatly to the suppleness of the negotiating process. Most negotiations ought to be conducted in such a way that policy differences can be confronted and compromises found. Considerations of personal ego or possible loss of face should not intrude on the process.[9]

Borins: Roger Fisher and William Ury of the Harvard Negotiation Project refer to this approach as separating the people from the problem. This involves concentrating on the problem, avoiding emotional outbursts, not ascribing malevolent motives, listening actively, and building personal relationships with fellow negotiators.[10]

Blakeney: Negotiations are frequently conducted under a glare of publicity. The people of the press very often decline to consider the policy elements of any compromise, and whether that compromise is good or bad for the country; instead, they put forward 'analyses' that focus almost solely on picking winners and losers among the premiers. This forces politicians to seek compromises that do not create a perception of defeat. This is why so many first ministers' conferences seem to start with so few issues decided and so many outstanding, and why the final settlement contains elements that each participant can point to and declare victory.

My fervent wish would be to see press coverage develop that focused much more on issues and potential compromises and solutions, and much less on the personalities involved. Most of the participants are simply stating the positions of their provinces, which have been derived from much more concrete considerations than personalities. People in public life deserve press coverage a cut or two above the level of *People* magazine. Sometimes we get it. Too often we do not.

Borins: What were the lessons of the 1980–1 constitutional negotiations?

Blakeney: There were several. I will mention three, and will preface them by stating that the approaches they suggest apply to many negotiating situations.

First, use every possible opportunity to build support for your position before the actual negotiations. The federal government does this in an orchestrated way, with speeches in advance, press kits, carefully crafted press releases, and the like. It is no easy thing to prepare a press release that states your position in successive paragraphs, the first with a reading time of thirty seconds for radio and television stations that still use clips of that length and the second and third paragraphs with reading times of twenty and fifteen seconds for the more staccato formats. Only a well-staffed negotiating team can manage this.

During conferences, I tried to put Saskatchewan's position in my opening statements and other televised statements. A televised opening statement at a federal–provincial conference is addressed to the chair in name only. It is in fact addressed to the public and seeks to explain to the public the issues being considered, from the speaker's point of view.[11] Saskatchewan frequently had pamphlets and other handouts for the press, although we could not match the sophistication of the federal government.

It is with the electronic media that a province like Saskatchewan is at its greatest disadvantage in dealing with the federal government.[12] When a conference was in progress, Ottawa had staff and other resources that we could not match. And when the conference was over, federal officials could, and did, mount media campaigns that we could not hope to match because we were not in a media centre.

A constitution is an agreement between governments as well as a framework by which people govern themselves. Agreement of provincial governments is required for many proposed constitutional amendments. Yet the media outside Quebec very often pay a great deal of attention to federal government proposals for constitutional change and often scant attention to provincial government positions. This is partly because the media do not accept the idea of federalism – that federal and provincial governments are partners, each sovereign in its own field – and partly because the media are not staffed to cover stories from Fredericton or Winnipeg or Victoria in the way they are staffed to cover the Ottawa scene. So, recognizing the handicaps under which we worked, we attempted to put our case before the public as often and as coherently as possible.

Second, have an alternative strategy if no agreement is reached. Anyone who enters negotiations believing that an agreement must be reached is in a very weak position and will have difficulty keeping the opposition from being aware of the situation. So a fall-back position is necessary. In the constitutional negotiations of 1979 to 1982, this presented no obvious difficulty: Saskatchewan could have managed quite well without any agreement on constitutional amendment in this period. Neither of the main elements in the package – patriation of the Constitution and a *Charter of Rights and Freedoms* – was high on the priority list of most Saskatchewan people. The Trudeau government tried hard to rally public support for the Charter, through the televised parliamentary committee hearings of late 1980 and early 1981, and had some success. But since the Trudeau government was so deeply unpopular in Western Canada because of its resource policies, the danger of public anger at a failure to reach an agreement was minimal. Indeed, there is a good deal to suggest that in pure, short-term political terms, we should have resisted reaching any agreement with the federal government.

Borins: Fisher and Ury call such a fall-back position the best alternative to a negotiated outcome, or BATNA for short.[13] They urge negotiators to strengthen their bargaining position by improving their BATNA as much as possible. Since this can only be done away from the bargaining table, negotiators who focus solely on what occurs at the bargaining table may be weakening their position.[14]

Quebec's refusal to sign the 1971 Victoria Charter is an example of a province deciding that the status quo is preferable to an agreement. Similarly, the Trudeau government then decided that the status quo was preferable to resuming negotiations.[15]

Blakeney: The fact that we did not feel obliged to reach an agreement did not dispose of all the possibilities. In this regard, we had two considerations. *First*, Trudeau might have been able to patriate the Constitution with a Charter of Rights without *any* provincial support. Indeed, in 1981 the Supreme Court of Canada said that such action would be legal but unconstitutional.[16] Had the Supreme Court confined itself to the purely legal aspects of the issue before it, the consent of provinces, including Saskatchewan, would not have mattered. *Second*, because we wanted to include in any constitutional package some provisions relating to resource taxation, and because we thought that unilateral action by the federal government would further sour federal–provincial relations, we did not wish to abandon the pursuit of an agreement. So we had a viable alternative to an agreement but not a desirable one.

The federal government, for its part, had at least two options if no agreement was reached.[17] It could have tried to proceed without provincial consent, with the blessing of the Supreme Court. A second option was to hold a referendum; if there was substantial public support, the agreement of provincial governments was not necessary.[18] The unresolved question was this: What would the Parliament at Westminster accept as sufficient to allow it to amend the British North America Act in the manner requested by Canada's Parliament? A nationwide referendum to approve constitutional changes proposed by the federal Parliament might have solved Westminster's problem, but it would have been a high-risk option for the federal government. The referendum might well have lost in Quebec, if the perception was that the proposed constitutional changes reduced the legislative powers of the Quebec government, which Trudeau had earlier promised to increase. And the referendum might have lost in Western Canada, if the public came to regard it as an endorsement of the Trudeau government, which was so unpopular that in the 1980 federal election it had failed to win a single seat in Saskatchewan, Alberta, British Columbia, Yukon, or the Northwest Territories.

My point is that when entering negotiations, a government should consider the possibility of failure and what options would then be open to it. These options should be preserved and, if possible, enhanced during the course of negotiations. If an agreement is reached, that will render unnecessary the pursuit of other options.

During the 1980–1 period, all of the negotiators were uncertain of the strength of their positions in the event of a failure to reach agreement. This laid the groundwork for a compromise agreement. The Quebec government opted not to accept the compromise and to pursue its other options. One was to assert in the courts that the Province of Quebec had a constitutional veto. This move failed. The second option was to pursue constitutional change by political means. Some might say that the Quebec government under Premiers Parizeau and Bouchard has been pursuing yet another alternative strategy: if normal political means of constitutional change fail, Quebec has another choice – separation. Without suggesting that separatism is *only* a bargaining strategy, it is certainly *also* that – and a powerful one.

The *third* lesson I regard as important in complicated negotiations is to put your draft agreement on the table and, if possible, get it accepted as the basis for negotiation. One can build into a draft many assumptions that are hard to change during the course of negotiations.

With respect to the negotiations surrounding the Charter of Rights, the federal government consistently kept its draft on the table. It did so by including a Charter in Bill C-60, its constitutional reform package of 1978. All subsequent drafts for constitutional change put forward by the federal government contained its version of a Charter.[19] Thus, if today you ask who drafted Canada's Charter of Rights and Freedoms, among those who know you will get the name of a federal public servant, Barry Strayer, now Mr Justice Strayer.

Borins: Fisher and Ury talk about the 'one-text procedure,' in which a mediator writes a text and then modifies it on the basis of criticisms made by the parties who are negotiating. After several rounds of this, the mediator asks the parties whether they are prepared to accept the final draft in its entirety. The Americans, acting as mediators between Israel and Egypt, did this in the negotiations that led to the Camp David Accord.[20] In multiparty negotiations, working from one text greatly reduces complexity. Of course, when there is no mediator, the key question is whose draft becomes the basis for discussion.

Blakeney: With respect to the amending formula, the government of Alberta waged a long and, at first, lonely campaign to get its amending formula accepted. Up until about 1979, almost all proposed amending formulas were built on a regional view of Canada. Thus, in the federal formulae the four regions – Atlantic, Quebec, Ontario, and the West – had to agree to any constitutional change. Alberta disagreed with this concept and favoured a formula by which all provinces were juridically equal. It kept pressing this idea. The result was that several formulae put forward by Alberta, bearing such names as the Toronto Consensus and the Vancouver Consensus, gained support from groups of premiers.[21]

Alberta's greatest victory in the process was that it convinced the Quebec government to accept the principle of juridical equality of provinces, which gives no province a veto. Some of Alberta's formulae had high population quotas as well – for example, a constitutional amending formula that would require the agreement of Parliament and the legislatures of seven provinces representing 80 per cent of the population of Canada. This gives a de facto veto to Ontario and Quebec at the present time, though this may change as populations change. Alberta's negotiating strategy paid off so that when the final compromise was made, the package included an amending formula that was structured along the lines of the Alberta draft. It calls for the agreement of Parliament and the legislatures of two-thirds of the provinces representing 50 per cent of the population of Canada.

We saw Alberta pursue the same strategy with respect to Senate reform. A few years ago, its idea of a triple-E Senate – a Senate that was elected, effective (that is, with real power), and equal (that is, with an equal number of senators from each province) – was scoffed at as hopelessly unrealistic. Through sheer persistence and through having this idea at least on the table at every discussion of Senate reform, Alberta succeeded in establishing the idea as one that must be seriously considered. Only future events will show whether the Alberta strategy has succeeded again.

Borins: You may not have pushed your point as long or as loud as Alberta. Even so, did Saskatchewan gain any direct benefits from accepting the Constitutional agreement of 1981?

Blakeney: Yes. Section 92A was added to the Constitution. During the negotiations, we used the tactic of having our draft of this provision on the table as the basis of discussion as often as we could. This constitutional change was important to us, since it will help blunt the effect of two adverse Supreme Court of Canada decisions rendered in the late 1970s dealing with the taxation of resource revenues by provincial governments.[22] I will say a little more about this important issue in Chapter 14.

Borins: Without speculating on the future course of federal–provincial relations, do you feel that the negotiations leading to the Meech Lake Accord and the Charlottetown Accord offer any lessons for future intergovernmental relations?

Blakeney: That is a large question. I will not try to answer it fully, but I will make a few comments.

Negotiators should not lose sight of the likely end point in the negotiations for the sake of achieving agreement at an intermediate point. In a sense, this is counselling perfection. But it is sometimes tempting to pursue the interim victory. Both Meech Lake and Charlottetown are examples.

Most of the elements of the Meech Lake Accord, including the distinct society provisions, required only the approval of Parliament and seven provinces representing 50 per cent of the population of Canada. S.41(d) provisions dealing with the Supreme Court and s.41(e) provisions dealing with the amending formula required unanimous provincial approval. If the provisions had been included in two resolutions, only the resolution dealing with s.41(d) and (e) would have failed when the legislatures of Manitoba and Newfoundland failed to ratify the resolutions within the prescribed time. But I presume that political imperatives dictated that the package be presented as one 'seamless web.' One cannot help but wonder whether an extra effort might have convinced the Quebec government to accept an arrangement to put the whole package to Parliament and the legislatures, but separated into two or three resolutions according to the level of support required for passage. This was an attractive alternative, particularly since it is quite possible that *all* the separated resolutions would have passed.

The Charlottetown Accord, it seems to me, reflected the desire of the negotiators to meet the concerns of many interest groups. Because it was so unwieldy, the final package was harder to support and easier for opponents to attack when referendum time came. The experience in Australia and Switzerland is that almost invariably, the more complicated the package the more likely it is to be rejected.

These musings are akin to offering advice on how to ride a bronco while I am firmly seated on the corral rail. But I hope I have identified the extra hazards that political leaders face when negotiating a package of constitutional changes which must then be accepted by parliaments, legislatures, or voters across Canada.

Another interesting development is the use of federal legislation to set out changes that it is hoped will later be accepted as constitutional changes. Perhaps the first example of this was the Canadian Bill of Rights introduced by Prime Minister Diefenbaker in 1960 – this law to apply in areas of federal jurisdiction only. This was followed in 1982 by the Charter of Rights and Freedoms, introduced as part of the Constitution Act. The Charter repeated much of the Bill of Rights.

More recently, Prime Minister Chrétien has introduced federal legislation designed to give a veto on constitutional change to each of the five regions of Canada (the new, fifth region being British Columbia). The strategy seems to be that if accepted over a period of time, even though its legal basis is federal legislation only, this veto will become something of a *fait accompli* and will therefore be easier to get accepted as an appropriate constitutional change. This is an interesting twist in federal–provincial constitutional relations.

In most federations, and certainly in Canada, intergovernmental relations is a favourite indoor sport.

Part Three

Government and Its Environment:
Lobbying, Crises, Communications, and Change

14

Lobbying: Advice to the Private Sector

The first two sections of the book approached public management primarily in terms of institutions, describing their characteristics and outlining the underlying principles governing their operation. This final section deals with a variety of topics, including lobbying, public consultation, the management of change, crisis management, media relations, and changes of government. Though the topics appear disparate, we think there are two common themes. First, these chapters all deal with the relationship between the government and the society it governs. Second, the topics are situational, in the sense that they pose a set of challenges to which public sector institutions must respond.

The first topic is lobbying. Government is the target of lobbying efforts by its own electorate, and when it attempts to influence the policies of other governments it is a lobbyist itself. This chapter presents a number of case studies of communities, universities, and businesses lobbying government. Described here are attempts to persuade government to do things favourable to the organization, such as spending money on desired projects; and attempts to dissuade government from doing something unfavourable to the organization, such as increasing taxation on the private sector. As the title to the chapter indicates, we use these cases to develop some principles that will guide lobbyists in their dealings with government. The principles include the importance of providing information to government, the necessity of avoiding entanglement in federal–provincial conflicts, the value of finding appropriate allies, and the relevance of communicating effectively with the public.

Borins: Let us start our discussion of lobbying with instances of organizations persuading government to do something that will advance the organization's interests, such as giving it a grant, a contract, or a mandate, or changing some rule or regulation in a favourable way.

Blakeney: I'll begin with my favourite case of what an academic would probably call grantsmanship. It concerns the Elrose hospital. Elrose is a town of about seven hundred people. It had a small nursing home and wanted a new hospital. The proponents of this project were therefore seeking a government grant to build the hospital and assurance of operating funds. It was a marginal case. The area the hospital would serve was barely large enough to be able to support a community hospital. Undeterred, the community mounted a campaign.

I need hardly say that delegations arrived at the minister's office from the proposed hospital board and the nursing home board. The town council then expressed its support, as did the local chamber of commerce. The campaign became a little more imaginative when surrounding rural municipalities were organized to support the project, but it was still a standard approach. Then the campaign moved to the provincial conventions of both the urban and the rural municipal government organizations, where resolutions in support of the project appeared. This was innovative. I thought, 'They are moving nicely.' I thought they were moving very nicely indeed when resolutions in support of the project appeared on the agendas of the provincial conventions of all three major political parties. The proponents had organized to the extent that groups representing all three parties had taken the issue to the local constituency conventions of each of the parties, received their endorsements, and had the matter moved to the provincial conventions. No stone was left unturned in the proponents' efforts to show that the project had support from every segment of the town and surrounding area.

This is the way to organize pressure. At one level a government will simply want to get rid of an issue like the Elrose hospital, which will be a minor item on the agenda of a provincial government. Marginal decisions will go to well-organized proponents, on the 'squeaky wheel' principle. On another level, governments want to be shown that if the project runs into any problems, a large number of apparently competent people will be there to solve them – in the Elrose case, to get the hospital built, built well, and operating successfully. Such people are likely to be happy citizens, and governments like happy citizens.

I recall the way two communities approached our government for special grants. One town that came in, outlined their pressing problem, and asked what the government could do to help. Another town came in and advised that they had a problem, and that the community preferred to solve it this way, and that the whole town was enthusiastic about the solution, and that the government would surely want to be part of this exciting, necessary, and broadly supported project.

The difference in the approaches was stark. The first town expected the government to analyse the problem and suggest some solution while the community raised all the difficulties with the proposed solution. In the second town, the problem had been assessed, a proposed solution arrived at, and public support for the solution mobilized *before* the appeal to the government was made. Clearly, a government feels more comfort, and more pressure, when the second approach is taken. It feels more comfort because its commitment is confined to giving the grant and not to solving the problem to the satisfaction of a perhaps disgruntled and almost certainly divided community. It feels more pressure because the second community has already organized support for the project, which has probably involved the raising of funds locally, and because there are many stakeholders who will be disappointed if the government decides not to join them in their, by now, pet project. The element of pressure, even a level of threat, is clearly present.

Elrose was not the only community that had developed the skills of lobbying government into an art form.

Borins: Going back to our previous discussion of budgeting, you mentioned that the Romanow government dealt with the deficits of the early 1990s partly by making cuts in health care. This included converting fifty-two rural hospitals to health clinics. Was Elrose hospital one of those which was converted?

Blakeney: Yes, the Elrose hospital and over fifty similar small hospitals are no longer in-patient health care facilities. Elrose has been converted to a health centre offering out-patient treatment only. It has fallen victim to technological progress. As medical equipment and technology advanced, the College of Physicians and Surgeons in Saskatchewan (as elsewhere, I am sure) strongly discouraged medical doctors from carrying out surgical procedures in hospitals that were not fully equipped, as no small hospital can be. As a result, surgery – except of an emergency kind that can be done at a health centre – virtually ceased in the small hospitals. So did the delivery of babies.

I recall the comment of one local in a community whose hospital had closed. Asked if the closure would mean a change in where women delivered their children, he replied 'No, no. As a matter of fact, the last baby delivered in our hospital was my daughter, and she's already totalled two cars.' Evidently, in that community totalling a car was a rite of passage.

The great improvements in highways, housing, and communications have meant that the small hospital as an in-patient facility now has very restricted usefulness. Often, a small hospital represented an important part of the local economy, but with the financial constraints of the 1990s, it was no longer possible to sustain them.

In the case of Elrose, the health centre has been combined with a nursing home. There are long-term care beds, respite beds, laboratory and X-ray services and nursing services on call on a twenty-four-hour basis. This is a good level of service, and the town of Elrose continues to thrive.

Borins: Returning to lobbying, the literature points out the importance of having substantial public support for a proposal.[1] The Elrose case goes beyond that to emphasize the importance of having a well-developed proposal.

My story concerns an experience of my own as a lobbyist.[2] In 1986 and 1987, when I was associate dean of the Faculty of Administrative Studies (now Schulich School of Business) at York University, we approached the federal and Ontario governments for a five-year, $6 million grant to establish a centre for international business. The centre would support research and executive development, and establish an innovative international business MBA program that would combine study in business with study of a foreign language. We exerted most of our efforts in Ottawa, but at the end of the day we received the $6 million from Queen's Park – and not a penny from Ottawa. Our efforts amounted to a controlled experiment for determining which tactics and circumstances will result in a successful lobbying effort.

In the case of the federal government, we presented our proposal to the two departments we thought were most likely to be supportive – External Affairs, which was responsible for international trade, and Regional Industrial Expansion, the precursor of Industry Canada, which was responsible for improving Canada's management capabilities. Unfortunately, the two departments were fighting a turf war at that time, and because our proposal was intended to improve trade through better management education, it got caught in the middle of the battle.

There was opposition from lower-level officials at External Affairs, who had only enough money for a small program of their own, which supported international business studies programs at five other universities. In their view, our proposal was an attempt either to take their money or to circumvent their mandate. DRIE had enough uncommitted money in its budget to fund our proposal, but an uncertain mandate, owing to the threat of opposition from External Affairs. We had some support from senior officials at DRIE, but because of the rapid rotation at the upper levels, they kept leaving before they could act. The proposal finally died in mid-1987, when it was discovered that DRIE had overcommitted its budget by $100 million for the fiscal year at hand, which resulted in a freeze on new initiatives.

When we presented the proposal to the government of Ontario, we had much more luck. I showed it to Don Stevenson, then Ontario's representative to the governments of Canada and Quebec. Stevenson, who had begun his career as a foreign service officer and who was one of the first senior public servants in Ontario to become bilingual, liked the proposal, especially the international MBA program combining business and language. He passed it on to George Radwanski, a consultant who was then completing a report on the service sector of the Ontario economy. Radwanski liked the proposal and recommended in his report that the government establish an international business centre at an Ontario university. This provided valuable credibility. We also presented the proposal to a mid-level contact in the Ministry of Industry, Trade, and Technology – the department we felt was most likely to be its champion.

In early 1987, Premier David Peterson's minority government was a few months from the end of its two-year alliance with the NDP and was preparing a pre-election Throne Speech. Ontario's Ministry of Industry, Trade, and Technology wanted to incorporate a series of initiatives into the Throne Speech to show that Ontario, while not supporting the Free Trade Agreement – which the federal government was then negotiating – nevertheless was taking action of its own to stimulate international trade. Thus, York's modest proposal became part of the solution to one of the government's priority problems. We knew things were moving along very nicely when the MITT deputy minister *summoned us* to discuss our proposal with him just before he went into a series of interdepartmental meetings to draft the Throne Speech.

Our proposal was incorporated into the Throne Speech. Still, we did not obtain an immediate grant. It turned out that the Ministry of Colleges and Universities had concerns about other departments giving large grants to one university, especially without other universities having an opportunity to compete for the funds. A compromise was worked out whereby both ministries presided over a competition among Ontario universities for the $6 million grant. The eventual winner was a consortium of York, the University of Toronto, and Wilfrid Laurier University. The Ontario Centre for International Business was established as a joint venture of the three universities.

From this story, I draw several conclusions for lobbyists. First, it is important for a proposal to be consistent with the government's *current priorities*. An international MBA program incorporating language studies fit very nicely with an Ontario government priority, which was trade expansion by means of alternatives to the Free Trade Agreement. In contrast, Ottawa's priority was the Free Trade Agreement. I emphasize *current* priorities, because government's priorities are always changing, and it is the responsibility of a good lobbyist to track the latest doctrinal shifts (that is, the 'flavours of the month').[3] In this instance, to say that the proposal would expand trade was not enough: the question was which *type* of trade. Another way to characterize our effort was that we had a solution in search of a problem; our challenge was to find the right problem.[4] The classic case, on a large scale, of a corporation aligning itself with government policies is Dome Petroleum, which in the 1970s and early 1980s succeeded in becoming the *instrument* by which the federal government pursued its policy of oil development on the Arctic frontier.[5]

The second conclusion is that the governmental context is important. For several reasons, Ottawa was unreceptive while Queen's Park was inclined to be supportive. The *timing* was right at Queen's Park, as the government was putting together a package of programs for an election that would be coming in a few months; conversely, a proposal to the federal government in 1986 and 1987 was too early for the run-up to an election anticipated in the fall of 1988.[6] Ontario's Throne Speech provided a *context* for departments to raise proposals for ministerial endorsement without having to undergo the detailed scrutiny of a submission to Treasury Board; the federal government provided no such opportunity at that time. In both governments, our proposal got caught in jurisdictional conflicts. In the case of Ontario, the Throne Speech process mitigated this conflict, since the question asked of any proposal by a committee of deputy ministers was only whether it would be an effective element in the government's program – turf fights could be sorted out later. In Ottawa there was no such process for minimizing turf fights, and our proposal remained a source of contention between External Affairs and DRIE.

The *budgetary context* is also relevant. Ontario was experiencing a strong economic boom, and tax revenues were growing rapidly. This allowed it to open its Treasury doors wider than usual, as many governments like to do in the run-up to an election. Proposals for one-time grants that do not involve an ongoing commitment for operating costs flourish in such circumstances. (See Chapter 10.) Conversely, in Ottawa, first External Affairs and then DRIE were being 'put through the wringer.'

A third conclusion is that rapid changes in personnel at the senior levels complicate a lobbyist's task. Not only does it create problems within the public service (see Chapter 8), but it also creates uncertainty for anyone who must deal with the public service. In addition, it pushes power farther down into the bureaucracy, because the less mobile lower-level officials have the advantages of continuity and expertise.

All that being said, you might wonder what happened to our centre. It was successful – in part. To its credit, York University's business school worked hard to develop the international MBA, and was ultimately rewarded when that program received base budget funding beyond the centre's five-year time frame from the Ministry of Colleges and Universities. The executive development and research programs were never able to become self-sustaining, and as a result, when the original grant ran out the centre died. Back at the beginning of the book we referred to a university as a collection of entrepreneurs held together by a common grievance over parking; if this is so for *one* university, you can imagine how hard it is to get several universities to co-operate.

We now turn to cases where the private sector lobbies to avoid the negative impact of increased taxation.

Blakeney: During my time as Premier, we had to deal with three major resource industries: potash, uranium, and oil. In each case, world market prices were rising dramatically. In each case, there was a tough three-way fight for resource revenues involving the provincial governments (which under the British North America Act of 1867 have legal jurisdiction over the resources), the federal government (which has a mandate for economic equalization), and the industries producing the resources. You will recall that I touched on these issues in Chapter 4.

During the 1970s, Western provincial governments of all political stripes followed a strategy of abrogating in letter or in spirit their long-term contracts with producers, and instituting various new and higher resource royalty charges. For example, Saskatchewan instituted a royalty surcharge on oil in 1973 and a tax on potash reserves in the fall of 1974. In addition, we were considering various forms of joint ventures with private companies as a way of ensuring that we would receive an appropriate return on our resource heritage.

In its May 1974 budget the federal government introduced an amendment to the Income Tax Act to the effect that provincial resource royalty payments would no longer be deductible from the taxable income of corporations for the purpose of calculating federal corporate income tax payable. Since royalties on oil and potash had increased, and since these royalty payments were not accepted as deductible expenses by the federal government for corporate income tax purposes, the corporations were clearly being squeezed. The federal amendment was meant to force provincial governments to lower royalties so that companies would enjoy higher corporate earnings, which would then be taxed by the federal government. The provinces felt that this tactic was an outrageous action in a federal country and that the provinces were entitled to the full economic rent that flowed from resource ownership and jurisdiction. Outrageous or not, the private resource producers were caught in the middle of an intergovernmental power play – clearly, it was an unfair position for them to be put in.

We saw three different industries – the oil industry, the potash industry, and the uranium industry – deal with this issue and with the provincial government in three different ways. I want to concentrate on the potash industry because, as I saw it, that sector presented a case study in how *not* to manage business/government relations.

In 1974, when the provincial government instituted a tax on potash reserves, to be paid in addition to the traditional Crown royalties, the industry at first paid the tax – or at least what they said was owing under the tax. The tax was in the nature of an income tax, and accordingly the province required the financial statements of the companies for administrative reasons. However, the companies refused to provide any financial statements.[7] Partly, this was to deny the government information that would have helped it invest in the potash industry, either by developing a mine of its own or by purchasing an existing mine.

I was surprised by the industry's approach to the reserve tax. Although the tax proposals were put forward early in 1974 to provide the industry with an opportunity to seek modification of the tax before it became law, no constructive dialogue ensued. We in the government made it clear that we were prepared to discuss the details of the new tax. The industry took the position that the tax was not legal and refused to negotiate the elements of the tax.

On top of this, in early 1975 the industry also declined to provide information on what quantity of potash was being mined. This made it impossible to calculate even the traditional Crown royalties owing, the legality of which had never been an issue.

By way of background, I should mention that the industry had, in early 1972, urged the Government of Saskatchewan to continue a scheme of regulating the production and price of potash established by the previous Liberal government of Premier Ross Thatcher, which we had succeeded in 1971. One potash company, Central Canada Potash – a subsidiary of the giant resource company Noranda – objected and in December 1972 commenced a legal action to upset this prorationing scheme, as it was called, on constitutional grounds. However, at that time all other companies supported the scheme and the government policy.[8]

I assumed that the potash companies were taking their very tough stand during 1974 and 1975 so that they would need to concede nothing while they awaited the outcome of the expected provincial election. After we were re-elected in June 1975, I expected that negotiations would then commence in earnest. That was not to be.

Nine days after the election, new legal actions were started. All the companies except Central Canada Potash joined in attacking the potash reserve tax on constitutional grounds, claiming that it infringed upon federal jurisdiction over interprovincial trade and commerce. In addition, they demanded that previous reserve tax payments be refunded, with interest, and refused to make any additional payments.

A few months later, all the companies that had previously supported the prorationing scheme so vigorously now joined Central Canada Potash in attacking it on constitutional grounds.[9] They were joined as a co-plaintiff by the federal government. This was not a case of the federal government intervening (to use a lawyer's word) to argue a point of constitutional law; rather, it was a case of the federal government joining with the potash mining companies, led by Central Canada Potash, to sue the provincial government. By welcoming the federal government as a co-plaintiff, the potash companies were sending a clear signal that in the then-current federal–provincial battle over sharing resource revenues, they were on the side of the federal government.

Our government countered this onslaught by announcing a policy of acquiring 50 per cent of the productive capacity of potash mines in Saskatchewan. This policy had two objectives. The first was to protect production from provincially owned mines from federal taxation – an answer to the federal corporate taxation moves. The second was to secure the revenues from the industry that the potash companies were unwilling to pay. The legislation authorized expropriation if necessary, although no expropriation took place or was threatened. Indeed, we ultimately purchased 40 per cent of the potash industry, at a cost of $520 million, paying what both potash producers and the American government agreed were fair prices.[10]

Eventually the Supreme Court of Canada ruled that some of the taxes were unconstitutional. The taxes were restructured, and compromise agreements were arrived at that gave the government a very large part of the revenues it sought.[11] From the Saskatchewan government's point of view, the favourable outcome of the negotiations owed much to the rising demand and price for potash, but at least as much to the fact that in their campaign against the government, the potash companies had made some crucial strategic and tactical errors. These had eroded public support for their cause.

The controversy not only assisted us at home in our dealings with the potash companies, but also helped us press our case for a constitutional amendment to soften the impact of the Supreme Court decisions in the Central Canada Potash and CIGOL cases. As I mentioned in the previous chapter, section 92A was added to the Constitution 1982.

Borins: Can you identify more clearly some of the errors made by the potash companies, as you saw them?

Blakeney: I think I can do this best by referring to the oil and uranium industries. The oil industry and the potash industry had been operating in Saskatchewan according to tax regimes of long standing. When the value of resources soared in the 1970s, our government moved to raise royalties and taxes to increase the return to the public. In this matter, the oil and potash industries had legitimate complaints. Both attacked the tax legislation as unconstitutional, as they were surely entitled to do. Both suggested that if taxes were not lowered, their industries would not expand production, which was also their right. But the oil companies realized that in the public eye they were foreign companies making large profits from resources in a relatively poor province. The potash companies, while similarly perceived, did not seem aware of how the public would regard them. Let me turn to specifics:

Their first error was *refusing to provide information.* The potash producers all refused to provide the financial and other data required by law for the calculation of taxes; they also refused to pay taxes due and owing – even those which were acknowledged to be legal. In contrast, the oil industry vigorously objected to the tax changes and pursued all their legal remedies, but always remitted the information required of them as well as the taxes payable under both the old and the disputed tax laws. Later, the uranium producers entered into vigorous negotiations with us about our proposed taxes and undertook to prove to us that the taxes were too onerous by fully disclosing their financial position and the impact of the proposed taxes on each producer. Following the exchange of a mountain of computer printouts, they convinced us to modify our proposed royalty schedules.

For producers of a 'political' mineral like uranium, the need for public support is always a consideration. Producers of oil have a world of experience at bargaining with governments and know how to protect their flanks. In stark contrast, the producers of potash felt aggrieved and reacted almost with petulance, and certainly without regard to their position with the public. In the search for public support, after the battle lines were drawn they were left trying to persuade ordinary citizens – who have to file their income tax returns and pay their taxes whether they like it or not – that it was all right for foreign-owned potash companies to refuse to file any returns or pay any taxes. As the public saw it, the companies merely thought the taxes were too high. As the companies found out, that was not an easy sell.

Borins: Taking the view, prevalent in the literature, that lobbying is in essence a process of exchange between government and interest groups, it is clear that one of the things that lobbyists can provide for government is information. This includes information about the impact of government policies. In the case of changes in economic policies, such as proposed tax changes, corporations always have more information than government and can be effective at arguing for changes in proposals.[12] Conversely, when companies are unwilling to provide information, governments and the public assume that corporations have something to hide, such as massive profits.

I have an example of how, by providing the right information at the right time, a lobbyist played a significant role in getting a desired program launched. Ontario's Ministry of Consumer and Commercial Relations (MCCR) and Ministry of Transportation (MoT) had jointly designed a Used Vehicle Information Package

(UVIP) in 1991, to be mandated for consumer protection when cars were sold privately.[13] While the program would bring in revenue, it would also require an initial investment to link data bases in MCCR and MoT. Given the Ontario government's deficit, they were having difficulty getting the approval of the Ministry of Finance. Enter the lobbyist. The Used Car Dealers' Association provided a study showing that the average resale price of used vehicles reported to the Ministry of Revenue was considerably below the average selling price of used vehicles. In other words, private resellers were underreporting their prices to minimize the sales tax they had to pay. It followed that by requiring people who sold cars privately to use the UVIP and to report the fair market value of the vehicle, the Ministry of Finance would receive more sales tax revenue.[14] When the Ministry of Finance realized this, it became a strong supporter of the proposed UVIP. As a result, the proposal was fast-tracked, and cabinet approval was received and legislation pased within three months. The revenue impact of the UVIP was an immediate 50 per cent increase in average tax collected per taxable transaction (from $129 to $195). The used car dealers' interest in having UVIP was that it levelled the playing field between them and private resellers.

Blakeney: That is a useful illustration of how lobbyists can provide governments with valuable information. Information from lobbyists is usually self-serving and should be assessed with caution, but it can nevertheless be helpful and important to a government. Returning to the unforthcoming potash industry, their second strategic error was *getting involved in federal–provincial fights*. As I have suggested, once the federal government in its budget of 1974 ruled that royalties and taxes paid to provincial governments were not deductible expenses for the purpose of calculating federal corporate income tax, the companies were in a very difficult position. They had every right to complain about what governments were doing to them. But public opinion in Saskatchewan and Western Canada would certainly place the blame on the federal government or, perhaps, on the two governments for not cleaning up the tax mess. The oil industry castigated both governments, saying that between them the governments had created the problem and that they should solve it forthwith. The uranium industry, which paid few taxes at that time, stayed out of the fray. But the potash industry took the position that their total tax burden was too high and that the provincial government should give way. They levelled few criticisms against the federal government, and indeed, as I've mentioned, joined with them as co-plaintiffs to attack Saskatchewan's resource taxation laws.

The moral of this story is that when intergovernmental conflict creates unreasonable demands on an industry or a company, it is dangerous to choose sides and prudent to attack both. Attacking both governments is reasonably safe even for industries that have difficulty pleading poverty. Siding with Ottawa against the government of the provinces where your operations are conducted was a foolhardy approach for a resource producer to take in the 1970s in Western Canada, and would be so in almost any circumstances.

The third error the potash companies made lay in *not finding the right allies*. The oil and potash industries used the tactic of announcing that if the proposed high taxes were introduced, they would suspend plans for expansion. This tactic, or a variation of it, is a standard response from industry to proposed tax increases. The potash industry put its position forward as a threat.[15] In contrast, the oil industry announced its position quietly, as a necessary outcome of government policy, and stopped drilling wells. Then the Oil Well Drilling Contractors Association, a group of local entrepreneurs, very effectively made the case to the government and the public that excessive taxation was costing its members their jobs. So far as I am aware, the potash industry made few efforts to raise support from local governments, trade unions, or contractors, all of whom might have seen their interests adversely affected and made the potash industry's case to the government and the public.

Borins: Gotlieb makes a similar point in his discussion of the Canadian embassy lobbying in the United States on behalf of Canadian exporters. When Canadian producers find trade action being threatened against them by competing American producers, their best course of action is to find allies, such as retailers and/or consumers of Canadian exports.[16] An example: when American lumber producers urged the U.S. government to increase its duty on Canadian softwood imports, the Canadian government worked with American lumber and building materials dealers and with mortgage lenders to build a consumer coalition to oppose the lumber producers.[17]

Blakeney: The potash industry's fourth error was its *failure to communicate effectively*. The industry attempted to carry its case to the public by buying television time and having potash executives answer questions phoned in by the public. The questions were often uninformed and incoherent. Not surprisingly, the company executives were less than deft at steering the questions around to ones they could answer and then answering them in a nontechnical way. Their answers were often excessively technical and hit the wrong points.

The government engaged a first-class interviewer, Patrick Watson, and gave him free reign to ask any questions he wished, and I tried to answer them as directly as I could. When both the interviewer and the person interviewed are experienced in using television, the impact is likely to be much more favourable.[18] The oil industry, and certainly the uranium industry, did not attempt to challenge the government's policies with a media campaign.

To conclude, the private sector often finds it difficult to combat a government policy. My basic advice would be to follow a three-part strategy. First, set out your objectives fairly and forcefully in the public domain and seek local allies to make your case. Avoid a slick presentation, but be sure it is a professional one. Second, co-operate with the government on technical issues so as to avoid being branded a bad corporate citizen; as well, avoid being drawn into intergovernmental fights. Third and finally, except in rare instances don't attempt to fight a holy war against the public sector. Rather, present your case in terms of the government's own values – things like creating a healthy economy, providing jobs, stimulating exports, increasing tax revenues, and the like. The public is usually much less ideological and much more pragmatic in its thinking than either government officials or business leaders.

Borins: It's interesting that your lessons are all aimed at the private sector. John Burton, a former public servant in the Potash Secretariat, developed some lessons for governments in their relationship with multinational resource-extraction firms. He argues that it is essential for government to have in-house expertise about the industry so that it can set royalty schedules that will recover resource rents, and prevent multinationals from using transfer pricing to avoid royalty payments. It is also necessary to have a credible threat of public ownership as a bargaining lever.[19]

Blakeney: I agree with John Burton that royalties over any longer period of time are best based on the value of the mineral extracted, and that this requires a method of evaluation other than the price at which a mining company sells the product to an associated company on a non-arm's-length basis. And in dealing with a mining company seeking to buy a province's minerals in the ground, it is often necessary that there be an alternative buyer. If the companies form a common front, effective bargaining may require the option of the Crown itself doing the job of extracting and selling the mineral.

Returning to private sector lobbyists, I'll give one last example of effective lobbying, with the lobbyist linking his own interests to the government's policy agenda. Leonard Lee, whom I came to know on the board of the Public Policy Forum, is an entrepreneur who owns a substantial mail-order tool business called Lee Valley Tools. Lee found that he was at a competitive disadvantage vis-à-vis American mail-order companies because Canadian customers who bought from them, while legally required to pay provincial sales tax and GST, in practice rarely did so. Lee launched a critique of the provisions and practices of the Free Trade Agreement that let these tools into the country duty free, and called his position FTA, or 'Fine Tuning Absent.' He conducted a vigorous campaign of letters to the media, and sent letters and briefs to the political and public service heads of the appropriate agencies. He linked his campaign with the rising public concern over cross-border shopping. He was rewarded early in 1992: the federal government made changes to its tax policies for mail-order shipments, changes that allowed Lee Valley Tools to compete without disadvantage.[20]

Borins: Returning to your advice to business not to fight holy wars, I should add that they did fight a holy war against the Rae government; as Rae wrote in his memoir, 'business as a class wanted our government to fail and was prepared to do whatever it could to make sure we did fail.'[21] While business as a class opposed the Rae government, there were lots of instances where individual businesses worked smoothly with it – for example, in publicly assisted restructurings such as Spruce Falls Pulp and Paper and Algoma Steel. This should not be surprising, given the weak economy and the imperatives of corporate survival. But electoral politics is another matter, and there the holy war succeeded.

15

Public Consultation

Public consultation is a very close cousin to lobbying. One might distinguish the two by arguing that the public initiates lobbying and the government initiates consultation; but regardless of who initiates, both involve a flow of information between government and the public, with the ultimate objective of achieving some measure of consent by the governed. In this chapter we look at various forms of consultation, including formal meetings with interest groups, Royal Commissions or commissions of inquiry, and task forces. We claim that commissions have had a substantial impact on public policy, especially in the long run. Finally, we argue that governments should be clear in their objectives when undertaking consultation.

Borins: In the course of discussing other topics, we have frequently mentioned politicians and public servants consulting with the general public and particular publics. Did you develop any special methods of public consultation?

Blakeney: I think the answer to that is, in general, no. When we came to office in 1971 we inherited the traditional methods that had long been in use in Saskatchewan. The New Democratic Party had annual conventions attended by a thousand people drawn from a total population of one million. These people represented a surprisingly complete cross-section of the public, although a few groups were seriously underrepresented. MLAs, particularly rural MLAs, knew their voters and were known to them. Lobbying the MLA formally and informally was a well-developed art. I recall having a discussion in my Regina office with a sophisticated political science researcher from Boston – from Harvard, I believe. He was astounded at the high recognition factor rural MLAs had. I recall his comment: 'In some of these constituencies, over 80 per cent of the people polled could give the name of their MLA. I could take you to places in the U.S. where fewer than 80 per cent of the people could give you the name of the President of the United States.' Regrettably, the same high name recognition was not evident in the cities, but MLAs were a useful and effective way to do some consultation.

Other long-established methods of consultation were used. The cabinet set aside a block of four or five days each year to meet, receive briefs from, and talk with a wide range of public bodies. These included local government groups like the rural and urban municipal associations and the association of school trustees; business groups like the Saskatchewan Chamber of Commerce, the provincial division of the Canadian Manufacturers Association, and other groups representing small business; the Saskatchewan Teachers Federation, the Federation of Labour, and other employee groups; the United Church of Canada, Roman Catholic organizations, and other religious groups; and many narrower interest groups such as pro-life and pro-choice groups.

Borins: In most of those encounters you would be listening to, and reacting to, the agendas of those groups.

Blakeney: Correct. Most of these activities might better be described as lobbying by public groups rather than the government seeking public comment on proposed government action.

Since the 1970s there has been a gradual change in what the public accepts as appropriate consultation. I could not document this conclusion, but it seems to me that there is less acceptance of the idea of representative democracy and more demand for some approach to direct democracy. MPs, MPPs, MNAs, MHAs, and MLAs are less and less seen as the appropriate people to seek out the public's reaction to any proposed government action. Governments are now doing everything from receiving briefs, to establishing premier's councils on (say) labour/management relations, to conducting polling and surveys, to organizing conferences, symposia, and televised town hall meetings, to having ministers appear on open-line shows, to setting up 1-800 numbers, e-mail addresses, and websites. And the list goes on.

Borins: I think there are a number of reasons for this. First, new information technology has created a number of these modes of consultation; those it has created involve direct contact with either the minister or the public service, rather than going through a local MP or MLA. Second, initiatives to improve the quality of public service include direct response by the front line worker, or the immediate supervisor, to client complaints. Thus, the role of the MP or MLA as fixer or advocate for constituents has been eroded. Third, polling is a faster and more scientific method for determining the state of public opinion than calling on MLAs to canvass the views of their constituents. MLAs are now perceived as a means of triangulating, or testing, poll results with subjective impressions. Finally, this is an age of expertise, and backbenchers rarely are experts. Consultations involving technical issues are likely to be handled by people with expertise in the subject. If we're right about the declining role of parliamentarians, this does raise questions about how they can add value to the democratic process, and even whether governments should be elected on some basis other than geographical constituencies. Those questions aside, we return to the issue of consultation in our current system of government. How would you classify the various means of consultation commonly used?

Blakeney: There are at least three variables at play when we try to classify methods of consultation:

• Level of formality.
• Duration. For example, is it a one-time consultation on a particular issue, or is there an ongoing consultative body?
• The degree to which consultation is an interactive exercise in joint decision-making, as opposed to a flow of information from the government to the citizen, and vice versa.

I am not going to try to rate all the methods of consultation we have mentioned by reference to the criteria for classification I've just mentioned. The discussion would become convoluted. But keeping these general categories in mind may be helpful.

The most traditional form of consultation is a Royal Commission; indeed, a case can be made that for at least the last half-century, Royal Commissions and their reports have been a dominant force in shaping public policy in Canada.

Borins: That contrasts with a widely held public perception that Royal Commissions are bodies that hold hearings and produce multivolume reports which thereafter occupy shelf space and gather dust.

Blakeney: That is because the public assumes, wrongly, that the chief function of a Royal Commission is to produce a report which contains recommendations for immediate government action. Very often the whole process of hearings, report, and recommendations is designed to shape public thinking so that, at some future time, a government may be able to take new initiatives and carry the public with it. I'll mention a few that have played this role.

Since the Second World War, one of the defining characteristics of Canadian federalism has been payments flowing from the federal government to the have-not provinces – so-called equalization payments. So well established has the idea become that when this principle was included in the Constitution Act in 1982, virtually no public debate resulted. This principle was a major recommendation of the Rowell-Sirois Royal Commission (on Dominion-Provincial Relations) which reported in 1940.

Another widely accepted public institution in Canada is universal, comprehensive, government-operated medical care insurance. The idea was introduced into the realm of practical politics by Saskatchewan Premier Tommy Douglas in 1960 when he appointed the Thompson Committee (the Advisory Planning Committee on Medical Care) to recommend a framework for such an insurance plan. While not strictly speaking a Royal Commission, it acted as one. Legislation followed, tracking the model set out in the Thompson Committee report. In 1964 the Hall Royal Commission (the Royal Commission on Health Services), appointed by Prime Minister John Diefenbaker, reported. Subsequently, Prime Minister Lester Pearson introduced legislation in Parliament that closely followed the Hall Commission report. So medicare, in principle and in many of its details, is a product of Royal Commissions or the equivalent.

Another dominant theme in Canadian political life in the past fifty years has been relations between French speakers and English speakers in Canada. Those relations has been heavily influenced by Royal Commission reports. On the federal scene, the Laurendeau-Dunton Commission (the Royal Commission on Bilingualism and Biculturalism) and the Pépin-Robarts Report (the Task Force on Canadian Unity) have played key roles. In Quebec, a highly influential report was the Belanger-Campeau Report (Commission on the Political and Constitutional Future of Quebec). In some cases legislation flowed from these reports; in all cases the reports shaped the public dialogue.

Many other Royal Commissions have shaped public perceptions of issues and informed the subsequent debate. I think of the Royal Commission on National Development in the Arts, Letters, and Sciences (the Massey Commission), which led not only to the Canada Council but to a much heightened awareness among Canadians of the distinctive nature of our culture. The Royal Commission on the Status of Women (the Bird Commission) introduced many issues concerning the place of women in Canadian society. The Royal Commission on the Economic Union and Development Prospects for Canada (the Donald S. MacDonald Commission) reviewed a huge range of economic issues and paved the way for the free trade debate. The Royal Commission on Aboriginal Peoples (the Erasmus-Dussault Commission) has opened for discussion many issues regarding the relationship between aboriginal and non-aboriginal peoples in Canada. The long-term impact of this report cannot yet be judged.

Borins: In almost all the examples you mentioned, the commission dealt with issues of broad public policy. They were Royal Commissions of the type John Courtney was referring to when he said, 'The modern royal commission has become, in effect, a vehicle by which individuals, groups and governments are permitted to state their views on matters of concern to the nation as a whole.'[1] They were not commissions of the 'what went wrong' variety.

Blakeney: True. The use of commissions to uncover what went wrong in a particular case of tragedy or failure of public policy is a good deal more troublesome. Canadians have not yet made up their minds how issues of this kind should be dealt with. They feel that when there has been a clear failure of public policy, the public is entitled to know promptly what went wrong and why. If someone is at fault they want to know who. But at the same time they also feel that if someone is likely to be charged with a criminal offence connected with the failure of public policy, that person should not be forced to testify under oath before a Royal Commission without the full range of legal protections that the accused would have in a court of law. These two desires are often not compatible. The result is often long delays in the commission's final report, and insufficient attention (in the eyes of some) to the interests of victims of the tragedy or of the failure of public policy. Recent examples of these delays and frustrations concern Nova Scotia's Westray Mine Public Inquiry (the Richard Inquiry) and the Commission of Inquiry on the Blood System in Canada (the Krever Inquiry). There is simply no satisfactory answer to this problem. About all that we can do is make as clear as possible at the outset of these commissions that if it appears that criminal charges might result from the work of the inquiry, then long delays must be expected while criminal matters are dealt with in the courts.

Borins: Commissions sometimes deal with this problem by separating their work from that of the courts. Thus, the commission would report on the public policy issue without attempting to find fault, at least at the individual level. This was the case with the Krever Commission.

We will revisit this point in Chapter 17 in our discussion of crisis management. We will argue that crisis managers should focus on solving the problem, not assigning blame. Once the problem has been solved, the next step is to prevent it from ocurring again. At the same time, it is natural for victims to want compensation.

You have talked about the purposes for which Royal Commissions are established. You were for a time a member of a Royal Commission. How do they operate in practice?

Blakeney: There seem to be a few rules to follow in making Royal Commissions operate successfully. The respective roles of the chair and of the executive director need to be sorted out at an early stage. In some commissions it is a relationship similar to that between a minister and a deputy minister. In other commissions the chair deals directly with many commission staffers and is, in effect, the chief operating officer. That model strikes me as less likely to give the best result – especially with Royal Commissions of the broad policy kind – than the minister–deputy model. A chair who deals directly with staff is undercutting the executive director. In addition, a chair who spends time in the commission's offices is not spending that time consulting interested parties, either formally or informally. Another issue relates to research. If too much of the research budget is committed to an early fact-finding stage, time and money are consumed that would often have been better spent in more directed research on the merits of particular recommendations that the commission is considering.

Janet Smith and Anne Patterson have set out some very useful ideas on the operation of Royal Commissions based on the work of the Royal Commission on National Passenger Transportation.[2]

Borins: Royal Commissions often publish lengthy reports as well as numerous volumes of background studies and research reports. I have some familiarity with the latter, having co-authored research reports for both the MacDonald Commission and the Royal Commission on National Passenger Transportation. If the commission was established mainly to stimulate debate, then it will have achieved its purpose, at least in part, if the report and background documents are reprinted and quoted and become part of the relevant literature. I have often seen this happen. Keynes's comment about practical people being guided by the writings of defunct economists is relevant here.[3] I suppose the outstanding example of ideas moving rapidly from a Royal Commission recommendation to a major public policy was when the Mulroney government embraced the advice of the MacDonald Commission to negotiate a free trade agreement with the United States.

Blakeney: I agree that the MacDonald Commission was enormously influential. I digress to another influential Canadian whose ideas were often expressed in Royal Commission reports – the late Mr Justice Emmet Hall of the Supreme Court. Among the major commissions he chaired or co-chaired were the one that produced the Report on Health Services in 1964, which led to national medicare; the Provincial Committee on Aims and Objectives of Education in the Schools of Ontario (the Hall-Dennis Committee) in 1968; and the Grain Handling and Transportation Commission in 1977. He was a man of prodigious energy. At the end of February 1973, Hall retired as a judge of the Supreme Court of Canada as he neared his seventy-fifth birthday. He returned from Ottawa to Saskatoon to enjoy his retirement.

The Minister of Justice in Saskatchewan, Roy Romanow, and I knew that he would soon be seeking some task for the public good, so once he was settled back in Saskatoon, we arranged for him to conduct an overview of the Saskatchewan court system, where he had served as a barrister, as president of the Law Society of Saskatchewan (in 1952), as a judge, and as Chief Justice of Saskatchewan before going to the Supreme Court. In April 1973 he had just got his small team organized and had just commenced his work when our government ran into a political storm.

At that time the University of Saskatchewan had its main campus in Saskatoon and a second major campus in Regina. There had been a good deal of friction between the two campuses, and the government proposed to set up a new organization whereby each campus would have its own president but there would be a single Board of Governors. There developed a good deal of opposition to this proposal in Saskatoon, with some allegations of government interference with the autonomy of the university and so on. It seemed to us that the opposition was being given support by the chancellor of the University of Saskatchewan, the Right Honourable John G. Diefenbaker, who was highly regarded by a great many Saskatchewan people. As we saw it, the situation called for a Royal Commission on University Organization and Structure. The person to head such a commission was clear: Mr Justice Hall, who was a graduate of the University of Saskatchewan and a former chancellor. I asked Judge Hall whether he would take on the task and defer his review of our court justice system, and he readily agreed.

He got this commission set up and had just commenced his work when in August 1973 there was a national railway strike that halted all movement of grain in Western Canada, which had a severe impact on the incomes of virtually all Saskatchewan farmers. The federal Minister of Labour asked Judge Hall whether he would serve as sole arbitrator in the dispute. He advised the federal minister that he could not undertake this without the agreement of the Government of Saskatchewan since he had previous commitments to us. He came and asked me whether I would agree to let him serve as arbitrator. If there ever was a pro forma meeting it was that one, since it would have been politically impossible for me to even appear to be holding up the settlement of the rail dispute. So by August 1973, less than six months after leaving the Supreme Court, Judge Hall was enjoying his retirement by first arbitrating a national railway strike, then dealing with and delivering his report on university organization and structure, and thereafter proceeding with his review of the Saskatchewan court system.

In his report on university organization Judge Hall said, in effect, that we had the right diagnosis – the campuses could not get along – but the wrong prescription. He recommended a separate university in Regina. We adopted his advice, and legislation for the new university was introduced in May 1974. I'm not sure that his was the right solution, but the Royal Commission had made it the only defensible solution. And that can be one of the purposes of a Royal Commission. Very often, Royal Commission activities and reports have a discernible impact on public policy over the long term.

Borins: Agreed. One commission of inquiry that provided the context for solving a hot political problem was the Commission of Inquiry into Bilingual Air Traffic Services in Quebec.[4] The issue was the desire of francophone pilots and controllers to use French in Quebec, and the resistance by anglophone pilots and controllers. It led to wildcat strikes in June 1976 by English-speaking pilots and controllers and to an increase in tensions between English and French Canadians, which contributed greatly to the election of the Parti Québécois the following November. Through research and public hearings, the commission oversaw the development of a bilingual air traffic control system for Quebec that was demonstrably as safe as an English-only system. Its report, delivered in 1979, was immediately accepted, which removed an important francophone grievance. In Chapter 16 I will discuss how the commission's research was a very effective way of managing change.

With respect to Justice Hall's commission about Saskatchewan universities, I'm not surprised at the outcome. As I've mentioned before, universities are very decentralized places. When two universities have only a common board, the pressure to sever that last link is overwhelming. While I'm generally supportive of competition among universities, there are times when some programs at a particular university are too small to be effective. Getting universities to pool resources – for example, in joint doctoral programs – is not easy. But to return from my digression, how would you distinguish between commissions and task forces?

Blakeney: I don't think it is helpful to distinguish between commissions and task forces. There are differences in the level of formality, in their capacity to subpoena witnesses, and in some other respects. But it seems to me that they are used for essentially the same purposes.

Borins: I would say that Royal Commissions are, or should be, used for big issues that affect the entire society; commissions of inquiry for 'what went wrong' investigations; and task forces or other less formal approaches for quick consultations on big issues or for ongoing consultations on sectoral issues. Perhaps I am revealing my professorial tendency to create a readily classifiable world in which every purpose has its own organizational structure and term of reference. I would also maintain that the informal types of public consultation have become more popular in recent years; but that is a hypothesis to be tested – by a doctoral student, of course.

Blakeney: It is useful to repeat that government is a political process and that good decisions by governments are ones that the public agrees with or at least can be persuaded to accept. And that in order to achieve this public acceptance, it is often highly worthwhile to offer the general public, and other special publics, the political space to make themselves heard. And that this involves consultation by a variety of means. There may well be other reasons to embark on public consultation, but improving the quality of decisions is a major one.

As we noted earlier, there are many ways to consult, and the Saskatchewan government in the 1970s used some of them. Succeeding governments have used others.

Borins: What dictates the method used?

Blakeney: A good deal depends on why the government proposes to consult. A paper by Patterson, Lohin, and Ferguson contains a useful way to organize one's thinking on this point.[5] It suggests that there are four types of consultations in which governments may engage (although there are doubtless more):

1. Consultation where the objective is to inform or educate the public participants.
2. Consultation where the objective is to gather information or views from the public participants.
3. Consultation where the objective is to involve public participants in making the decision.
4. Consultation where the objective is to have the public participants make a joint decision.

A look at that list will make clear that different approaches would be used to meet different objectives. As you would expect, governments often have more than one objective. Sometimes the objective will involve two or more types of consultation from the list above. Sometimes the objective will be to help put a decision into effect, or to explain a decision more broadly, or both. It is often totally appropriate for a government to attempt to line up support for a decision in the process of consulting to arrive at the decision. To repeat the obvious, the likely level of public acceptance for a decision is one of the tests of whether the decision should be made at all.

Borins: It seems to me that pre-budget consultation, as currently practised, exemplifies these points, and shows how the world has changed in the last twenty years. Traditionally, governments did not consult about the tax or economic policy

changes contained in budget statements, claiming that those consulted could receive inside information that would give them an unfair advantage in the market.
However, it soon became clear that consultation could be designed so as to avert
this problem – for example, by the government presenting a number of options,
some with contradictory economic effects. Now there is substantial pre-budget
consultation, often to line up support for the overall approach being taken.

Aside from varying complexity, what are some of the difficulties inherent in
the types of consultation you mention above?

Blakeney: Consultation can be time consuming, and consultation involving participation (type 3) or joint decision-making (type 4) can be extremely time consuming – possibly never-ending. Sometimes the situation demands a prompt
decision. If this is so, it is often better not to start a consultation process than have
to make the decision before it is completed. To ask someone for his or her opinion on an upcoming decision, and then make your decision before he or she has
had a chance to reply, does not win friends either for you or for the decision that
circumstances have forced you to make.

Another problem is that if the objective is to build consensus, it is often the
case that some of the participants cannot effectively participate. If the government is represented by a public servant, or even a minister, he or she may not be
in a position to make the compromise that consensus building often requires,
because the mandate from the minister, or the cabinet, or perhaps the Legislature,
does not permit it.

Borins: I agree with you that for types 3 and 4, having representatives lacking
delegated authority is not very effective. On the other hand, that should not be a
problem for types 1 (informing) and 2 (gathering information), since the representative can make clear the limitation on his or her authority; having done that,
he or she is free to listen sympathetically.

Blakeney: That may be, but when it comes to representatives of some interest
groups, listening sympathetically can be a real challenge, because they are required to hew to a narrow 'party line.' As a cabinet we used to meet with and
receive briefs from pro-life and pro-choice groups. It was next to impossible to
get their representatives to discuss any move from the hard-line positions set out
in their briefs. 'We are unable to compromise on fundamental principles,' or a
like response, was the position usually taken. Many other groups whom we met
regarded themselves as message carriers rather than consensus seekers. 'Taking
a stand' is almost always a great deal easier than hammering out a compromise.

It is important to establish as carefully as possible what the purpose of the consultation is so as to make as clear as possible what expectations participants should have. Let me illustrate why. I had met with a small group and heard their views and proposals on a particular problem. Later I saw a leading member of the group and asked if he had a point of view on another issue. His answer was, 'What's the good of talking to you? You don't listen.' I demurred and replied that I did listen and that I had listened last time: 'I can tell you now what you said when I met your group.' To which he replied: 'You may have heard what we said but you didn't do what we asked you to do.' Clearly, to him, *listen* meant *agree*. He had too high expectations of what should flow from consultation.

When a government consults with groups about a proposed initiative there is a range of outcomes that the group consulted may expect. They may expect the government to:

1. Listen to the group's presentation.
2. Listen to the presentation and enter into a dialogue as to its merits.
3. The same as 2, but with explanations of why the government is proposing to proceed with the initiative.
4. The same as 1 or 2, but with an undertaking by the government to reply in writing to the group's submission.
5. The same as 1 or 2, but with an undertaking by the government to forward them a revised proposal following consultation.
6. The same as 5, but with an undertaking to discuss with the group any revisions to the government's proposals.
7. The same as 5, but with an undertaking to send to the group the draft of any legislation or regulations that follow the consultation.
8. The same as 5, but with an undertaking, qualified or not, not to proceed with the initiative without their approval.

This list is not exhaustive, and the order can be somewhat different. But it is clear that there is a continuum of roles that the group consulted can play. It is important that the government be clear in its own mind what it intends, and even more important that the group consulted understand its role. Confusion on this point often breeds frustration and allegations of bad faith.

I repeat a point I have already made. The type of consultation selected, and the role assigned to the group consulted, may depend upon the role you see the group playing in implementing the decision and in explaining it to the larger public. If the group is going to be a continuing player and a quasi-partner of the government, this is best recognized at the consultation stage so that the group has some ownership of the decision and of the process of putting it into effect.

Borins: I have two responses. First, with regard to any particular group, it could be that the government may want to involve them in different ways in different decisions. If the group has something approaching a veto (that is, a higher number in your list) in one decision, they may come to expect it in a later decision, when in the latter situation all you are willing to do is listen. If you try to go from a higher number in one matter to a lower number in another, the group may accuse you of betrayal; if you try to go from a lower number in one matter to a higher number in the next, the group may not believe you.

My second comment is that many policy decisions involve multiple stakeholders having conflicting interests: consumers, producers, environmentalists, and labour to name a few. Any consultation regarding the economy almost invariably brings several of these groups to the table. Given the groups' conflicting interests, it is unlikely that you could offer any one group a high level of influence. Essentially, I think a government has two choices. First, it can offer to listen to all the conflicting groups and then make the decision itself. Second, it can design a process whereby the conflicting groups attempt to hammer out a compromise. In the latter model, the government would act as mediator and design the rules of the game (such as the deadline for a decision and the degree of consensus required). An example of the latter model was a multi-stakeholder consultation regarding the regulation of pesticides, which was facilitated by Agriculture Canada.[6]

Blakeney: I think those are useful distinctions. But it sometimes happens the people regard 'consultation' as a stand-alone objective. It rarely is. It is almost always part of arriving at a decision about what to do about an issue, or part of the process of putting the decision into effect, or both. That should be realized and taken into account at the beginning.

Borins: Are there any other benefits flowing from consultation?

Blakeney: There are perhaps some psychic benefits from the process that help a government deal with the newly perceived responsibility of governments to be 'accountable.' I'm unclear what this word is supposed to mean when I hear it from public figures or read it in the media. Cabinets and ministers were once responsible to legislatures. Members of legislatures were accountable to voters, and voters could thus demand accountability.

That is still true. But there is a growing feeling that somehow cabinets and ministers are directly accountable to voters for particular decisions. If the call is for more complete explanations, for more transparency, this is usually not a problem. If the call is for some way that the public can express agreement or disagreement with a particular decision, this is a problem. Problems facing governments are rarely simple. They are complex and getting more so. It is bad government to somehow submit a problem to the public and seek to receive an oversimplified black-or-white answer when what is almost certainly required is a solution best described as a nuanced shade of grey.

Borins: Of course, technology – from polling to the Internet – makes it easier to submit individual issues to the electorate. It is difficult, though I would argue not impossible, to capture nuances by presenting questions in the right way. Of course, if the presentation is highly nuanced, and thus complex, most of the public will lose interest. What is even harder to capture is the tradeoffs across issues that a cabinet must consider but that the public never sees. The public is concerned about specific issues in isolation from other issues. You are concerned about the overall direction of policy and – as you ought to be – with keeping enough of society on-side that you can be re-elected.

Blakeney: Perhaps consultation, with the objectives of giving information and receiving it from groups and the public, generally could lessen the feeling among the public that they are detached from their government – that we are no longer free people governing ourselves, but people being governed by a faceless 'them' who govern 'without even talking to us.' But the alienation from government felt by many citizens is a larger theme. I doubt if increased consultation, as we have discussed it, can be the primary tool in dealing with that issue.

16

Managing Change

This chapter begins with a discussion of the factors which Blakeney feels were important to the successful implementation of change in Saskatchewan. These include being pragmatic rather than ideological; introducing change early enough in the political cycle to iron out the bugs before the next election; assigning responsibility for both planning and implementation to a lead agency rather than an interdepartmental committee; and preventing bureaucratic foot-dragging. It will be seen that consultation and simulation are two important aspects of the implementation process. We then look at the factors that led to the success or failure of a number of new programs in Saskatchewan, including the Wascana Centre Authority, the children's dentistry program, the occupational health and safety program, the Land Bank, and the Southwest Saskatchewan Pilot Project. The latter was a precursor of the trend toward 'one-stop shopping' or 'single window' service delivery, of which we provide several recent examples.

Borins: As we discussed in Chapter 4, which dealt with the process of setting priorities in your government, yours was a very creative government, one that introduced many new programs. What is surprising is that you did this in the context of what, in that same chapter, you described as 'a rural, conservative, and somewhat racist province in the 1970s.' How did you and your government persuade such a society to go along with your program of social activism?[1]

Blakeney: My approach was to downplay the novelty and importance of what we were doing and to present changes as good common sense. We never talked to the electorate about socialist ideology, democratic socialism, and the like. I regarded Saskatchewan's people as being generally solid and pragmatic – as open to change but suspicious of political ideology as such. If the ideology was couched in terms of

Saskatchewan people being self-reliant and 'doing it ourselves,' or in terms of fairness and being our neighbour's keeper, then it struck a chord. As I judged it, appeals to free enterprise or socialism as transcending ideologies did not. Of course, this didn't endear me to the left wing of the party, but that's not where the new votes were. Nor is it best for governments to emphasize the divisions in society. Without abandoning ideology, it is possible to stress the common goals that society shares. When I insisted upon a concrete and pragmatic justification for any changes proposed, ministers, party people, and public servants were forced to present the case for changes in terms that the voters could understand and support.

Borins: Your former cabinet colleague Elwood Cowley also made this point very clearly, as follows: 'If ideology rides rough-shod over the deeply held prejudices, beliefs, and ideals of the community, in the end the community will always win. Before you proceed with a reform, you should believe that, at some time in the future if not right away, you could obtain public support, or at least acceptance for what you are doing.'[2]

Blakeney: Agreed. Still, I sometimes wonder whether I understated the reasons of principle, or ideology if you will, for some of the things we did. I think that reflects my approach to public issues. I regard arguments about whether something can be classified as 'socialism' or 'free enterprise' as sterile. Such arguments proceed on the basis that these terms have some precise meaning. In fact, they are almost always designed to elicit unthinking support or opposition. I was asked many times by reporters whether I was a socialist. My answer was always the same: 'If you let me define the term, yes; if you define the term, probably no.' If I was being more argumentative, I would say 'If "socialist" means what my opponents said it meant twenty-five years ago – "yes"; if it means what my opponents say it means today – "no."' I think we do no service to the democratic system by attempting to get the public committed to words and slogans. We should seek their commitment to specific changes whose value they have an opportunity to assess. Ideological labels should be arrived at by a process of induction after examining specific changes that have been tried, rather than be a process of deduction from first principles. Most of us apply our private first principles when we are assessing the worth of government programs – and of our own actions as well. But it is unwise to try to incorporate those first principles into an ideology, and then use that ideology as the basis for judging government programs without reference to the particular circumstances of time and place.

Borins: When is the best time in a government's mandate to introduce change?

Blakeney: As early in the mandate as possible. The reason is that the costs of change in terms of disruption happen first and the benefits come only later. It takes time to iron out the bugs and get new programs working well. You want your new programs to be working well by the next election, so the time to introduce them is right after the most recent election. This means that planning has to occur early as well, either before a government takes office or, for an existing government, before the election. When you have an election, catch your breath, and then begin to plan. Programs are often launched too late.

Borins: The classic case of a government doing just that involved the federal Liberal government that was elected in 1974. During the election it had promised not to introduce wage and price controls, but with little notion of what it *would* do. It spent the first year of its mandate in a 'priorities exercise,' which involved relatively junior public servants interviewing each minister about what they felt the government's priorities ought to be. What emerged was a shopping list of sixteen nebulous priorities that provided no direction at all for the government. Indeed, the government spent most of its mandate reacting to externally driven events such as inflation, the increase in energy prices, and the election of the Parti Québécois.[3] However, the Liberals learned from experience, and in their following mandate established a small number of priorities, on which they made significant progress.

Blakeney: The best story I know of effective timing is the one told of Tommy Douglas and the Saskatchewan Hospitalization Plan. When the Douglas government was elected in 1944, one of its objectives was to introduce a hospital insurance plan covering all provincial residents. An able group of public servants was pulled together to plan the new program, and a starting date of 1 January 1947 was set. There were horrendous problems: no reliable data to work with, not enough hospitals, no precedent to draw upon in North America or anywhere else that had much relevance to a poor prairie province in Canada. The team struggled, persevered, and made great strides. But when the starting date grew near, the team leaders came as a group to Douglas and said that they could not have the plan ready to launch on 1 January. It is reported that Douglas told them how much he had appreciated their work, and how much he had enjoyed working with them. He expressed his regret that he would be losing them. Since they did not feel they could be ready by 1 January and since it was imperative that the start date be adhered to, he would have to seek another team.

I could well believe this story. It signalled that Douglas did not intend to debate with the team the reasons why the starting date had to be delayed, and that he intended to stick to the date and risk potential administrative upheaval. The team members reconsidered their position, and the starting date was, in fact, 1 January. There were administrative kinks, and they were worked out. Thinking in political terms, Douglas knew that these problems had to be solved well before his intended election call for June 1948 and that a delay in the starting date would only delay resolution of the problems and might risk the future of the plan. The Douglas government was re-elected, and the hospital plan turned out to be the prototype for all of Canada's provincial health care insurance plans. These plans have since become a badge of our common Canadian citizenship.

Borins: Both Malcolm Taylor, in his book about health insurance, and the McLeods, in their biography of Tommy Douglas, refer to that story.[4] Now I've also heard it from you. I think this is an example of what Peters and Waterman call a 'Bill and Dave' story. There are many stories about Bill Hewlett and Dave Packard told by people who now work at Hewlett-Packard. Most of those who now tell these stories have never spoken to or even seen the two founding fathers.[5] Even so, these stories encapsulate very powerfully the organization's culture and values.

I think that story about Tommy Douglas plays a similar role for the Saskatchewan NDP. It illustrates the importance of introducing change at the appropriate time in the mandate, the importance of making thorough implementation plans, and the need for sufficient political will to override the reservations of the public service. This third point especially is highlighted, in that the public servants involved were not the lethargic holdovers of the previous regime but the outside experts, the best and the brightest, brought in by Douglas himself.

When a government is planning new programs, is there an organizational structure that you think is most effective?

Blakeney: In terms of organization structure, there are some real choices to make. Al Johnson expressed a basic choice very well in an article titled 'Public Policy: Creativity and Bureaucracy,' published some years ago in *Canadian Public Administration*.[6] He argued that there are two different ways to plan new programs. One is to give a lead agency the responsibility for the program, and give it the responsibility for consulting all other interested departments in the course of designing the program. The other is to give responsibility for policy formulation to an interdepartmental committee of all interested departments.

Johnson argues very strongly for the former, because it provides ownership and championship. The lead agency, or champion, can build up momentum; other agencies are involved in that they are consulted, but they are not given veto power over the program. The second approach provides no ownership, no momentum, and multiple vetoes. It thwarts creativity by introducing the constraints of interdepartmental bargaining much too soon in the policy development process. It is hard to make change happen in those circumstances.

Borins: I see a parallel here to two points you made earlier on. One of the reasons you argue that ministers should not get involved in policy development is that officials may persuade them to accept constraints of administrative feasibility right at the outset of the process, which thwarts creativity. Similarly, you decided against moving the Saskatchewan Bureau of Statistics from the cabinet planning unit to the Department of Finance in large part because the conservative mentality of a finance ministry would have influenced its work. What I am seeing in your comments and those of Al Johnson is a government that put a value on creative policy development and tried to remove organizational barriers to it.

Blakeney: I support Johnson's view completely, with the following addition. While a mandate can often be given to an existing lead agency, it may be necessary to create a new agency whose mandate is to bring that change about. Again, I go back to the notion of special-purpose central agencies. Such an agency clearly works best when the change is important and, as a concept, is supported by cabinet. It is important that the individuals seconded to the new agency from the regular agencies feel that their commitment is to the project and to the new agency, and not to the defence of the agencies from which they have come.

Special agencies provide a convenient way for a premier and cabinet to oversee projects under development. As I have suggested earlier, when a special agency or secretariat is established to launch a new project, a premier or a cabinet committee can be closely involved in the project without appearing to slight a minister, which is how it would look if the project were given to an existing department. It is one thing to have a project – for example, developing a comprehensive potash policy and introducing it – removed from the ambit of the Department of Mineral Resources and given to a secretariat that has been established for the purpose and that reports to a cabinet committee on potash and its chairman. It is quite another to assign the task of developing the policy to the Department of Mineral Resources but have a cabinet committee headed by another minister supervising the progress of the minister and Department of Mineral Resources. Loss of jurisdiction is one thing. Over-the-shoulder supervision of one minister by another is quite another thing when we are considering the dynamics of harmony in cabinet.

Borins: I can think of a lot of experience that would reinforce Johnson's point about the importance of having a lead agency responsible for policy development. In their research about excellence in the private sector, Peters and Waterman found that a surprising number of innovations were made by champions – by small groups of tenacious and highly motivated individuals, often located out of the organizational mainstream in 'skunkworks.'[7]

Though policy development processes in the public sector are rarely as covert as these private sector skunkworks, the notion of highly committed champions is certainly applicable. Some years earlier, Anthony Downs, in *Inside Bureaucracy*, identified several personality types of officials, two of which are the 'zealot' and the 'advocate.'[8] The lead agency model provides a way of combining the focused energy of the zealots, who do policy development, with the broader vision of the advocates, who take the lead in consulting with the other departments.

In 1990 we were both on the jury for the first Institute of Public Administration of Canada (IPAC) Award for Innovative Management. Afterwards I wrote a paper that classified and analysed the various entries. Of the fifty-seven entries in the competition, ten were interdepartmental partnerships that had undertaken initiatives which could be implemented only if the departments involved worked together. The usual task force structure was a group of not more than a dozen middle-level public servants, housed in one department, with ready access to that department's deputy minister, and with links – sometimes through secondments, and sometimes through formal consultative committees – to other departments. In short, they followed the lead agency model rather than the interdepartmental committee model.[9] The fact that they had ready access to the deputy minister indicates that the initiatives had support at the top. I think that is also crucial if a new initiative is to move out of the skunkworks to become policy.

Blakeney: Yes. Some of the most enthusiastic champions have been thwarted by administrative problems, or by the inertia (and occasionally active opposition to change) that is found in the administrative structure of any large organization. The security of doing the same thing tomorrow that we did yesterday has some appeal for all of us – certainly, public servants are not immune from this. We all know that the requirements of our clients change constantly, if almost imperceptibly, and therefore that organizations must adapt. So we try to promote gradual adjustment. But sometimes this gradual adjustment is not enough and a general rethinking of what we are doing is required. This is often painful but often also exciting.

Sometimes public service opposition to change can be very deep, so much so that it is impossible to find anyone who is willing to champion innovation. It seems to me that this most often happens when a new government comes into office with some very different approaches to an important issue. I think public servants sometimes feel, perhaps unconsciously, that they have a duty to protect the public against the impetuousness and inexperience of the new administration.

I can recall a clear example of this. When we came to office we had decided to make major changes in our policy toward northern Saskatchewan. The people who lived in the north were largely of aboriginal origin and enjoyed fewer opportunities and a lower standard of living than the rest of the province. It was the familiar problem – the population was outgrowing the resource base for the traditional aboriginal pursuits of trapping, hunting, and fishing, and there was no alternative employment. We decided to create a single agency, a Department of Northern Saskatchewan, that would deliver most provincial government services to the area, and to set up elected local councils and elected school boards to administer local government matters.

Previously, the tasks of local government in the north had been carried out by the staff of the Department of Natural Resources. They were to be displaced by the new department and by staff of the newly elected municipal councils and school boards. Some of the DNR staff were obviously leery of the new approach. They had done as well for the north as anybody could have done within the paternalistic, quasi-colonial framework that prevailed, and they doubted whether the new approach would be as effective. They developed a pronounced lack of enthusiasm for completing the transfer of functions to the new bodies. What I judged to be covert resistance continued for several months. Finally I had to shuffle the cabinet and give the Minister of Natural Resources responsibility for the new Department of Northern Saskatchewan as well. He held both portfolios until the transition was complete. Through personal intervention, he was able to get across the idea that the government was firm in its resolve, that we believed we knew what we were doing, and that the time had come to get on with it. The participants were convinced, or at least acted as if they were, and the job was done.[10]

Borins: Have you other notable examples of change management, successful or unsuccessful, from your years in government?

Blakeney: I have many. I'll start with one that illustrates the power of a motivated and energetic champion. It concerns the establishment of a park authority in Regina – the Wascana Centre Authority – in the early 1960s when I was Minister of Education. This project related to lands, some developed and some not, owned by the Government of Saskatchewan, the City of Regina, and the University of Saskatchewan at Regina (as the latter was then called). The proposal was to develop these lands into a unified park area of some 1,000 acres (400 hectares) and to provide the authority with base funding set out in legislation. The city's contribution was fixed at 2 mills on its assessment base. The contributions of the other two partners were based on a percentage of the city figure. There was general enthusiasm for the park project in principle – and a great deal less enthusiasm for any statutory formula for financing and administering it. We resorted to the familiar special agency, but this one was meant to be permanent.

The government recruited Dr A.K. Gillmore to organize the project. It was my job as Minister of Education at that time to get cabinet to support the project, and it was Gillmore's job to get the Regina City Council to support it. There was resistance, since a large number of park maintenance people employed by all three partners would be transferred to a new agency responsible to a free-standing board that no one partner controlled.

Gillmore's strategy – to popularize the vision – was a work of art. We had engaged Minoru Yamasaki, the architect of many well-known projects, to draw up a master plan. Gillmore made slides of the model, of the master plan, and of projects around the world that might be copied. He took his slide show to countless meetings in Regina, generating a groundswell of support among the public. When it came time for the city council to vote on the project, their hands were all but tied. With formal support from the city and the university, a bill was tabled in the Legislature. This technique of mobilizing public support as a method of influencing legislative bodies should be in the arsenal of anyone who wants to bring about change in government programs.

We adopted the unusual technique of having an informal meeting of MLAs in the Legislative Chamber. There, the park model was displayed and Dr Gillmore gave his presentation. The legislation, which bound the government to contribute an amount set by statute – a statutory appropriation – was passed. The merit of having the funding set out in statute was proven when the project escaped unscathed from across-the-board cuts instituted by all three partners at different times. As of the 1990s there had been only one occasion when the provincial government brought in legislation to reduce the budget provided in the governing statute, and this was only for a short period. There is no doubt that the project benefited from the stability that a statutory budget provided and would have suffered considerably if any one partner could have reduced its contribution, since this would likely have triggered a pro rata reduction by the other partners.

The Wascana Centre Authority served as the model for riverbank parks that our government established in Saskatoon and Moose Jaw in the early 1970s.[11] Despite the success of these projects, they did not escape the draconian cuts required by the fiscal constraints of the early 1990s. The cuts were defined, since they had to be set out in specific terms in legislation. All three projects survived and continued to attract wide public support. We can hope that better days will allow a restoration of full funding.

Borins: It sounds like Dr Gillmore was a very effective marketer. The model was a great way of getting people to envision the product. His lining up of support is reminiscent, albeit on a larger scale, of the campaign by the people in Elrose that you wrote about in the previous chapter.

Blakeney: In government, and I suspect in any large organization, change cannot come only by a top-down process of getting an idea, formulating it into a policy, and putting it into place. I have already spoken of getting people on side by the art of persuasion. It is also important to consult with those who will be affected. One reason is that consultation can be a form of persuasion. People whose opinion has been sought frequently take a proprietary interest in the project. But a more important reason is that no idea emerges full blown, however creative its originator. The seed of the idea must be identified in the originator's mind and then nurtured through consultation with the people who would be affected by any resulting government policy. So long as the people who are consulted do not think they have a right to veto the idea, consultation is both necessary and desirable. The lead person with the task of elaborating the idea is almost certain to find out how to make it more generally acceptable without surrendering its core. And often new and valuable allies for the next phase of the endeavour can be found.

Once an idea has been modified to respond to concerns by those likely to be affected, the next move is to make a detailed and thorough implementation plan. This involves two main steps. The first is to sort out who will be affected by the proposal – more specifically, who will be pleased or displeased – and then attempt to neutralize opponents and encourage those who support the plan to do so actively (and sometimes publicly). There seems to be a need to explain constantly what you are going to do. Almost any proposal involving a lot of contact with the public causes initial confusion. This is particularly the case if opponents of the policy are seeking to generate doubt and confusion among the public.

The second step is to sort out the program's operating procedures. If there are likely to be objections on policy grounds, then procedural details such as the design of forms, the guides to users, and arrangements for responding to the public's questions must be given special attention. It is always sad to see a good program turn sour in the public mind because of sloppy administration.

To deal with some of the start-up problems of new programs, we used a device now quite common: we had a provincial inquiry centre with a toll-free line that operated during but also outside normal business hours. The people dealing with the calls were highly trained to respond to public requests for information. Careful records were kept of the subject areas raised by callers. We quickly developed norms for the number of calls we could expect on, say, workers' compensation, or social assistance payments, or the like. Whenever a new program was introduced, we armed the centre's staff with as much information as we could so that they could answer the simple questions themselves without the need to refer the caller to the agency launching the new program. If the number of calls about a program, new or old, persisted, it told us that we needed an information campaign – a brochure, or a better brochure, or some information advertising in weekly papers, or as the case may be. Introducing a new program to the public is not a casual exercise. The merits of a new program do not automatically announce themselves. It is necessary to figure out who does what, when, where, and with what resources. If the program is a major one, problems of budget and staffing have to be anticipated and a margin of error allowed for. The initial launch of a major program is no time for pinching pennies.

Borins: Highway 407 provides some examples of marketing for the launch of a program. In addition to an advertising campaign to create awareness of both the highway and the transponder technology, we established a 1–800 number that people could call to ask questions and order transponders. We also established a website to provide information and to enable people to ask questions and order transponders. Website technology permits a government to measure 'hits' as a way of seeing if its message is reaching people.

Blakeney: It is also advisable to perform some mock runs of how administrative procedures will work, and of what the citizen will be required to do. In short, if you are 'running a tracer' on an administrative program, don't start with, say, a completed application having been received from the citizen. Rather, start with the citizen hearing about the program and wishing to apply. What forms will he or she need to fill out? What instruction books are available? Whom can he or she call for help? What about the MLA's office staff? Are these people also well informed? These are really very obvious precautions, but sometimes the obvious is overlooked.

Even more obvious is the need to be sure that government employees who will be dealing with the public are informed, and are not tempted to blame the extra work and any public confusion and hostility on 'those people in Regina' or the 'head office crowd.' Almost every new program reminds us that people generally don't like change – they like the results of change but not the process. Taking irritants out of the process is vital to good administration.

Borins: I have an example of a program that illustrates both your points. In 1976 the federal government tried to put in place bilingual air traffic control in Quebec. As I mentioned in our discussion of commissions, this initiative was vociferously opposed by English-speaking pilots and controllers. To end their wildcat strikes in June 1976, the government agreed to establish a commission of inquiry to determine whether bilingual air traffic control could be implemented safely in

Quebec. One of the key elements of the commission's work was a set of simulation exercises. In these, bilingual controllers using radar scopes and aircraft simulators simulated the handling of traffic in Quebec airspace under both unilingual (that is, English only) and bilingual rules. The objective of the air traffic control exercises was to compare the safety and efficiency of the unilingual and bilingual air traffic control systems. At the end of the day, it was found that the two systems were equally safe and efficient.[12]

These exercises did the two things you suggested. They provided an opportunity for consultation, in that the pilots' and controllers' unions were involved in designing the exercises. The unions tried to make the exercises as difficult as possible, in order to see whether bilingual air traffic control would work. This was certainly a more productive activity than fighting bilingual air traffic control on the picket lines or in the op-ed columns of the newspapers. Furthermore, such testing could only improve the safety and efficiency of a bilingual air traffic control system. The context for consultation was a computer-based simulation – a sophisticated version of your second point, 'running a tracer.' So I think you are urging public servants to simulate the operation of their programs before implementing them. I would just add that the availability and sophistication of computer technology makes simulations of this kind very practical.

Blakeney: Obviously, it is important to do some planning to head off administrative foul-ups. Next we need to remind ourselves that sometimes circumstances demand that a change be driven forward in spite of administrative problems, which can be solved as the program proceeds. Tommy Douglas's insistence that the hospital insurance plan go ahead in spite of unresolved administrative problems is an example. There are often conflicting pressures. That is what makes public administration an art form.

I can recall other examples of successful and unsuccessful programs.

The children's dentistry program was a great success.[13] It was based on the New Zealand model. It involved training a new profession of dental nurses, setting up dental offices in most of the major schools in the province, and having the dental nurses examine the children's teeth and give any needed treatment. We started with students in the lower grades and gradually included most students. There was general supervision by dentists. We started work on the program a few months after we were elected. This involved organizing a school for training dental nurses, delivering a two-year training course, and having nurses in the schools in well under four years. The nurses were a big hit with the children, and the program was a big hit with the parents. When a child comes home and points to a filling in her tooth and says the nice lady fixed it for her and it was fun, a parent who recalls her dread of the dentist's office knows something is going right.

The plan had particular appeal in rural areas, where the nearest dentist might be 100 kilometres away and where, as a consequence, many parents didn't take their children to the dentist for regular checkups and felt guilty about it. Nurses spent much of their time teaching the children dental hygiene. When I was touring the province, the high level of public satisfaction with the dental plan was very obvious. And there was hardly an administrative hitch. The program grew in an orderly way as each year a new class of nurses graduated from the school. There were some grumbles from the dental profession, but since there was an acute shortage of dentists and they were heavily concentrated in major urban centres, their mild opposition was of little consequence. I remember saying to a rural MLA that we might run into some opposition from the dental profession. He replied that if all the dentists in his constituency objected he would not worry. When I asked him how may dentists he had in his constituency, he replied, 'None.'

We ran quality tests, comparing work done by the nurses with work done by dentists, and there was no evidence that the nurses' work was inferior. Besides, based on anecdotal evidence we believed they were better at teaching dental hygiene to children than most dentists.

Borins: I was reading Barker's article about the program, and I see some pretty clear factors leading to its success. The data compiled by the project team made it clear there was a real demand for dental care that was not being filled by the dentists. The Minister of Health, Walter Smishek, made this program one of his top priorities. The department set up a project team to champion the program. Interested parties were consulted. The implementation work was done. In short, all the pieces fell into place very nicely.[14]

Blakeney: The children's dental program was discontinued by the Devine government after the election of 1982. I've never fully understood why, and I continue to believe it was a mistake. It might not have survived the financial hurricane of the early 1990s, but it might have been revived in some form to live again another day.

Another experiment that was a clear success was the occupational health and safety program. Since about 1911 Saskatchewan has had a Worker's Compensation Board and a Bureau (later a Department) of Labour. Each of these sets safety standards for the workplace and enforces them. The occupational health and safety program, introduced in 1972, was in addition to these.[15] Under its provisions, every employer with ten employees or more was required to set up a health and safety committee, on which workers and managers had equal representation, to review safety issues in the workplace. If a dangerous situation was identified, the committee dealt with it. If the committee was deadlocked regarding the degree of danger, an official from the Department of Labour was summoned to break the tie. In addition, if an employee believed a situation to be immediately dangerous, he or she could walk off the job without being subject to discipline by the employer.

We decided to see if we could get unions and employers to accept this regime. I was not optimistic. Unions were called upon to accept it with the understanding that under no circumstances would actions taken on health and safety grounds be used as a bargaining or harassment tactic. If that happened, we could not defend the program. Employers were expected to take an honest look at the issues raised, and stay calm if one or two employees raised a silly complaint, and not assume that the department would always side with the workers. Employers were very apprehensive, but most followed the law – grudgingly at first. To their surprise, they found that there was no harassment, that remarkably few unreasonable positions were being taken by employees, and that a rapport on the issues was gradually building between employees, employers, and the Department of Labour. Employers saw success as favourably affecting employee morale, not to mention their Workers' Compensation Board assessments; employees saw success as giving them some control over conditions that threatened their well-being; and the department saw success as fostering co-operation in an area where, conceptually, all three parties had a common interest in success.

My worries were unfounded – as the gamblers say, one should give the cards a chance. This time, after an only mildly difficult start, they came up aces.

An example of a program that enjoyed mixed success was the Land Bank.[16] The idea was that a government agency, the Land Bank Commission, would buy farmland from owners wishing to sell and lease it to young people wishing to enter farming. The lessee would have an option to buy the land after five years. Alternatively, the lessee could lease the land until he or she was sixty-five years old. Several benefits were anticipated: it would provide a way for farmers who wished to retire to sell their land for cash, and allow young people to enter farming even though they did not have the large sums of money needed to buy land.

As the government saw it, the plan was a way to deal with the intergenerational transfer of land and with the inevitable consolidation of some farm units that were too small to be commercially viable. We hoped the commission would at least slow down any unnecessary drift toward concentrated ownership of farmland.

The plan was only a partial success. A substantial quantity of land was purchased and leased to young people. The large majority of these lessees were successful in establishing themselves as farmers. Since they did not incur large debts to buy land, they survived better than most during the period of very high interest rates in the early 1980s, and during the period of very low commodity prices in the late 1980s and early 1990s. Judged on this basis, the program was a success.

But there was a good deal of opposition to the idea of a Land Bank. There was a deep-seated unease about the government owning the land. It conjured up images of tenant farming in eastern Europe – a land-holding system that tens of thousands of people had come to Saskatchewan to escape.

There were other problems. The leasing arrangement established rents that were related to the purchase price of the land but kept the rental payments low. Land would be sold at prevailing market prices at the time of purchase to those who exercised their right to purchase, and this allowed the Land Bank Commission to offset low rents with possible capital gains if land prices increased. During the 1970s land prices did rise sharply. Lessees who wanted to buy felt that the government should not receive the market price for the land sold to lessees but something close to the cost to the government. And those who were unsuccessful in leasing land from the Land Bank – and there was never enough land to go around – felt that the lessees were already a favoured group and should not be permitted to buy land at less than market value. There was no way to reconcile these points of view.

The selection of lessees became a greater and greater problem. As rising land prices made the Land Bank the only way to get into farming for an increasing number of young people, the number of applicants grew. Elaborate point systems were devised to select the lessees, and appeal boards were set up to review decisions on the allocation of land. But we found that when ten young people apply and one is successful and nine are not, there is no way to convince all of the nine that the selection criteria were fair and fairly applied.

There was another problem. We had assumed that as young farmers got established they would be anxious to buy the land they were leasing. The young farmers were anxious to buy land, but they bought what was on the open market and continued to lease the Land Bank's land. In this way they increased their land base and were able to achieve the economies of scale that can be gained in prairie grain farming. Because we weren't making sales, we had less money to buy more land and were unable to establish a regime of steady buying and selling that would have dispelled the fear that the government wished to accumulate large holdings of cropland. This was certainly not the case, since accumulating land could only create major headaches for any government in Saskatchewan. We eventually got some sales by offering very attractive terms to lessees, but this policy served to alienate many people who were unable either to buy land on the open market or to lease it from the Land Bank Commission.

The Land Bank is a good example of a program that responded well to a real problem but also created a level of dissatisfaction with how it operated that was sufficient to erode public support. The public agreed that older farmers should be helped to retire and that young people should be helped to start farming. But there was no agreement on the method for deciding which young people would receive the land, particularly as rising land values priced more and more young people out of the regular markets for farmland. And in contrast to the childrens' dentistry program, which was accepted as an addition to the health insurance plans, of which Saskatchewan people were proud and possessive, the Land Bank program involved the government owning farmland – a concept that on first consideration generated apprehension and opposition. The idea came to be accepted at the intellectual level, but once the problems of land allocation arose, the earlier visceral objections were revived, or so it seemed to me. The moral seems to be that government activities must not only make logical sense but must also be congruent with the deeply held and perhaps illogical beliefs of the public. The Land Bank might have continued to be popular and accepted if rising land prices had not created new pressures. On the other hand, problems basic to its administration might have made it unacceptable in any case.

The Land Bank program operated until our government was defeated in 1982. After that, no new leases were entered into. A mortgage loan plan was set up by the new government to replace the Land Bank, but it had many problems and was soon terminated.[17] Land Bank lessees still lease land and weathered the most recent recession well. Many people who strongly opposed government ownership now find themselves as tenants on land that had been in their family for generations but is now owned by the chartered banks or mortgage companies. These farmers have no assurance that they will be able to continue to lease the land (and perhaps buy it back one day); the Land Bank lessees do.

An example of an experiment that was a clear failure is the South West Pilot Project. It centred on the small city of Swift Current and the area around it, which is home to about 5 per cent of the province's people. The continued march of technology and specialization has had its impact on government administration. There is always a basic question of organization that governments face: Should the organization be functional or geographic? There is something to be said for each principle. For example, a case can be made that the federal government should have ministries, say, for British Columbia and for Alberta rather than Ministries of Fisheries and Agriculture. This approach has largely been rejected except in the North, where a Northern Affairs Ministry often handles several functions that are handled by functional ministries elsewhere in Canada. Functional ministries make good sense: transport problems in British Columbia are more like transport problems in Ontario than they are like fisheries problems in British Columbia. But this does not mean that no consideration should be given to co-ordinating the transport and fisheries problems in British Columbia.

Trends in technology and specialization have tended to make bureaucracies more centralized. Transport Ministry and Fisheries Ministry people in British Columbia are now more closely linked with the senior ministry people in Ottawa. This seems to make it harder to co-ordinate policies of the two ministries at the local level and to move the locus of co-ordination up the bureaucratic tree.

We felt that the public expected the government of Saskatchewan to have a coherent policy to serve the people in a given area and that one group of government employees should be acting in a manner consistent with what another group of government employees were doing in the same area. So far as the government is concerned, its left hand should know what its right hand is doing, and each, in a general way, should know what the local governments are doing to serve the people in a given area. This is a reasonable expectation for the public to hold, but harder to fulfil in this age of technology and specialization than one might think.

We designed our experiment with all this in mind, to see if we could alleviate what we saw as a problem. In the jargon of a 1972 memorandum prepared for me by planning agency staff, 'the South West Saskatchewan Pilot Project has been created in an attempt to systematically encourage the co-ordination of all provincial government services in a selected area. The Project will facilitate the active and creative participation of the recipients of government services by the regular interaction of the public and the government employees working in the area.'

You will note that the role was not only internal co-ordination but also interaction with the recipients of the services. This involved working with local governments like city councils, with hospital, school, and nursing home boards, and with advocacy groups outside the government.

In the experiment, a very small staff would pull together representatives of all government agencies to form a co-ordinating committee and would invite representatives of local government and nongovernment groups to form an external project board. The intra-government first steps proceeded well. Again in the language of the memo, 'representatives of the various departments have shown an interest in coming to an understanding of the totality of government services.' Language like that used in these memos should have alerted some of us to potential trouble, but books cannot always be judged by their covers nor ideas by the tortured prose in which they are expressed.

The idea was that the nongovernment project board and the government employees' board would produce 'workable, concrete suggestions as to how government services could be made more efficient and beneficial.' At one point consideration was given to involving MLAs from the designated area in the discussions.

The project lasted a year or so and then was abandoned. It failed because it assumed that people outside the circle of public servants would have a major interest in making the delivery of public services 'more efficient and beneficial.' This proved not to be the case. Their concern with government services was not the efficiency of their delivery but rather the amount of money that was spent on them. Almost all external suggestions involved spending more provincial government money; at the same time, the small co-ordinating staff could not influence the level of spending by the Department of Highways, or Health, or as the case might be. The regional departmental representatives, not the co-ordinating staff, spoke for their departments, as had been made very clear at the outset. And the regional representatives who served on the co-ordinating committee were little better off: they too were in no position to commit their deputies and ministers – not to mention Treasury Board and cabinet – to extra spending. So the public consultation on how to deliver programs degenerated into a series of lobbying efforts for more program money, aimed at people who had only a minor capacity to deliver.

In retrospect, the project failed because it tried to do either too little or too much – perhaps, as well, because it was abandoned too soon. The Project produced expectations that ideas from local governments and citizens' groups would be considered, but the staff who ran the project did not get across to these groups at the outset that there would be no more budgetary money, and that what was being considered was methods of delivery, not spending levels. The project might have achieved more if a very senior person from each program department had been involved, but that simply could not have been managed. So in this sense the project did too little to respond to the expectations raised.

If the project had confined itself to dealing only with issues among provincial government agencies that were bound by the government's budgetary restraints, it might have been a modest success. Its attempt to reach beyond these boundaries proved fatal. In this sense it may have tried to do too much.

Perhaps, just perhaps, we might have been able to interest not only government employees but also local government and nongovernment people in issues of program co-ordination if we had defined the issues clearly at the outset and had persevered. But I think some of our people were caught up in the idea of involvement and participation by the public in developing and delivering government programs without being clear in their own minds what form this involvement and participation would take. I see today some of the same recourse to these same undeveloped concepts, along with calls for consultation and accountability. These are all fine concepts but are unhelpful in establishing appropriate government organizations to serve the public until they are defined far more precisely than is usually the case.

The South West Pilot Project was not a success.

Borins: As you suggest, the project probably failed mainly because it attempted to do too much, or at least raised expectations to an unrealistic level. In recent years there have been quite a few very successful service delivery initiatives that are similar in spirit to the South West Saskatchewan Pilot Project. These have gone under the rubrics of 'one-stop shopping' and 'single-window service delivery.' They are less ambitious than the South West Saskatchewan Project, in that they don't attempt to deal with all government services in a given area; but they attempt to provide in one location as many as possible of the services delivered by one or more departments to a common group of clients. There is no expectation that these programs will get any extra money; indeed, these initiatives were undertaken to reduce the administrative costs of existing programs in the deficit-dominated reality of the 1990s. Finally, these projects have a crucial component that was not yet available at the time of the South West Saskatchewan Project – namely, information technology. One example of integrative information technology is the electronic kiosk. Once governments have established electronic kiosks, it is relatively inexpensive to program them to do an increasing number of transactions for many departments.[18]

Here are a few examples of 'one-stop shopping' in the Canadian public sector:

- British Columbia's Government Agents provide registrarial, revenue collection, and information services on behalf of eighteen client ministries throughout the entire province, other than in Vancouver and Victoria.
- The City of Montreal's Accès Montreal project created fourteen neighbourhood offices at which residents could perform most transactions with the municipal government, and established a citywide telephone information and access line. It took the Gold Medal in the Institute of Public Administration of Canada's first Innovative Public Management Award, for which you and I were among the judges.
- Bob Rae's government in Ontario created a single-window approach for business registration that, using information technology, reduced the processing time for registration of a new business from eight weeks to less than one. Frances Lankin, then Minister for Economic Development and Trade, made this program one of her key priorities. However, as discussed in our chapter on lobbying, it did not win the support of the business community in the 1995 election.
- The federal government is providing single-window delivery of its programs for business at Canada Business Service Centres. Three pilot projects were very successful. These centres have since been established throughout the country, in many cases jointly with provincial governments.

- Human Resources Development Canada, established in the federal government reorganization of 1993 to combine the Canada Employment and Immigration Commission, the parts of Health and Welfare Canada dealing with income security, and the Department of Labour, has established a Service Delivery Network throughout the country. Its offices perform labour market functions, such as providing information about vacancies and counselling, and handle transfer programs, such as Employment Insurance, Canada Pension Plan, and Old Age Security. Many services are provided at electronic kiosks.

I think this trend to one-stop shopping is now well established and has great potential. Individuals and businesses want convenient, one-stop service, and they don't care which department or level of government delivers the service. Information technology has made it possible to integrate services in ways that hadn't been imagined at the time of the South West Saskatchewan Pilot Project. So your project may not have been a success on its own terms, but it was a precursor for today's innovations in service delivery.

17

Crises and the Media

This chapter illustrates a number of principles of crisis management, including media relations during a crisis. These principles include the importance of having an operational group to implement actions at the scene of the crisis, as well as a strategic group to plan the response to the crisis. These groups must be closely linked. We also discuss how the strategic group can avoid a bunker mentality or 'group think.' The most important goals in media relations are to get your message out in a clear and confident way and to emphasize what your organization is doing to cope with the crisis. We also discuss issues such as the timing and location of press conferences and the use of technical experts. We then provide a detailed analysis of media relations for a fictional case involving a ship colliding with a drawbridge in the St Lawrence Seaway.

From this, we move to media relations in general, discussing the choice of media, the type of message to communicate, the need for preparation and the importance of honesty, in terms both of what you say and how you present yourself.

Borins: In recent years, crisis management and media relations have become important issues for many organizations. In the private sector we have seen some crises managed superbly – for example, the Tylenol scare – and others, such as the *Exxon Valdez* oil spill, handled miserably. Here is a rather amusing example of bad crisis management. The owner of a company producing a new chocolate bar, the Cold Buster, was told by the media that animal rights activists were alleging that the bars contained animal parts and claiming that they had sabotaged the bars by adulterating them with caustic oven cleaner. The owner responded to the story as though it was a prank, replying, 'To our knowledge, we don't grind up any mice to make our bar.' Then he had a real problem.[1]

As long as we have managers making remarks like that, there will be work for consultants in crisis management and media relations. There have been a fair number of articles in the popular press about these consultants, and many organizations have been preparing brochures or guidebooks for their employees.[2] Why don't we, in this chapter, go into competition with the consultants? They have the advantage of providing personalized service, but our price is a good deal more reasonable.

What were the more memorable crises you saw while in public life?

Blakeney: Crises seem to be of two kinds: those caused by a natural disaster, such as an earthquake, fire, or flood, and those caused by some sort of human struggle, such as a major strike or a war. Saskatchewan has had its share of the first type – forest fires and floods. As for the latter type, the doctor's strike of 1962 against the introduction of health insurance was the most serious I have had to deal with. You will recall that on 1 July 1962, almost all Saskatchewan doctors withdrew their services and as a result almost all our hospitals closed. There was great public consternation, and a very high level of tension between those who favoured and those who opposed the introduction of government-sponsored medical care insurance. By a wide margin it was the most acute crisis I encountered in my political career, dwarfing disputes about the public ownership of potash, or patriating the constitution.

Borins: And what are the main lessons to be learned from some of these crises?

Blakeney: The first relates to the need for a highly competent operational group, a team of people who are at the front line doing what is needed to solve the problem. I remember a dramatic battle to save the town of Lumsden from a small river that had become a raging torrent, flowing at over forty times its normal rate. In this case a group of engineers and highway construction staff tried frantically to build dikes and earthworks to hold back the ever-swelling river. In the case of the doctor's strike, a core group of people in the Health Department worked at redeploying doctors who were willing to serve in small hospitals that were having trouble staying open.[3]

The operational group needs to be close to the scene of the crisis. It needs to be able to commandeer instantly any resources it thinks are necessary. This means there must be immediate, direct links with the top level of the organization to make sure that the needed resources are available.

Borins: You mention the top level of the organization. Where should they be in all this?

Blakeney: The top level of the organization is what I would call the strategic group, or the 'War Cabinet.' It is the responsibility of the leader of the organization to choose the group or, alternatively, to choose the group leader and allow him or her to assemble the team. For example, Premier Lloyd chose the strategic group that dealt with the doctors' strike. He was its leader. Health Minister William Davies headed the operational group, which kept the system functioning and recruited doctors from Britain and elsewhere to provide services in place of striking doctors.

Another team, which reported to the Premier and to the strategic group, dealt with legal challenges to the medical care insurance legislation, and also assisted the Premier in dealing with the press and with outside groups who wished to meet with the government.

The strategic group must not be entirely engaged in immediate crisis management. When the crisis is, say, a strike – that is, when the adversary is not nature but other people – the strategic group must be assessing constantly what the adversaries' objectives are, what their next moves will be, and how they will react to your moves. The operational group also needs to keep its objectives clearly in mind. This seems self-evident, but it is entirely possible for one side in a bitter dispute to change its objective from achieving the original goals to defeating the adversaries.

The strategic group needs good strategists capable of clear thinking and of planning several moves ahead. It also needs some contact with people who will give clear and totally honest advice – for example, with senior public servants who will speak frankly, or with impartial outsiders (if such people exist). It is vital to avoid developing a bunker mentality, or 'group-think,' which so easily emerges under the stress and fatigue that a crisis generates. People also have a tendency to be unyielding for fear of appearing indecisive. We always tried to have public servants – and where we could, outside advisers – on hand who could view any situation with a sceptical eye and look for creative solutions. During the doctors' strike, Tom Shoyama was totally unflappable under fire and could come up with a rational analysis of almost any situation. I noted later that during some hard-hitting federal–provincial disputes over energy pricing during the 1970s, the federal government, for whom he then worked, called upon Shoyama to pour the oil of calm rationality on some very troubled matters.

During the medicare dispute, Premier Lloyd consulted with such pillars of icy reason and clear analysis as David Lewis of the federal New Democratic Party and Montreal lawyer and mediator Carl Goldenberg.[4] As a result of these consultations, a British peer and physician, Lord Taylor, arrived on the scene as a mediator. Lord Taylor, behind a theatrical exterior, was very shrewd at assessing what the underlying concerns of each party were. He crafted a compromise that ended the strike and launched the medicare plan with that minimum level of accommodation between the parties that allowed the plan to work.[5]

In human conflict, unconditional surrender by the adversary is rarely an objective worth pursuing. This is particularly true when a government will have to live with the adversary group in the future and where each of the contesting groups felt that it had some merit of its side. The need to provide some methods of face saving is not a principle confined to the Orient.

A final point: It is important to maintain close links and transparently clear communications between the strategic group and the operational group so that the latter is on line with what the former intends. One might first think that in a crisis, when everybody is enormously busy, there would be an inclination to hold fewer meetings. This is not the case. Meetings to confirm strategy and meetings to keep the lines open between the strategists and the front-liners are in fact a profitable use of time. When those in charge of the front-line operations understand fully the strategic objectives of their side and how it is proposed to achieve them, comfort levels are raised and a context is provided in which tactical, hour-by-hour decisions can be made.

Of course, tactical moves are sometimes designed to confuse the adversary. The decision as to how many of your people are to be made aware of these tactics, and how many are to remain as confused as you hope your adversaries are, is always a difficult one to make. For such tactics to be effective, verbal communications as opposed to written messages are almost always necessary.

Borins: Some studies are available that illustrate this approach to crisis management as used by other governments. For example, Michael Brecher, in his detailed, minute-by-minute study of the Israeli cabinet's decisions during the 1967 and 1973 wars, found that the Israelis intensified their search for information, considered many alternatives, consulted widely, and expanded the decision-making group.[6]

Graham Allison, in his study of the Cuban Missile Crisis, recounts how President Kennedy formed and then relied on the advice of an ad hoc group of fifteen, which included several members of his cabinet, senior officials, members of his staff, an expert on the Soviet Union, and a former Secretary of State.[7] Kennedy and this group gave direct orders to the Navy commanders who were implementing the blockade of Cuba – which caused a great deal of consternation among the admirals in Washington who were by-passed.[8]

You've spoken about strategy and operations. What about media relations during a crisis?

Blakeney: The most important point is to get your message out. This involves being responsive to the media, but much more besides – it also means establishing your own agenda as the basis of discussion to the greatest extent possible. This can be done with different levels of finesse. I had a friend who was a controversial farm leader. When asked an awkward question during an interview, he would reply, 'That's not the issue,' and then state the issue he wanted to discuss and speak to it. In a time of crisis, this is usually the result you want to achieve, but you hope to go about it a little less obviously.

During a crisis the media will usually want to dwell on why the crisis happened, how it could have been avoided, and who is to blame. They start from their familiar who, what, when, where, why approach. The government almost never wants to talk about who is to blame except as a means to deflect attention, if possible – which it usually isn't, so why try? The reason why the origins of the crisis are usually not what you want to talk about is that with the wisdom of 20–20 hindsight, it can almost always be shown that something could have been done that would have been better than what was, in fact, done. For example, if there is a forest fire it can almost always be shown that, given the location of the fire, the firefighting equipment could have been better positioned than it was. The fact that there was no possible way anybody could have predicted the location of the fire, and accordingly where the equipment should have been positioned, is often overlooked.

The best interests of the government are almost always served by concentrating on what is being done to deal with the crisis. Television makes this a little easier. It's a lot easier to get television shots of what is happening now than what happened last week. I recall seeing the stories of a major fire in Manitoba. There were virtually no stories on how the fire started or, more pertinently, how it managed to grow to such a huge size that many communities were threatened. There was not even much coverage of the firefighters. Coverage concentrated on the people who were evacuated, the way they were being billeted in schools and homes, how food and clothing was being supplied, and so on. What we saw was the epitome of purposeful activity – people coping with a crisis caused by uncontrollable natural forces.

Almost always, your message should be that there is a crisis but that the authorities are on top of it and performing well. You do not normally wish at this stage to send the message that we're looking into how the crisis happened, and who was to blame, and how we can prevent it from happening again. The 'we're coping' message can usually be upbeat and can be seen to reflect favourably on the government; the 'we're looking into what mistakes were made and by whom' message can often be turned by the political opposition and the media so that it reflects unfavourably on the government.

As I have suggested, it is easier to get your preferred message out with television reporters than with the print media, because the latter are more likely to spend more effort on the 'why' of an event, and correspondingly less on the who, what, when, and where.

When dealing with the media in times of crisis, many questions arise of a more technical nature, such as when and where to hold a press conference. There are no fixed answers, but there are some general propositions that are usually valid. Here is one: Have a press conference as soon as possible, even if you haven't all the facts. It is important that your version be in the public domain as soon as possible. There will be other stories published, and if you are late you will be playing catch-up from the beginning. It is always possible to give some idea of what happened and of what steps are being taken to deal with the crisis, and to promise more facts tomorrow. There are almost always some experts who can be either consulted or lined up to come to deal with the problem. This can be reported in 'the doctor is on the way' style.

The location of the press conference will depend on many factors, including where the reporters are whom you wish to reach, and whether there are good visuals that could dramatize the unpredictable nature of the crisis or the way the government has begun to respond.

If you are sufficiently well informed, you can deal at the press conference not only with the general public but also with particular publics. Suppose there is a railway accident involving a train carrying dangerous chemicals that derails and blocks an important local road. Regarding the public generally, you will state what happened, and that equipment is on the way to remove the chemicals from the derailed cars and to clean up the wreck.

To the regional reporters, you will direct the message as to when the local road will be open again.

To residents of the immediate crash area, you will direct the message that the rail cars are or are not leaking. If the cars are leaking, you will also inform them that the threat from the chemicals is substantial so they should evacuate, or that the threat is minimal and will be confined to a small area, or as the case may be.

To railway shippers, you will direct the message that the railway companies have advised that they can reroute shipments and that only minor delays are anticipated, or as the case may be.

All of this simply involves you and your staff listing quickly the special publics that will be affected and attempting to give some preliminary facts to each special group, as well as to the larger public, who may regard the accident as just another sensation to be savoured.

For many press conferences, I favour a team – a senior policy person and one or two technical experts. For example, during the electrcity blackouts caused by an ice storm in January 1998, Premier Bouchard and Hydro-Québec CEO André

Caillé gave daily press conferences together. The senior person should manage the conference and introduce her experts and their areas of expertise, but at first should answer all questions herself. She can ask advice from the experts and relay the answers. If the leader has confidence in the policy sensitivity of the experts, she can hand over a question and let them reply to it directly. It would usually be unfair, however, for her to steer them questions with a tough policy content. If a difficult question is asked, it is sometimes possible for the senior person to split it into a pure technical element and a policy element and ask the expert to deal with the purely technical elements first. That way, she has a minute or so to formulate a reply to the policy element, which may require a careful selection of words to avoid misinterpretation.

Another key point in dealing with crises relate to what I would call the 60/40 principle. During a crisis there are tough decisions to be made, tough judgment calls.

I think it was Yogi Berra who said, 'When you come to a fork in the road, take it.' Unfortunately, life does not offer such neat verbal solutions to difficult dilemmas. Once a close decision has been made in a crisis situation, then at a press conference dealing with the crisis, it is usually best to say that you considered the options and that the one you chose appeared to be *clearly* the best. Unless you feel that the decision might be reversed, it is usually best to leave the impression that you have selected the best one – clearly the best one – and that you are pursuing it with vigour. This is an application of the principle that one bad general is better than two good generals. Those who are looking for leadership from the crisis manager must feel that a course of action has been decided upon and will be followed, and that they can act accordingly. As a crisis manager, you will find it a difficult feat of mental discipline to pursue your decision as if it was 100 per cent right, while staying receptive to facts that might show the original decision at the forks was wrong. Often your decision should not be revised in any case, because events have intervened. But even the *possibility* of a U-turn must not be completely eliminated. The trick is to make sure that your receptivity to contrary facts does not undermine your confidence in your judgment and thereby your single-minded determination, which is so desirable in a crisis situation. Decisiveness is necessary, not only to energize your team but also to show the public that things are in hand. Indecisiveness is almost always the wrong signal to send.

Borins: Allison also has a principle that totals 100, which he calls the 51/49 principle. He observes that in a hectic and competitive world, politicians and senior officials will argue even marginal cases with the confidence and certainty of advocates.[9] In a crisis, this ability helps them send the necessary signals of self-assurance.

In our public management class, we used a case titled *The St. Louis Bridge Incident*.[10] In this fictional case, on a mid-November morning a ship collided with a drawbridge on the St Lawrence Seaway near Montreal. The bridge was damaged and would take six weeks, which was past the end of the shipping season, to repair. While repairs were going on you could either leave the drawbridge raised, which would allow the fifty ships still in the Seaway to get out to sea but would force road and rail traffic using the bridge to detour, or you could lower the drawbridge, which would allow road and rail traffic to pass unimpeded but close the Seaway to shipping. After considerable thought, you decided that the potential disruption to maritime traffic was more serious than the potential disruption to road and rail, and that the better course of action was to raise the drawbridge during repairs. How would you explain your decision to the media?

Blakeney: This case illustrates some of the points I was attempting to make earlier. This is clearly a 60/40 judgment call, or perhaps 70/30. In any case the decision is not entirely clear and self-evident and some balancing has to be done. As I recall the 'facts' in the case, at the time of the collision there was an ongoing dispute between the Seaway Authority and the Seaway pilots and their unions, and there was the real possibility of a strike. This added to the complexity of the decision, since if the drawbridge was left in a raised position so as to cut off all ground traffic and leave the Seaway functioning, a pilots' strike might shut down the Seaway in any case, the result being the worst of both worlds.

But a decision having been made, I would explain it this way: The key issue as we see it is to keep the Seaway open, to keep the ships moving and Canada's reputation as a reliable trading partner intact. In this way we will save jobs in Montreal, not only during the remaining weeks of the shipping season but also in the future, as a result of our enhanced reputation for reliability among shipping interests.

I would attempt to get the railway company to state that the closing of the railway bridge would not cause serious disruption, because traffic could be diverted to other lines.

As for the possibility of a pilots' strike, I would suggest that I felt it unlikely that the pilots would proceed with a work stoppage when others had been asked to make major sacrifices to keep the Seaway open and to protect all those whose jobs depended on the Seaway. This would not seem to be in the long-term best interests of the pilots.

Mainly, I would emphasize that Canada is a great trading nation, and how much cargo is carried by the Seaway, and how massive the costs for shippers would be if ships were trapped in the Seaway for many months. I would also point out that there would be long-term damage to Canada's reputation and Canada's economy if the Seaway were closed prematurely.

And I would also point out that the Seaway serves American ports and American shippers and that our obligation to our American partners is to keep the Seaway open. The Great Lakes region, on both sides of the international border, is one of the great industrial regions of the world, and it is vital to Canada that the transport of goods to and from this industrial heartland be, to the greatest extent possible, by the Seaway and not by rail to and from east-coast American ports. These arguments have the advantage of being true, believable, and not easily quantified (and therefore not easy to refute).

If I were staging a press conference, I would have the first one – in any case an early one – at the site of the ship accident. The visuals would include the ship, flying a foreign flag, being towed from where it rammed the bridge. To the extent possible, I would try to cast the ship as the villain of the piece. The message would be that we are talking about foreign trade, and that this huge ship caused the damage, and that the clean-up process is clearly under way. I would try to focus attention on the experts who were working to get the drawbridge repaired as quickly as possible, and away from what caused the accident. Doubtless, with the wisdom of hindsight, somebody will find something that Seaway officials should have done to prevent the accident, at which time – a greater hazard – attention might focus on a possible error by the pilot. My judgment would be that when the Seaway is in a bitter dispute with its pilots, it is not the time to be seen to be casting blame on the pilot. There will be time enough to determine how the accident happened after the glare of publicity has abated.

I would also make sure that the minister responsible for the Seaway was briefed so that he could parry questions dealing with the cause of the accident by reference to ongoing investigations as to how the ship could have struck the bridge. He too could emphasize the Seaway's importance to the entire Canadian economy and to our relations with the United States and with shipping nations around the world. I would ask the minister to stress the steps that were being taken to get the bridge repaired quickly so as to lessen the inconvenience to the area's residents. I would advise the minister to commend the railway company for arranging rail diversions, the crews for working so hard to repair the damage, and the officials of the Quebec government for their prompt and thorough action in dealing with the environmental issues. The overall thrust would be that the accident could not have been predicted, that it threatened Canada's reputation as a trading nation and endangered short-term and long-term jobs, and that it was gratifying to see the crisis being handled with a spirit of co-operation and determination.

Borins: The media will be keenly interested in any crisis. Why don't we go on from here to media relations in general? Have you any maxims about the media to share with our readers?

Blakeney: A few. The first relates to the choice of media: if you are initiating a story, choose the medium and/or journalist whose approach is most consistent with your message.

Borins: Another case we used in our course was *The Four Million Dollar Typo*,[11] which recounted actual events. Mr St Laurent, a senior public servant in the Canadian Employment and Immigration Commission, discovered that because of a clerical error the commission had overpaid 16,000 Employment Insurance claims throughout the country by a total of $4 million. A decision was made to announce the mistake frankly and collect the overpayment. St Laurent gave the story to Canadian Press, since he could rely on that news service to treat it factually. (The *Toronto Sun* would have used it as an opportunity to editorialize about public service incompetence.) The announcement had the desired effect – the story was nothing more than a two-day wonder.

Blakeney: As I suggested earlier, if you know the reporters and their media well enough, you can emphasize those parts of the story that will interest them. I referred to this in the context of managing a crisis, but it applies equally to more routine stories for which you are seeking coverage. If a government is announcing a list of, say, cultural grants, the information you circulate to local community newspapers and local radio stations should highlight the grants in the area. Don't depend on the media people to dig them out of the release; indeed, add any additional information you can. If you can give the media a local contact who could voice a positive comment on the grant for the local radio station and the local newspaper, so much the better. The community media very much like stories with a 'neighbourly' angle; if you cast your press release with this in mind, the chances of coverage are greater. This perhaps parochial approach to news is not confined to small newspapers. The tales about headlines in the *Toronto Star* like THREE METRO RESIDENTS INJURED IN MONTREAL BLAZE, and, in smaller print, 57 DIE IN MONTREAL APARTMENT BLOCK FIRE, are only slightly apocryphal.

My next maxim relates to the *type* of message: When questions are asked, try to answer them within the framework of your message. Don't answer 'When did you stop beating your spouse?' questions designed to embarrass you. Rephrase them and respond, again within the framework of your message. It is important to get your message out. If the news is bad, get it out quickly for damage control. Bad news looks much worse if it comes out bit by bit.

Here is a third maxim: Don't falsify. It is not defensible. Most people are uncomfortable when they don't tell the truth – I'm glad to say – and the discomfort shows. The effect is often very bad indeed. There is the further problem that if you are caught, the issue becomes not the original story but your integrity. This can be devastating. Richard Nixon was forced to resign from the White House not because he engaged in some reprehensible practices to gain information but because he lied, was caught, and lost his credibility with Congress and the public. Most people get into trouble almost innocently: they are asked a question to which they don't have the answer, and then wing an answer that proves to be wrong, and then continue to make elaborate explanations rather than simply admit the error. My experience is that if you are straight with the press they forgive the odd error of fact; they might report that you were wrong on your facts, but they don't accuse you of lying. There is no harm in admitting you don't know, and you are not compelled to answer all awkward questions. It is far better to say 'no comment' and take the heat for that than to falsify an answer. If you have a real problem, you should consider your position with care. A 'no comment' will work for a brief period: after that, an admission of the difficulty is usually the best approach. If you are a cabinet minister or a senior official, a premier can support you if you have made a serious error and disclosed it. It is next to impossible for a premier to stick by you if you have made a serious error and lied about it.

I recall an incident that may illustrate this. A day before budget day the Minister of Finance had an embargoed press conference explaining the budget. Somehow our senior cabinet press officer left a copy of the detailed press release in the press room after the conference and the information became public on the morning of budget day. The Minister of Finance, who was in no way at fault, offered to resign. The press officer came to me, explained what had happened, and tendered his resignation. I asked him to send me a letter detailing the circumstances and putting his resignation in writing. Fortunately, no information of commercial value had been released, so the chief result of early disclosure was embarrassment to the government. In this case there was immediate disclosure, no effort at concealment, and a written recital of the facts in my hands and in the hands of the minister so that our stories would be consistent. Consequently, I was able to refuse to accept the minister's resignation. I was also able to direct attention to the error made by the press officer and almost immediately refuse to accept his resignation.

Fortunately for us, the official was held in high regard by the media reporters, from whose ranks he had been drawn, and by the opposition. The story was a two-day wonder and then was gone. Any attempt to be anything less than frank could have turned all of this into a nasty problem. I might have been forced to accept the resignation of a highly competent official and possibly even the minister.

I have a fourth maxim, which relates to preparation: If you are not experienced, do a trial run of your press conference, with someone playing the devil's advocate, asking tough questions. Think about how various media might want to play the story, and whether your presentation will facilitate or undercut their approach. Practise prepared remarks; read them over and underline the points you want to stress, and try to put special emphasis on the thirty-second clip you would like the media to use.

Borins: As we discussed in the previous chapter, rehearsal is also a form of simulation.

Blakeney: My fifth maxim is this: Beware of colourful phrases unless you are sure of how they will be used – which is next to impossible. C.D. Howe suffered from an off-hand comment he is said to have made, 'What's a million?'; Pierre Trudeau paid heavily for a remark to a group of Western farmers: 'Why should I sell your wheat?' Brian Mulroney would long regret referring to constitutional negotiations as 'rolling the dice.' In each case the phrases were repeated, out of context, endlessly by the media and by political opponents. Unless you are very skilled, develop a straightforward media style that is free of irony and that avoids colourful phrases.

My sixth maxim, and last, is this: Be yourself. You may not be the greatest media personality in the nation. And you may need to improve some of the externals – things like keeping your hands away from your face, dressing so as not to distract the viewer's eyes from your face (and your message), and learning not to punctuate your remarks with *umms* and *aahs*. You can spot these problems by playing back tapes of your press conference presentations and noting which things reduced the effectiveness of your message. You can also watch tapes of other people's press conferences. But I caution against attempting to copy anybody else's style. If you are going to be convincing, you have to be comfortable with your presentation.

If you are a senior person in the public or private sector, you will have enough problems dealing with the media without having to remake yourself when the cameras are rolling. You will be dealing with the press frequently and will want to develop an easy and natural relationship with them. They will appreciate it if you speak in front of the camera in a clear, crisp, comprehensible way, using language their viewers will understand. They want a good, usable clip. But they are usually suspicious of anyone whose on-camera presentation is totally different from his or her off-camera style. And, more importantly, if you use an unnatural style before the TV cameras, the viewers will notice it and regard you as insincere, unless you are very good indeed.

18

Managing a Change of Government

This chapter discusses the management of a change of government from several points of view. An incoming premier has to choose a cabinet, find trusted and effective staff for the Premier's Office, work out a relationship with the public service (which may involve replacing or moving some civil servants), decide which policies and practices of the previous government to reassess and which to maintain, find ways to get caucus involved, and develop a system for making order-in-council appointments. We also discuss the role of the public service in a change of government, in particular the briefings they should prepare for the incoming government and its ministers. We then look at the transition from the point of view of a defeated premier, and the steps that must be taken to establish an effective office of the Leader of the Opposition. Finally, we consider the question of whether more should be done to provide an institutional memory from one government to the next, and consider the role the public service could play in enhancing institutional memory.

Borins: Allan, you've been on both sides of a change of government, coming and going. For the premier taking power, I suppose it must be daunting to come into office with the desk empty, no files, and a host of pressing decisions to make. So Bob Rae described it in his memoir: '[David Peterson] and his staff slipped away without sharing very many tips of office organization, management, or pending provincial issues. When we moved into our offices on October 1, 1990, the room was completely bare. Inside the empty desk were the words, "Good luck, David Peterson."'[1]

Blakeney: Arriving to an empty desk is a shock. This happened to me in full measure only once, when I took over as Premier in 1971 from the previous Liberal administration. I had moved into and out of ministerial positions several times before that, but in each case my predecessor was a cabinet colleague who was still available for consultation and who left for me all the files that covered ongoing matters in the Department of Education, or Health, or whatever. Not so in 1971 – Premier Thatcher had removed all his files, and since he operated in a highly personal style, some matters had been recorded in his files and nowhere else. I remember getting a letter from a school asking whether they would get their grant. I recall writing back saying that we had not yet located the file and asking them to send a photostat of any letter of commitment. It came back bearing Thatcher's signature, and we honoured it. The original file was never found. This happened several times with minor items.

These minor items aside, the problem was that my desk soon filled with items calling for decision and I did not have any context in which to make them. On many issues large and small, I had to ask, or my office staff had to ask, what the practice had been. This is a major problem for any new government – all manner of people who were unhappy about how the previous government dealt with a particular issue try on the new government for size. People approaching the new government usually set out plausible and sometimes convincing reasons why they are right and the previous government was wrong. There is a temptation to think you should do things differently than the previous government did them. This must be firmly resisted. I started with the assumption that if the previous government handled a problem in a particular way, it was probably with good reason. I assumed they were right until someone had the opportunity to assess their methods. All of the extra activity associated with reassessing the policies of the previous administration makes the first few months of a new administration particularly busy. The press of affairs is heightened if you reach the conclusion that the public service you have inherited is prone to defend all practices of the previous government or, perhaps worse, to be overcritical of those practices in order to ingratiate itself with the new government. At times like this you appreciate professionalism in the public service.

After 1971 we quickly identified in the existing public service, or recruited from outside, key public servants on whom we felt we could rely fully. It was not *only* a case, or *mainly* a case, of their desire to be loyal to the new government; more often it was a question of competence. Once we had a reliable core group, they could deal with the requests for revision of policies and also identify for us the many competent and professional public servants who were already working for the province. In 1971 we were fortunate to have already in place some senior public servants – the deputy provincial treasurer was one – in whom we had total confidence from day one, and who knew many of the most able people within the service.

Some early problems were a little more complicated. We believed that the highway tendering practices, particularly with respect to allowances for extras, were being used as a vehicle for patronage. We had to make a judgment call about whether the public servants were part of that problem. After some consideration, we concluded that they were not and that if we mandated different policies they would follow them faithfully and effectively. It turned out we were right.

Patronage comes in many forms, and may be politically inspired or arise from contact between suppliers and public servants. One of the more subtle forms involves the drawing up of specifications for the purpose of purchasing equipment – say, road graders – by tender. The specifications for the graders can be so drafted that only one or two manufacturers can meet them. The public servants who draw up the specifications may genuinely believe that one brand of equipment is clearly the best. And they may be right. But that does not mean that a government should always buy the best grader – an inferior but substantially cheaper one may be the best buy. A new government may soon find itself attempting to learn just why most of the graders had been purchased from one supplier. This problem can be dealt with quickly on an interim basis with a declaration that tenders which do not meet the specifications will nevertheless be received and evaluated. This is not a good long-run system, because the subjective element is too great and charges of favouritism will certainly result. But it does serve to concentrate attention on the drafting of the specifications and to identify this step as a possible point of patronage.

These are only some of the issues that confront a new government immediately after taking office.

Borins: What can the leader of an opposition party do to prepare for power?

Blakeney: One thing an opposition party can do is prepare a detailed election manifesto. Before the 1971 election we published our *New Deal for People*, which contained a surprisingly comprehensive and detailed outline of what we hoped to do in office. To arrive at these policies, the party spent two years making detailed studies of issues such as environmental regulation; education financing; the expansion of health insurance programs into chiropractic services, prescription drugs, and children's dentistry; northern development; and labour practices. In the course of these studies we identified and tentatively resolved the principal issues, and gained some idea of what the costs and available revenues would be. Our manifesto stood the test of office, and most of the policies we stated in it were introduced.

It is unfortunate that the days of election manifestos that are sufficiently detailed to serve as the basis for legislation are gone. It seems to me that the forward planning necessary to write a manifesto has become more difficult in recent years because the information in the public domain seems to be less reliable than before. Also, as I argued in Chapter 7, the substitution of image for policy – particularly in the electronic media – has meant that detailed election manifestos are perceived as irrelevant. Both these trends are regrettable.

Borins: More recently, there have been two instances of detailed election manifestos, namely the Liberals' Red Book of 1993 and the Ontario Conservatives' Common Sense Revolution of 1995. Greenspon and Wilson-Smith recount that in the 1993 campaign, Chrétien 'made a point at almost every campaign stop of reminding voters that, four years on, they could come back to him and tote up the promises kept and the promises broken.'[2] The 112-page Red Book was a way of showing accountability to the electorate at a time of deep distrust of politicians. It also provided a clear contrast with Prime Minister Kim Campbell's increasingly desperate policy improvisations. The platforms in the federal election of 1997 probably had less of an impact. Perhaps election manifestos are more useful in winning power than in retaining power. Also, the process of drafting a manifesto may be a helpful discipline for a party that is preparing to take power.

Blakeney: A party in opposition can also begin thinking about the key employees it will need and who they might be. The amount that can be done here is quite limited. The election date is not in your control. You are not sure you will win. The result is that you do not know whether the people you have your eye on will be available when you need them. Top people often make career changes, and with each move their possible availability changes.

Of course, the leader of an opposition party can do some preliminary planning about who will be appointed to cabinet. I will refer to this a little later.

Borins: What should the bureaucracy do to prepare for a new government?

Blakeney: The bureaucracy should do two major things. They should prepare to give the incoming government complete information on the current state of affairs – the current programs, the state of finances, the trends in both. This is usually arranged by the permanent heads, whose staff prepare briefing books for the incoming ministers. As I have said before about policy analysis done by public servants, the quality of the staff is indicated by the quality of the briefing books. Each book should have an overview section and sections for each major activity. The main messages should be set out succinctly and with a minimum of detail. There should be detailed backup material. The minister should not have to read all the backup details to gain a reasonable appreciation of the issues to be confronted.

As with all other public service communications, the briefing books should be written in appropriate lay language. It is not the job of the minister to learn the jargon of a government department. It is the job of the public service to frame the issues in the language the minister can understand and share with his colleagues. As an aside, whenever I heard a minister at cabinet using departmental jargon, I knew that a problem was developing: the minister was in danger of not being able to communicate with the public about the work of the department.

The other major thing the public service can do is acquaint itself with the incoming party's election platform and its approach to public issues, and start thinking about what new policy directions are likely to be pursued and how they will be carried forward. I think it was Richard Crossman who recounted that when the Labour Party came to power in Britain in 1945, its ministers were supplied, soon after being sworn in, with draft legislation prepared by the public service based on the Party's election manifesto. In Canada, we are not likely to see so sophisticated a response as this, but some thinking on, say, how to expand the public sector, or contract it, might be considered by public servants. Along the same lines, the public service can consider where additional key staff may be found to assist the incoming party in implementing its program. The public service should do its preparation for any party that might form the next government. It seems to me that this may not have been the case when the Rae government assumed office in Ontario in 1990.

Borins: I agree completely that the British response you describe captures the *ideal* of what a professional public service should be doing, both before and during an election campaign, and that the performance of Ontario's public service in 1990 fell far short of the ideal. The public service did not anticipate that the NDP would win the election, and did not prepare for an NDP government. Similarly, the party did little to prepare for office, and did not have a detailed program that the public service could have worked from. The NDP transition team was disappointed with the quality of briefing materials provided and with the bureaucracy's attempts to translate their program into concrete policies.[3]

I was recently at a conference where the British Cabinet Secretary, Sir Robin Butler, described the preparations for the transition between John Major and Tony Blair.[4] In early 1996, then–Prime Minister Major authorized permanent secretaries to begin confidential talks with Labour Party shadow ministers. The public service was enjoined not to advise the Labour Party on policy, but rather to discuss how the machinery of government would be designed to implement Labour's policies. These discussions became more intense as the election approached, to the point where the Cabinet Secretary was meeting fortnightly with Blair. Shortly before the election, the Cabinet Secretary provided Blair with a list of key appointments as well as a critical path for meetings in the early days of his ministry.

Blair provided a list of priorities and legislation, as well as the timing of the budget. In the U.K., unlike Canada, the practice is that if a majority government is elected, it takes office the day after the election. As a result of this careful co-ordination, Prime Minister Blair was able to hit the ground running. For example, the public service responded to Labour's promise to conduct referenda on devolution in Scotland and Wales by establishing your preferred mechanism – a special secretariat for devolution. It was staffed and operating the day after the election. Prime Minister Blair was able to implement this and many other policies and priorities in his first hundred days in office, not only because the civil service did its work, but because the Labour Party had its policies and priorities worked out well in advance of the election.[5] In addition, Labour had established a commanding lead in the public opinion polls long before the election, and maintained it throughout the campaign, which added both urgency and certainty to the transition work. Sir Robin described this process as a 'conjuring trick,' whereby the public saw a group of politicians take power one day and the very next day start producing wise and dynamic policies.

One could argue that an ideal transition is most likely to occur when, as in the recent British election, one party is expected (or as oddsmakers would say, 'heavily favoured') to win. The real challenge is to have an effective transition when the outcome is more uncertain.

What are any premier's priority areas upon taking over – the things that must be tended to immediately?

Blakeney: There is a long list of things that must be done almost immediately. The urgent one is to select a cabinet. This must be done within a few days of the election, even though the opportunity to plan in advance is limited. In most jurisdictions cabinet building is, as we noted in Chapter 2, a complex job that involves balancing experience and competence with regional, gender, ethnic, religious, and ideological considerations. A premier does not know who will be available in his caucus until the election is over. Usually he knows perhaps half of the likely choices, but not necessarily the portfolios each should occupy. So in the first few days after an election victory he is occupied with a round of fast and furious consultations to cobble together the best team. When a government first assumes office, the premier would be wise to choose a small team; this way, he can strengthen it later by adding members.

Other immediate problems are to organize the Premier's Office to deal with the flood of mail, telephone calls, and the like from well-wishers, from those who wish to raise issues of substance, and from those who wish to pay courtesy calls – a wild misnomer, since the callers wish to use your most valuable resource, which is time, to exchange pleasantries for their benefit. Time planning becomes crucial.

Very quickly, getting key personnel in place becomes urgent. Getting some-body to act as a liaison with caucus is vital. New members of the Legislature have little idea of what their role is and how they can act for the benefit of their constituents. Some have little idea of how a large organization works. Someone is needed who can meet with them, guide them, and keep them off the backs of the premier and the new ministers.

Borins: The Kennedy School at Harvard runs a very successful program for newly elected members of Congress, which does just that. Perhaps an equally entrepre-neurial Canadian university will do likewise.

Blakeney: The next problem is to find key personnel for your office and for some central agencies. The senior people from the Premier's Office will almost cer-tainly have left with the previous administration. Regular employees from the Executive Council (which is called the Privy Council Office at the federal level) are almost certainly still in place. The cabinet secretary may or may not be there. Gaps will need to be filled, often on a temporary basis so that the machinery can operate while recruiting takes place.

Any new premier is amazed to learn how many routine matters of government require formal orders of the Lieutenant-Governor-in-Council. This was force-fully brought home to us when Lieutenant-Governor George Porteous died in office. That is when we discovered that while the Constitution permits an admin-istrator – normally the Chief Justice or a retired Chief Justice – to act on behalf of the Lieutenant-Governor when he or she is absent or unable to act, it does not allow the administrator to act when there is no Lieutenant-Governor. We found ourselves unable to pass orders-in-council and had to press the federal govern-ment for an early appointment of a new Lieutenant-Governor. There should be a constitutional change to permit an administrator to act for, say, sixty days after the death of a Lieutenant-Governor so as to allow time for selecting a successor. This small item falls through the cracks at the time of our great constitutional debates.

Another urgent matter is to review appointments to boards and commissions. The premier, or a minister on his behalf, needs a comprehensive list of all gov-ernment-appointed boards, commissions, and committees, along with the names and terms of office of the present incumbents and the reasons they were appointed. There are hundreds of such boards and commissions, some more political than others. Many are special-purpose bodies with members nominated by farm, la-bour, or business organizations or by organizations of teachers, trustees, or health professionals. Rarely should these bodies be disturbed. Other bodies have mem-bers who are appointed for their competence but with some attention to their political hue. Lists of suitable people to sit on these boards and commissions need to be compiled. These people can then be appointed or reappointed as the existing appointments expire. The more choice a government has in this process – that is, the longer the candidate lists – the better the result is likely to be. This is not usually urgent, however.

There will, however, be some boards and commissions that are so important to the operations of government that moves must be made promptly to assume control. For example, an electric power utility uses huge amounts of capital, makes commitments with long-term implications, and is often called upon to make controversial, policy-laden decisions. A new government will need to get some people on the board of directors of such a utility almost immediately, or at least make sure that key decisions are subject to ministerial review. How urgent this matter is depends on how much confidence the new administration has in the people already directing such bodies.

Borins: I noticed that one of the first things Roy Romanow did upon taking office in 1991 was to fire the president of Saskatchewan Power, in whom he did not have confidence.[6]

Blakeney: The president was a lawyer with no background in operating a power utility but who had been president of the Saskatchewan Progressive Conservative Party. I have referred to the search for key people. That should be a high priority and assigned to a minister or cabinet committee with whom the premier can keep in touch. The quality of a government depends greatly on the quality of the public service and the relationship that develops between public servants and elected officials. So getting in place or confirming in place senior public servants is a top priority for any incoming administration.

Borins: We move on now. What is the transition like when *leaving* power?

Blakeney: When leaving office, I took the view that I would soon be back. That was not based on statistics, since most governments in Canada last at least two terms. But it was not a bad working premise.

When we left office in 1964, I sent a personally signed letter to every employee of the Department of Health thanking them for their service on behalf of the public and asking them to co-operate with the new government for the benefit of the public. It was received very well. I regretted that the fast transition when we were defeated in 1982 did not allow me to follow that course again.

Once out of power, the challenge is to set up an effective team in the Opposition Leader's office. This is a difficult job. It is not too hard to get people with an interest in partisan politics. There are people who don't mind being dependent on the choices of the electorate. But good economic and social researchers are harder to get. They usually like to work in a government environment rather than a political one. They don't want to be labelled partisan, as they often are if they work in an Opposition Leader's office. And they find it more rewarding to work on new policy initiatives as opposed to critiques of government programs new and old. Money and other resources are always tighter for parties in opposition. In addition, the Opposition Leader is likely to be spending a lot of time on overtly political activity, such as talking to prospective candidates. This leaves less time for the leader to work with the staff in developing alternative policies to deal with public issues. All of these factors make it harder to recruit top staff.

The problems of transition are difficult for the Leader of the Opposition, but they are not as urgent as the ones the new Premier faces. Aside from the mundane problems, such as making sure that election records are saved and filed – problems that are usually dealt with by the party officials – and aside from doing some debriefing to see whether lessons can be learned from the defeat, most problems can be tackled at a more leisurely pace than when the election results in victory. This is just as well, since victory stirs the adrenalin while defeat rarely does.

Borins: Let's look at the transition issue from a broader perspective. Is it not valuable to pass on some institutional memory – which is different from continuity of policy – from one government to another? Are there any reforms that could be undertaken to improve the information that is passed from one cabinet to the next?

Blakeney: It is not easy to devise methods for passing along to the incoming government the fruits of experience of the defeated one. Ideally, an election defeat would be regarded as a rejection of one group of policies in favour of another, and there should be little sense of personal rejection. But if this was ever true, it isn't now in today's climate of personalized politics.

I have tried to put this point of view to the media. I have explained that I might be selling Ford cars and think they are the best. Another person sells Dodge cars. My customer usually buys the Fords I sell but on one occasion may decide to try a Dodge. This is not a reflection on me or even on my product, and if I think my car is best I should not try to change it to be more like the Dodge, which I think is inferior. I am confident that the customer will soon agree with me. This line of argument does not convince the media: they regard politics as a contest of salesmanship rather than a comparison of products. Accordingly, they perceive an election defeat as a failure of salesmanship. Clearly there is some of both elements in elections, but they are increasingly becoming contests of personalities rather than policies. Canadian politics is poorer for this.

There is always a need for a core of senior public servants who will carry on from one administration to the next. And a new government must have policy advisers who are in tune with its objectives. In some provinces, and in Ottawa, all of this is achieved by the assembling of large ministerial staffs that are overtly partisan to work at policy formulation. In other provinces it is achieved by recruiting a few senior public servants who are officially part of the bureaucracy but who are also in tune with the new government's philosophy. Neither model works without problems in providing institutional memory on many policy issues. A strong nonpartisan public service should be maintained, and where this is done, a reasonable measure of institutional memory on administrative and some policy issues is provided. If the public votes for a change, things must be changed. This will often disturb the even tenor of the public service world. A balance must be struck between the need for stability and continuity, and the need for ways to initiate meaningful change. It is sometimes not easy.

I favour the idea of outgoing ministers getting their departments to prepare comprehensive briefing books. All outgoing ministers should then take a copy with them. The public servants may wish to supply the incoming ministers with additional information. Fine. But the briefing book is the basis for the research work that the office of the Leader of the Opposition will be commencing. The Opposition will find it useful to know what facts were drawn to the attention of the incoming government. Incoming ministers normally blame all problems on the mess left by their predecessors. If this excuse is used many months after assuming office, and if the Opposition can speculate with confidence that this problem was drawn to the attention of the minister on his or her first day of office and that nothing has been done for months and months, the Opposition has gained a tactical advantage.

I have sometimes felt that if legislative committees could operate in a less partisan way – as they sometimes do – serious questions of policy could be discussed by considering the proposals of the new government in light of the comments by members of the Opposition, who are often very well informed on the issues involved. It would be a sign of the maturity of both the new government and the Opposition that they could carry on such a discussion. Most new ministers fear that they will not be as well informed as some opposition members – which is often the case – and that this will be demonstrated and will reflect unfavourably on them. This is especially a problem when the media report any exchange of views as a contest between individuals. Regrettably, this state of affairs deprives a new government of much of the benefit of the experience gained by the outgoing government.

Borins: I will conclude with the experience of the Rae government in Ontario when it left power. To his credit, Bob Rae prepared his successor for a smoother transition than he had experienced. Some months before he called the 1995 election, Rae directed his Cabinet Secretary, David Agnew, to meet with representatives of the opposition parties and then to co-ordinate the production by each ministry of a comprehensive briefing book for its incoming minister. The books included information about the ministry's programs, legal framework, organizational structure, budget, and short- and long-term issues. In addition, some ministries went the extra mile and analysed and costed out the policies proposed by both the Liberals and the Conservatives. This work was appreciated by the incoming Conservatives, and they were effusive in their praise for the professionalism of the outgoing government and the public service.[7] It is good to see that, with respect to transition planning, the Ontario public service learned from experience. We can hope that future transitions look more like 1995 than 1990.

Conclusion:
A Philosophy of Statecraft and
Some Directions for Inquiry

In this concluding chapter we return to the common voice with which we began. We begin by reviewing some of the themes concerning public sector management that run through this book. We believe that these themes, taken together, form the outlines of a philosophy of statecraft. By statecraft, we mean the effective use of the power and resources of the public sector. We conclude by pointing out some directions for inquiry that our work might encourage others to undertake.

We think of the philosophy of statecraft we outline as a set of ideals about how, in certain circumstances, the public sector should be organized and how public officials – both ministers and public servants – should act. That they are ideals indicates that they are not always achieved, but we believe they are worth striving for. Here, then, are seven key themes which, like the leitmotifs in a Wagner opera, appeared and re-appeared throughout our discussion. The order of presentation should not be taken as a ranking of importance. *All* the themes are important, and are interrelated, and taken together comprise the philosophy we have been expounding.

1. Co-ordination through Teamwork

A cabinet should be a team of politicians attempting to achieve a collective vision of a better society. Ministers should strive to communicate this vision to their departments, instead of serving as the voice of narrow departmental interests. Ministers should be judges before they are advocates.

Similarly, senior public servants should also be a team, helping cabinet implement its collective vision of a better society. Deputy ministers are both the chief executive officers of their departments and members of a team that is working to ensure that all departmental programs are consistent with the overall policies of the cabinet.

Unlike a private sector corporation, government does not have a general manager. It is up to the cabinet collectively to set the policies of government, and up to the public service collectively to implement them. When ministers and public servants take seriously their responsibilities as members of the team, they can do a great deal of the necessary co-ordination of government on their own, without having to resort to external central agencies. We advocate a minimal use of formal central agencies and as much informal co-ordination as possible.

2. Policies and Programs That Are Responsive to the Public

Ultimately, political power in a democracy depends on the approval of the electorate, and a government must always be asking whether its policies and programs are receiving that approval. This axiom has numerous implications. Ministers should spend as much time as possible in contact with the electorate, attempting both to understand what the electorate wants and to persuade the public of the appropriateness of the government's policies. If, after a time, the electorate doesn't approve, then the policies must be revised. 'Selling' policies to the public requires presenting them in terms of values the public can identify with, rather than in terms of formal political ideologies. Politics is in this sense an immensely pragmatic enterprise. Despite recent trends in Canada and elsewhere to a politics of image and generality, we are most comfortable with political platforms that lay out a party's program in some detail.

Not only should a government's overall policies be responsive to the public, but so should be its specific programs. Implementation plans should include either 'running tracers' or doing simulations, so that the reactions of the citizens who are affected by the program can be noted and understood. Similarly, the public should be able to access information about the programs – for example, through toll-free telephone lines and on the Internet. In order to determine whether policies are being accepted, politicians and public servants need to be skilled listeners. We think the service excellence component of the New Public Management is extremely important. If it succeeds, more responsive programs will be delivered to a more satisfied citizenry.

3. Organizational Structures That Encourage Intelligence and Creativity

A government is constantly making decisions. They will make the best ones if the process is infused with as much information as possible and if the people participating in the process use as much of their intelligence and creativity as possible. Bureaucracies tend to reduce available information, because it takes too long to gather and process, and to ignore creativity, because it upsets routine and threatens conformity. It is important, therefore, to design organizations and establish practices with a view to overcoming these tendencies; doing so will increase the possibilities for intelligent and creative decision-making.

This can be done in numerous ways. Cabinet meetings and retreats must include opportunities (such as Blakeney's 'state of the nation') for unstructured discussion, the goal being to eliminate each minister's defensiveness regarding his or her department's programs. The traditional speaking order in cabinet – junior ministers first – is designed to encourage frankness. Reassigning ministers, ensuring a flow of temporary assignments, and bringing new people into cabinet are all ways of ensuring that cabinet is constantly being revitalized. Cabinet crisis-management teams can avoid taking on a bunker mentality by maintaining continuous contact with sympathetic but intellectually sceptical and creative outsiders.

We support Al Johnson's argument that policies are likely to be more creative if they are developed by a group of dedicated champions housed in a lead agency, rather than by interdepartmental committees that have no 'ownership.'

In the matter of handling key priorities, we see temporary special-purpose agencies – or secretariats, as they were called in Saskatchewan – as one way to ensure creative policy development. At the bureaucratic level, secretariats create the championship that Johnson considers so important. At the cabinet level, giving the responsibility for overseeing a secretariat to a small committee, headed by a lead minister, opens policy development up to the ideas of all ministers, more so than if policy development of the key priority were handled by only one minister.

Another example of our emphasis on creativity is that we are against imposing the constraints of administrative feasibility at the policy development stage. Such constraints often arise when ministers become too involved too early in the process.

4. An Excellent Public Service

Critical to effective policy-making is the establishment of an excellent public service. This involves the pro-active recruitment of high-fliers and early assignments for them that provide both the overview that comes from working in a central agency and the experience in dealing with the public that comes from working in a department that delivers programs. Management development is also extremely important; it should include opportunities to learn about one's own government, and about the society that government serves – which is especially vital for public servants recruited from outside. Later on, it should include contact with the profession in Canada and throughout the world; this can be arranged by making it possible for public servants to study for advanced degrees, and to participate in professional organizations. The particular achievement of the Saskatchewan government was that it succeeded in following this approach in a hinterland location.

Developing an excellent public service requires more than recruiting and retaining high-fliers. It also requires establishing programs to realize the potential of people who, for whatever reason, didn't have the opportunity to be identified by the educational system as high-fliers. It requires investment in training. The burden of central agency controls must be relaxed, so that public servants have more flexibility to find innovative ways to provide better service.

5. Performance and Accountability

We have outlined an approach to public sector management that makes both individuals and organizations aware of their level of performance. We have been critical of upward delegation, whether by individual ministers to cabinet as a whole or by public servants to their ministers. One way of avoiding it is by emphasizing the separation of the cabinet's role in decision-making from the public service's role in policy analysis. When public servants are required to make clear recommendations, opportunities are created to judge their effectiveness at policy development. Similarly, Blakeney's intention in taking office in 1971 with a very small cabinet was that the most effective performers in caucus could be appointed to the cabinet over the following months.

We have also emphasized the value of having measures of organizational performance. Detailed election platforms create standards against which a government's performance can be evaluated. A budget system that focuses on outputs rather than inputs allows politicians to determine how to spend program dollars most effectively. Accompanied with a reduction in central agency controls, this enables public servants to allocate resources most efficiently in producing outputs. The Crown Investments Corporation was designed to measure the performance of public sector investments. Our approach to the monitoring of entrepreneurs who are funded by the public sector emphasizes the entrepreneur's accountability, both personal and financial, for the venture's performance.

6. Appropriate Timing

In a number of contexts, we have emphasized the importance of timing. A government's priorities should be set early in its mandate so that cabinet can become comfortable with them and so that programs resulting from these priorities can be implemented soon enough that the bugs can be ironed out before the next election. Tommy Douglas's insistence that hospital insurance be implemented eighteen months before he expected to call the 1948 election is the classic example of this.

There is a cycle for government spending. Immediately after an election is the appropriate time to 'put government through the wringer' – that is, to identify and cut the least effective programs, so as to free resources, which can then be utilized more effectively as the next election approaches. The spending patterns of the Blakeney government make it clear that such an approach was followed during his tenure.

Timing also involves modifying plans in order to take advantage of opportunities. Blakeney's calling of an early election in 1978 so as to take advantage of a window of opportunity before the 1979 federal election is one example of this.

7. Persistent Inculcating of Values

As often as possible, Blakeney gave *the speech* about collective responsibility, and a similar speech about the importance of critically reviewing government programs. At cabinet meetings he took great pains to go carefully through the reasons for decisions, to ensure that all ministers would be strong in their public support. To some of his ministers, Blakeney sounded didactic. Even so, we maintain that this persistence was highly necessary. One of the key elements of leadership is to inculcate the key values of the organization, and Blakeney was simply doing that, both for ministers and for public servants. This element of our philosophy reinforces all the others.

Some Directions for Inquiry

We hope this book will be a point of departure for other people's research and thinking. There are some questions we have not answered, which other students of public management might address.

Blakeney has been careful to qualify his advice as applying to a small provincial government. Can the conclusions we have drawn be applied to larger provinces, or to nations? In Blakeney's Saskatchewan it was possible for politicians, including the Premier, to spend a good deal of their time in face-to-face meetings with citizens. The public service was small enough that even management trainees had opportunities to attend meetings with and learn from deputy ministers and politicians. The cabinet was small enough that all its members could engage in serious policy discussions.

Is this possible in a larger province or a nation? Is public opinion polling the only way for politicians to find out about the public's reaction to policy proposals? Can a public service be inculcated with the values of ministers it rarely sees? Is it possible to manage a large public service by adapting the principles we have outlined here?

These questions are analogous to private sector managers asking whether firms that have been successful enough to grow large can maintain the entrepreneurial vigour and flexibility of their early years. Private sector managers have made great efforts to combine the managerial advantages of a small enterprise with the economies of scale of a large organization. Can the public sector do the same? Trends such as reducing the size of cabinet, reducing central agency controls, and designating relatively autonomous units in government as special operating agencies are all evidence of a will to reorganize the public sector in similar ways.

A second area of research relates to the concepts applied to Blakeney's experience. Borins came to this project with an eclectic background, combining the perspectives of comparative public administration and private sector management, the latter in the areas of organizational behaviour and strategic management. Undoubtedly there are other intellectual perspectives that could be applied. What would a political theorist make of Blakeney's approach to public management? For example, how would a student of Machiavelli interpret it?

We hope this book will encourage similar collaborations between practitioners and academics. Our project involved sustained collaboration: we started by team-teaching a course, and that experience led to the writing of this book. In that sense this project was an example of *action learning* – a methodology that involves people learning by reflecting on their experiences while participating in a common project.[1] Another example of action learning would be managers in different organizations who are all responsible for a particular function (for example, information technology or human resources) meeting regularly to share experiences and learn from one another.

In our case, the discipline of teaching a course and then writing a book gave us an opportunity to explore public management questions in depth. Taping our class and then transcribing the tapes was very important, because it gave us a basic text – raw material that could then be shaped. From the transcripts, we branched out with additional research about the Blakeney, Douglas-Lloyd, and federal governments, and about management theory.

There are many ways that management practitioners and academics can collaborate. For example, academics might give executive development courses, and practitioners might give guest lectures; or academics might serve as consultants, and practitioners might advise about curriculum. Executive-in-residence or scholar-in-residence programs are another means. All of these have their place. However, our experience suggests that the most learning occurs when practitioners and academics are involved in a common endeavour that plays to their unique strengths and that is sustained over a long period of time. We hope this venture will encourage other ambitious action-learning projects between management practitioners and academics.

We hope this book will also have an impact on other people who have held elective office. There are currently five Canadians who have served as Prime Minister, excluding Mr Chretien, well over two dozen ex-Premiers, and probably hundreds who have been cabinet ministers. It would be splendid if this book would move some of them to talk about their practice of statecraft. An example of what me mean is a plenary session that was held at the Institute of Public Administration's 1993 conference with Borins as moderator and former premiers Blakeney, Peterson, and Ghiz as speakers. They discussed both management issues, such as the management of cabinet, and policy questions, such as the implications of the failure of the Charlottetown Accord. This session was very well received by conference participants. We hope this book will encourage other ex-Premiers and cabinet ministers to share their experiences, either in writing or in public forums.

Our governmental heritage is parliamentary democracy. As a society, we have a common interest in using it to provide good government. If our work advances that common interest, our efforts will have been amply rewarded.

Using *Political Management in Canada* to Supplement a Textbook

One type of reader for whom this book was written was students of public administration and/or political science. While we did not write a textbook, this book can be used as a supplement to a textbook. To facilitate this, we list below the major public administration and political science textbooks currently in use in Canada, and show which chapters in this book can supplement various chapters in those. For each book, we have listed its chapters first, followed by the corresponding chapters in this book.

Keith Archer, Roger Gibbins, Rainer Knopf, and Leslie Pal, *Parameters of Power: Canada's Political Institutions* (Scarborough: Nelson, 1995)
Chapter 2 ('The Constitution: Canada's "Master Institution,"' pp. 27–64): Chapter 13
Chapter 4 ('The Modern Era of Megaconstitutional Politics,' pp. 111–64): Chapter 13
Chapter 5 ('Parliamentary Democracy and the Legislative Process,' pp. 165–212): Chapter 6
Chapter 6 ('The Political Executive,' pp. 213–54): Chapters 1,2,3, and 5
Chapter 7 ('The Administrative State,' pp. 255–302): Chapters 8, 9, and 15
Chapter 9 ('Elections and Voting,' pp. 357–410): Chapter 7
Chapter 10 ('Political Parties,' pp. 411–58): Chapter 6
Chapter 11 ('Interest Groups and Representational Institutions,' pp. 459–506): Chapter 14

James Bickerton and Alain Gagnon, eds., *Canadian Politics*, 2nd ed. (Peterborough: Broadview Press, 1994)
Chapter 14 ('The Prime Minister and Cabinet,' pp. 267–87): Chapters 1, 2, and 3
Chapter 15 ('Central Agencies: Making a Mesh of Things,' pp. 288–306): Chapter 9
Chapter 16 ('Bureaucracy,' pp. 307–27): Chapter 12

Chapter 19 ('The Dynamics of Canadian Federalism,' pp. 366–88): Chapter 13
Chapter 25 ('Reading Prairie Politics,' pp. 491–505): Entire book applicable

Stephen Brooks, *Canadian Democracy*, 2nd ed. (Toronto: Oxford University Press, 1996)
Chapter 5 ('Federalism,' pp. 119–20): Chapter 13
Chapter 6 ('The Machinery of Government,' pp. 156–71): Chapters 1, 2, 3, 4, 5, 8, 9, 10, and 11)
Chapter 8 ('Interest Groups,' pp. 225–39): Chapter 14

Rand Dyck, *Canadian Politics: Critical Approaches*, 2nd ed. (Scarborough: Nelson, 1996)
Chapter 17 ('Parties and the Election Campaign,' pp. 405–24): Chapter 7
Chapter 18 ('Pressure Groups and Lobbying,' pp. 425–69): Chapter 14
Chapter 20 ('The Executive,' pp. 471–506): Chapters 1, 2, 3, and 5
Chapter 21 ('The Bureaucracy,' pp. 507–36): Chapters 8, 9, 12, and 15
Chapter 22 ('Parliament,' pp. 537–74): Chapters 5 and 6

Roger Gibbins, *Conflict and Unity: An Introduction to Canadian Political Life* (Scarborough: Nelson, 1994)
Chapter 3 ('The Institutional Landscape,' pp. 43–95): Chapters 1, 2, 3, and 6
Chapter 4 ('The Politics of Language and Québécois Nationalism,' pp. 96–151): Chapter 13
Chapter 5 ('Regional Politics,' pp. 152–207): Chapter 14
Chapter 6 ('Redistributive Politics,' pp. 208–58), Chapter 16
Chapter 8 ('Intergovernmental Relations and Constitutional Politics,' pp. 309–62): Chapter 13
Chapter 9 ('The Canadian Party System,' pp. 363–430): Chapters 7 and 14

Robert Jackson and Doreen Jackson, *Politics in Canada: Culture, Institutions, Behaviour, and Public Policy*, 3rd ed. (Scarborough: Prentice-Hall, 1994)
Chapter 6 ('Federalism and Its Challenges: Finances, Nationalism, and Regionalism,' pp. 239–78): Chapter 13
Chapter 7 ('The Prime Minister, Ministry, and Cabinet: Policy-Making at the Centre,' pp. 279–316): Chapters 1, 2, 3, 4, and 5
Chapter 8 ('Legislative Politics: Symbolism or Power,' pp. 345–52): Chapter 6
Chapter 9: ('Bureaucracy and Democracy: Public Servants, Budgets, and Controls'): 'Structures of the Federal Bureaucracy,' pp. 373–86: Chapter 9; 'Bureaucrats and Budgets,' pp. 397–402: Chapters 10 and 15; 'The Public Service,' pp. 387–96: Chapter 12

Chapter 11 ('Elections and Electoral Behaviour: Letting the People Decide,' pp. 479–91): Chapter 7

Chapter 12 ('Interest Groups and Political Movements: Influencing Public Policy,' pp. 515–48): Chapter 14

Kenneth Kernaghan and David Siegel, *Public Administration in Canada*, 3rd edition (Toronto: Nelson, 1995)

Chapter 5 ('Communications, Leadership, and Motivation,' pp. 92–125): Chapters 1, 9

Chapter 7 ('Implementing and Evaluating Public Policy,' pp. 155–79): Chapter 16

Chapter 8 ('Government Departments and Central Agencies,' pp. 183–208): Chapters 5, 8, and 9

Chapter 9 ('Public Enterprise,' pp. 209–47): Chapters 4 and 11

Chapter 11 ('Other Nondepartmental Organizations,' pp. 286–303): Chapter 15

Chapter 12 ('Institutional and Value Frameworks,' pp. 307–24): Chapter 12

Chapter 13 ('Power, Politics, and Bureaucracy,' pp. 325–51): Chapters 8 and 12

Chapter 15 ('The Executive and the Bureaucracy,' pp. 377–92): Chapter 3

Chapter 16 ('Interdepartmental and Intradepartmental Relations,' pp. 393–411): Chapter 8

Chapter 17 ('The Legislature and the Bureaucracy,' pp. 412–32): Chapter 6

Chapter 19 ('Intergovernmental Administrative Relations,' pp. 451–74): Chapter 13

Chapter 20 ('Pressure Groups, Political Parties, and the Bureaucracy,' pp. 475–94): Chapter 14

Chapter 21 ('The Public, the Media, and the Bureaucracy,' pp. 495–516): Chapters 16 and 17

Chapter 22 ('The Management of Government Programs,' pp. 519–44): Chapter 4

Chapter 23 ('The Management of Human Resources,' pp. 545–66): Chapter 12

Chapter 23 ('Representative Bureaucracy and Employment Equity,' pp. 567–587): Chapter 12

Chapter 26 ('The Budgetary Process,' pp. 609–39): Chapter 10

Chapter 27 ('The Management of Financial Resources,' pp. 640–57): Chapter 10

Chapter 28 ('The Future of Public Administration in Canada,' pp. 661–73): Chapter 12

Michael Whittington and Richard van Loon, *Canadian Government and Politics: Institutions and Processes* (Toronto: McGraw-Hill Ryerson, 1996)

Chapter 10 ('Intergovernmental Relations: The Federal Process,' pp. 247–76): Chapter 13

Chapter 17 ('Interest Groups: Access and Influence,' pp. 457–78): Chapters 14 and 15

Chapter 20 ('The Political Executive: Function, Composition, and Structure,' pp. 543–64): Chapter 1

Chapter 21 ('PM, Cabinet, and Support Agencies,' pp. 565–94): Chapters 3, 5, 9, and 15

Chapter 22 ('Bureaucracy: Function and Structure,' pp. 595–636): Chapters 8, 9, and 12

**Michael Whittington and Glen Williams, eds., *Canadian Politics in the 1990s*
(Toronto: Nelson, 1995).**
Chapter 13 ('Pressure Groups,' pp. 252–75): Chapter 14
Chapter 14 ('The Federal Bureaucracy: Reinventing the Links Between State and
Society,' pp. 276–91): Chapters 9, 12
Chapter 19 ('The Federal Cabinet in Canadian Politics,' pp. 382–401): Chapters 2, 3,
and 5
Chapter 20 ('Federalism and Intergovernmental Relations,' pp. 402–23): Chapter 13
Chapter 21 ('Politicians and Bureaucrats in the Policy Process,' pp. 424–40): Chapters
1, 8, 9, 10, 11, and conclusion

Notes

Preface

1 For those interested in a biography, we suggest Dennis Gruending, *Promises to Keep: A Political Biography of Allan Blakeney* (Saskatoon: Western Producer Prairie Books, 1990).

2 For example, the collection of articles edited by Pierre Trudeau and Thomas Axworthy (*Towards a Just Society: The Trudeau Years* (Markham, ON: Viking, 1990) deals entirely with the policies of the Trudeau government. For discussions of organizational change during the Trudeau years, we suggest Richard French, *How Ottawa Decides: Planning and Industrial Policy Making, 1968–1984*, 2nd ed. (Toronto: Lorimer, 1984), Colin Campbell and George Szablowski, *The Superbureaucrats: Structure and Behaviour in Central Agencies* (Toronto: Macmillan, 1979), and the sections of Colin Campbell, *Governments under Stress: Political Executives and Key Bureaucrats in Washington, London, and Ottawa* (Toronto: University of Toronto Press, 1983) dealing with Canada. Similarly, the management practices of William Davis, Premier of Ontario from 1971 to 1985, are described by his former Cabinet Secretary in Edward Stewart, *Cabinet Government in Ontario: A View from Inside* (Halifax: Institute for Research on Public Policy, 1989). Two more recent political biographies, both of which concentrate on policy rather than management, are Bob Rae, *From Protest to Power: Personal Reflections on a Life in Politics* (Toronto: Viking, 1996) and Mike Harcourt with Wayne Skene, *Mike Harcourt: A Measure of Defiance* (Vancouver: Douglas and McIntyre, 1996). Evert Lindquist and Graham White, 'Analyzing Canadian Cabinets: Past, Present, and Future,' in Mohamed Charih and Arthur Daniels, eds., *New Public Management and Public Administration in Canada* (Toronto: Institute of Public Administration of Canada, 1997), wrote that the first edition of our book was the

'only account [that] provides a serious and creative analysis of issues of design and management of cabinets from a first minister's perspective' (p. 119).

3 One recent book that embarked on an exercise similar to ours is Allan Gotlieb, *'I'll Be with You in a Minute, Mr. Ambassador': The Education of a Canadian Diplomat in Washington* (Toronto: University of Toronto Press, 1991), which, based on a discussion of a number of the issues Gotlieb was involved in as ambassador, draws some lessons as to how the Department of External Affairs should manage Canada's relations with the United States. However, the scope of that book is much narrower than ours.

4 Albert W. Johnson, 'Biography of a Government: Policy Formulation in Saskatchewan, 1944–1961,' (PhD dissertation, Harvard University, 1963), 294–5, and Albert W. Johnson, 'Efficiency in Government and Business,' *Canadian Public Administration* 6, 3 (September 1963): 245–60, argue that the public perception of inefficient public sector management is a political liability.

1: Making Collective Responsibility Work

1 Gruending, *Promises to Keep*, 91.

2 This organization chart would also be applicable to the federal government. Even though it greatly simplifies the organizational structure, the fundamental principle of collective responsibility is just as relevant as it would be in a small provincial government.

3 There has been a long debate over how much policy direction private sector boards actually provide. Some authors, initially Berle and Means and later Galbraith, have claimed that boards of directors merely rubber-stamp decisions taken by management. See A.A. Berle and G.C. Means, *The Modern Corporation and Private Property* (New York: Harcourt, Brace and World, 1932), and J.K. Galbraith, *The New Industrial State* (Boston: Houghton Mifflin, 1967). It is not our intention to participate in this debate. Suffice it to say that we are referring to the theory of private sector management in which the board does exercise policy direction. In addition, recent trends such as increased global competition, improvements in management information systems, greater shareholder activism, and increased legal liability for directors are forcing corporate directors to take a more active role in policy direction. See James M. Gillies, *Boardroom Renaissance: Power, Morality, and Performance in the Modern Corporation* (Toronto: McGraw-Hill Ryerson, 1992). David Leighton and Donald Thain in *Making Boards Work: What Directors Must Do to Make Canadian Boards Effective* (Toronto: McGraw-Hill Ryerson, 1997) characterize 'old style' boards as deferential to management and formalistic at meetings, and 'new style' boards as more loyal to the company than to management and open, frank, and participatory at meetings.

4 See Allan Blakeney, 'The Relationship between Provincial Ministers and Their Deputy Ministers,' *Canadian Public Administration* 15, 1 (Spring 1972): 42–5, and 'Goal-setting: Politicians' Expectations of Public Administrators,' *Canadian Public Administration* 24, 1 (Spring 1981): 1–7.

5 Sir Ivor Jennings, *Cabinet Government*, 3rd ed. (Cambridge: Cambridge University Press, 1959), 117–18.

6 Richard H.S. Crossman, *The Myths of Cabinet Government* (Cambridge: Harvard University Press, 1972), 63.

7 Jonathan Lynn and Anthony Jay, *Yes Prime Minister: The Diaries of the Right Hon. James Hacker*, vol. 1 (London: BBC Books, 1986), 200.

8 Allison, in outlining the organizational process model, cites 'the fact that a government consists of a conglomerate of semi-feudal loosely allied organizations, each with a life of its own.' Similarly, the governmental politics model 'sees no unitary actor but rather many actors as players ... players who act in terms of no consistent set of strategic objectives but rather according to various conceptions of national, organizational, and personal goals; players who make government decisions not by a single, rational choice but by the pulling and hauling that is politics.' See Graham T. Allison, *Essence of Decision: Explaining the Cuban Missile Crisis* (Boston: Little, Brown, 1971), 67, 144.

9 Robert Reich, *Locked in the Cabinet* (New York: Knopf, 1997), 150.

10 Kim Richard Nossal, based on case studies of Canadian foreign-policy decisions and of the selection of the F18A as Canada's new fighter aircraft in 1980, concluded that while decision making in the federal government is characterized by some of the 'pulling and hauling' that Allison described, conflict is muted by certain characteristics of the Canadian system, including cabinet solidarity, strong political control of the bureaucracy, powerful central agencies, the cohesiveness of the senior bureaucracy, and a highly institutionalized system of interdepartmental consultation. See Kim Richard Nossal, 'Allison Through the (Ottawa) Looking Glass: Bureaucratic Politics and Foreign Policy in a Parliamentary System,' *Canadian Public Administration* 22, 4 (Winter 1979): 610–26, and Michael M. Atkinson and Kim Richard Nossal, 'Bureaucratic Politics and the New Fighter Aircraft Decisions,' *Canadian Public Administration* 24, 4 (Winter 1981): 531–62.

11 See A.W. Johnson, 'Biography of a Government,' 237–44; S.M. Lipset, *Agrarian Socialism: The Cooperative Commonwealth Federation in Saskatchewan. A Study in Political Sociology* (New York: Doubleday Anchor, 1968), 269–306; and T.H. McLeod and I. McLeod, *Tommy Douglas: The Road to Jerusalem* (Edmonton: Hurtig, 1987), 126–8.

12 Walter Smishek, Chair, Treasury Board, memorandum to permanent heads re. 'Relations between Treasury Board and Outside Agencies or Interests,' 18 August 1977. Blakeney Papers, Collection R–800, file XXXII, 89.

2: Choosing a Cabinet

1 See Gruending, *Promises to Keep*, 84–6.
2 Ibid., 56–76.
3 See McLeod and McLeod, *Tommy Douglas*, pp. 169, 281.
4 In 1972 the Treasury was renamed the Department of Finance. Since the latter was used for most of Blakeney's time as Premier, we will use the terms Department of Finance and Finance Minister.
5 See Edward Greenspon and Anthony Wilson-Smith, *Double Vision: The Inside Story of the Liberals in Power* (Toronto: Seal, 1997), 53–71 and 253–78.
6 Jennings, *Cabinet Government*, 117.
7 Harold Wilson, *The Governance of Britain* (New York: Harper and Row, 1976), 31.
8 See Johnson, 'Biography of a Government,' 172–6, 434, for a similar discussion of Tommy Douglas's choice of his first cabinet in 1944.
9 See Rae, *From Protest to Power*, 134.
10 See Harcourt and Skene, *Mike Harcourt*, 118.

3: Managing Cabinet

1 Jeff Sallot, 'Top Court Becomes Supreme Player.' *Globe and Mail*, 6 April 1992, A1, A4.
2 Greenspon and Wilson-Smith, *Double Vision*, 302.
3 In the first Douglas Government, one of the ministers, Woodrow Lloyd, took notes. In 1948, a Cabinet Secretariat was established and the first Cabinet Secretary appointed. See Johnson, 'Biography of a Government,' 277, 377–8. Ontario's first Cabinet Secretary was also appointed in 1948. See Stewart, *Cabinet Government in Ontario*, 10.
4 Kenneth Bryden, 'Cabinets,' in David Bellamy, Jon Pammet, and Donald Rowat, eds., *The Provincial Political Systems: Comparative Essays* (Toronto: Methuen, 1976), 310–22, discusses our cabinet committee structure as being a resumption of the committee structure of the Douglas–Lloyd government after the much less structured Thatcher cabinet (pp. 311, 318). While this interpretation is correct, my emphasis is on how we carried out a much more activist agenda than the Thatcher government with as few cabinet committees as possible. Christopher Dunn, in an article a few years ago, 'Changing the Design: Cabinet Decision-making in Three Provincial Governments,' *Canadian Public Administration* 34, 4 (Winter 1991): 621–40, and in his more recent book, *The Institutionalized Cabinet: Governing the Western Provinces* (Montreal: McGill-Queen's University Press, 1995), identifies our government as part of a trend in provincial governments to replace what he

calls the 'unaided' or traditional cabinet with an institutionalized or structural cabinet. In response to this thesis, I reiterate my point that the traditional cabinet has the virtue of maintaining cohesiveness and solidarity. As a consequence, we kept our institutionalization to a minimum by restraining the number of committees and the staff that served them. Dunn's book is useful in giving an outsider's view of how well different styles of cabinet government worked when practised in three Western provinces.

5 For an extended discussion of the Planning Committee, see Dunn, *The Institutionalized Cabinet*, 66–72.

6 See Tom Waller, 'Framework for Economic Development: The Role of Crown Corporations and the Crown Investments Corporation of Saskatchewan,' in Eleanor Glor, ed., *Policy Innovation in the Saskatchewan Public Sector, 1971–82* (North York: Captus Press, 1997), 29–48.

7 Peter Aucoin, 'The Machinery of Government: From Trudeau's Rational Management to Mulroney's Brokerage Politics,' in Leslie Pal and David Taras, eds., *Prime Ministers and Premiers: Political Leadership and Public Policy in Canada* (Toronto: Prentice-Hall, 1988), 50–68.

8 During the period from 1980 to 1984, there were cabinet committees for Social Development and Economic Development; both of these had resource allocation responsibilities, and also had secretariats of their own. These secretariats were dissolved by Prime Minister John Turner.

9 Katherine Graham, 'Discretion and the Governance of Canada: The Buck Stops Where?' in Katherine Graham, ed., *How Ottawa Spends: 1989–90* (Ottawa: Carleton University Press, 1989), 19. Cf. Kenneth Kernaghan and David Siegel, *Public Administration in Canada*, 3rd ed. (Toronto: Nelson, 1995), 188–9.

10 One example of a large provincial government that has reduced the size of its cabinet and simplified the committee structure is the Harris government in Ontario, which has a cabinet of twenty and only three committees – Legislation and Regulations, Management Board, and Priorities and Planning. Also, it appears that Harris has substantially centralized power in the Premier's Office. See Guy Crittenden, 'The Harris Kremlin: Inside Ontario's Revolutionary Politburo,' *Globe and Mail*, 1 November 1997, D1, D9, and David Wolfe, 'Queen's Park Policy-Making Systems,' in Sid Noel, ed. *Revolution at Queen's Park: Essays on Governing Ontario* (Toronto: Lorimer, 1997), 151–64. For a discussion of the difficulties of managing larger cabinets, see Graham White, 'Big Is Different from Little: On Taking Size Seriously in the Analysis of Canadian Governmental Institutions,' *Canadian Public Administration* 33, 4 (Winter 1990): 534–40.

11 For a published version of this report, see Gordon Osbaldeston, *Organizing to Govern* (Toronto: McGraw-Hill Ryerson, 1992).

12 For a discussion of how and why Australia restructured its cabinet by consolidating

ministries and differentiating between cabinet and non-cabinet ministers, as well as the implications of these reforms for Canada, see Peter Aucoin and Herman Bakvis, 'Consolidating Cabinet Portfolios: Australian Lessons for Canada,' *Canadian Public Administration* 36, 3 (Fall 1993): 392–420. For a discussion of Chrétien's cabinet after the 1997 election, see Hugh Winsor and Edward Greenspon, 'PM bets on familiar faces,' *Globe and Mail*, 12 June 1997, A1, A5. In their analysis of recent trends in Canadian cabinets, Lindquist and White conclude that smaller cabinets with fewer committees are here to stay ('Analysing Canadian Cabinets: Past, Present, and Future,' 123).

13 In Canada's federal government, Clerk of the Privy Council is the title of the Cabinet Secretary and deputy minister to the Prime Minister.

14 Gordon Osbaldeston, *Keeping Deputy Ministers Accountable* (Toronto: McGraw-Hill Ryerson, 1989), 44–6. See also John Chenier, 'Ministers of State to Assist: Weighing the Costs and the Benefits,' *Canadian Public Administration* 28, 3 (Fall 1985): 397–412.

15 See Patrick Gordon Walker, *The Cabinet: Political Authority in Britain* (New York: Basic Books, 1970), 35–8; Jennings, *Cabinet Government*, 228–32; J.E. Hodgetts, *The Canadian Public Service: A Physiology of Government, 1867–1970* (Toronto: University of Toronto Press, 1973), 45; and Margaret Banks, 'Privy Council, Cabinet, and Ministry in Britain and Canada: A Story of Confusion,' *Canadian Journal of Economics and Political Science* 31, 2 (May 1965): 193–205.

16 Crossman, *The Myths of Cabinet Government*, 61.

17 See Richard Rose, *Ministers and Ministries: A Functional Analysis* (Oxford: Oxford University Press, 1987), 16–24, 73–92, 245–50.

18 Richard Mottram, Permanent Under-Secretary of State for Defence, letter to Sandford Borins, 28 October 1997. The theme of rivalry between junior and senior ministers occasionally appears in British political fiction – for example, an ambitious junior minister attempting to supplant his or her senior minister. In C.P. Snow's *Corridors of Power*, the protagonist is a junior Minister of Defence who intrigues with interest groups to ease his senior minister out. See C.P. Snow, *Corridors of Power* (Harmondsworth: Penguin, 1984). John Mortimer, in *Titmuss Regained* (New York: Viking, 1990), wrote about an ambitious junior minister in the department of 'Housing, Ecological Affairs, and Planning' who passed up to his senior minister a political hot potato in the form of a decision about whether to approve an application to build suburban housing in an old village in which the senior minister's mother owned a house. Ultimately, this decision led the senior minister to leave the cabinet, but not before he ensured that his unduly ambitious junior minister was demoted to the post of junior minister in the Northern Ireland Office. Before concluding that, in this case, life imitates art, we should remember

that whereas conflict is intrinsic to plot development in a novel, effective managers minimize potential conflict.

4: Setting Priorities

1 Thomas Axworthy, 'Of Secretaries to Princes,' *Canadian Public Administration*, 31, 2 (Summer 1988): 247–64.
2 For additional information on initiatives during Blakeney's premiership, see Eleanor D. Glor, ed., *Policy Innovation in the Saskatchewan Public Sector, 1971–82* (North York: Captus Press, 1997).
3 A.W. Johnson, 'Biography of a Government,' 172–235.
4 Bob Rae, *From Protest to Power*, 3, 236–7.
5 J. Richards and L. Pratt, *Prairie Capitalism: Power and Influence in the New West* (Toronto: McClelland and Stewart, 1979), 288.
6 Ibid., 287–303.
7 The Douglas government began having planning conferences such as these in the late 1940s. See Johnson, 'Biography of a Government,' 400.
8 See Gruending, *Promises to Keep*, 136–50; Richards and Pratt, *Prairie Capitalism*, 257–78; and Elwood Cowley, 'The Art of the Possible,' in J. Richards and D. Kerr, eds., *Canada: What's Left?* (Edmonton: NeWest Publishers, 1986), 24–33.
9 Johnson, 'Biography of a Government,' 414, 457–63.
10 Sandford Borins, *Innovating with Integrity: How Local Heroes Are Transforming American Government* (Washington: Georgetown University Press, 1998).
11 Sandford Borins, 'Innovating for High Performance,' unpublished manuscript, 1998.
12 Gruending, *Promises to Keep*, 136, 142, 186.
13 Dunn, 'Changing the Design,' 634, sees these ad hoc cabinet committees and their secretariats as indicative of the general trend toward overshadowing the traditional cabinet. On the contrary, I see them as a way of facilitating the involvement of all ministers in key government initiatives.
14 Osbaldeston, *Keeping Deputy Ministers Accountable*, 57–8, observes that most federal deputy ministers see the Prime Minister very infrequently, but that those working on key priorities see him much more frequently and feel a strong day-to-day sense of accountability to him.
15 Axworthy, 'Of Secretaries to Princes,' 261–4.
16 G. Bruce Doern and Glen Toner, *The Politics of Energy: The Development and Implementation of the NEP* (Toronto: Methuen, 1985), 39–43.
17 David Zussman, personal communication with Sandford Borins, 25 October 1997.
18 Gilles Paquet and Robert Shepherd, 'The Programme Review Process: A

Deconstruction,' in G. Swimmer, ed., *How Ottawa Spends, 1996–97: Life under the Knife* (Ottawa: Carleton University Press, 1996), 39–72.

19 Gordon Ritchie, *Wresting with the Elephant: The Inside Story of the Canada–US Trade Wars* (Toronto: Macfarlane Walter and Ross, 1997), 62–3.

20 G. Bruce Doern and Brian W. Tomlin, *Faith and Fear: The Free Trade Story* (Toronto: Stoddart, 1991), 165. The organization of the Trade Negotiation Office is discussed on pp. 40–1 and 163–7.

21 Ibid., 178–201. Burney and Wilson became involved because of the impasse between Reisman and his American counterpart, Peter Murphy; because of the tensions between Reisman and Trade Minister Pat Carney; and because of their strategy to have the Americans bring in higher-level players, in particular the Treasury Secretary, James Baker.

22 Greenspon and Wilson-Smith, *Double Vision*, 207–27.

23 Malcolm Taylor, *Health Insurance and Canadian Public Policy*, 2nd ed. (Montreal: McGill-Queen's University Press, 1987), 102; McLeod and McLeod, *Tommy Douglas*, 145–55.

24 The classic work in this area is Alfred Chandler, *Strategy and Structure: Chapters in the History of the American Industrial Enterprise* (Cambridge: MIT Press, 1962).

5: The Responsibilities of Ministers

1 Gruending, *Promises to Keep*, 90.

2 T.W. Plumptre, *Beyond the Bottom Line: Management in Government* (Halifax: Institute for Research on Public Policy, 1988), 72.

3 J.L. Granatstein, *The Ottawa Men: The Civil Service Mandarins, 1935–1957*, 2nd. ed. (Toronto: University of Toronto Press, 1998). The end of the mandarin era during the Diefenbaker government is discussed on pp. 253–82.

4 Thomas J. Peters and Robert H. Waterman, Jr, *In Search of Excellence: Lessons from America's Best-Run Companies* (New York: Harper and Row, 1982), 279–91.

5 Gareth Morgan, *Images of Organization* (Beverly Hills: Sage, 1986), 120–6.

6 See Blakeney, 'The Relationship between Provincial Ministers and Their Deputy Ministers,' 43, and Blakeney, 'Goal-setting,' 3.

7 See Osbaldeston, *Keeping Deputy Ministers Accountable*, 87–91, who urges ministers to have a clear and focused agenda, and discusses how ministers set their agendas. Donald Savoie, in *The Politics of Public Spending in Canada* (Toronto: University of Toronto Press, 1990), 185–201, would describe these ministers as 'mission' or 'policy' oriented; others who are in cabinet to enjoy the status, or to win support for projects that benefit certain constituencies, are 'process' oriented.

8 R.H.S. Crossman, *The Myths of Cabinet Government*, 66.

9 Gruending, *Promises to Keep*, 96–7, and Evelyn Eager, *Saskatchewan Government: Politics and Pragmatism* (Saskatoon: Western Producer Prairie Books, 1980), 140.

10 Blakeney, 'The Relationship Between Provincial Ministers and their Deputy Ministers,' 43–4; Blakeney, 'Goal-setting,' 3–4. Also see Osbaldeston, *Keeping Deputy Ministers Accountable*, 18, for a deputy minister's statement of the same view.

11 Crossman, *The Myths of Cabinet Government*, 65.

12 Osbaldeston, *Keeping Deputy Ministers Accountable*, 38–42, raises similar concerns about the management of political staff.

13 See Morgan, *Images of Organization*, 77–109.

6: Managing the Caucus, the Legislature, and the Party

1 See Paul F. Barker, 'The Formulation and Implementation of the Saskatchewan Dental Plan' (Ph.D. diss., University of Toronto, 1985), and Paul F. Barker, 'Decision Making in the Blakeney Years,' *Prairie Forum* 19, 1 (Spring 1994): 65–79.

2 Charlotte Gray, in 'Caucus Charisma,' *Saturday Night*, July/August 1990, 15–18, described Mulroney's approach in detail. It included delivering pep talks at caucus, involving backbench MPs in caucus committees and task forces, and showing interest in and concern about the well-being of MPs and their families.

3 Gruending, *Promises to Keep*, 99–100.

7: The Election Trail

1 Georgette Gagnon and Dan Rath, *Not Without Cause: David Peterson's Fall from Grace* (Toronto: HarperCollins, 1991), 161–204, 305–9.

2 Johnson, 'Biography of a Government,' describes the 1944 (pp. 129–69), 1952 (pp. 475–6), 1956 (pp. 515–16), and 1960 (pp. 611–13) platforms in some detail.

3 Gruending, *Promises to Keep*, 77–83, and David Smith, *Prairie Liberalism: The Liberal Party in Saskatchewan* (Toronto: University of Toronto Press, 1975), 316–20.

4 Gruending, *Promises to Keep*, 126–35.

5 Ibid., 169–77.

6 Ibid., 213–25; James Pitsula and Ken Rasmussen, *Privatizing a Province: The New Right in Saskatchewan* (Vancouver: New Star Books, 1990), 23–38; and Cowley, 'The Art of the Possible,' 39.

7 Gruending, *Promises to Keep*, 229–30; Pitsula and Rasmussen, *Privatizing a Province*, 102–19.

8: The Responsibilities of Deputy Ministers

1 Jonathan Lynn and Antony Jay, *Yes Prime Minister: The Diaries of the Right Hon. James Hacker*, vol. 2 (London: BBC Books, 1987), 229.

2 Peters and Waterman, *In Search of Excellence*, 279–91, 306–17.

3 Concerning the use of co-ordinating mechanisms by Japanese businesses, see William Ouchi, *Theory Z: How American Business Can Meet the Japanese Challenge* (Reading, MA: Addison-Wesley, 1981), 71–94, 131–60, and Richard Pascale and Anthony Athos, *The Art of Japanese Management: Applications for American Executives* (New York: Simon and Schuster, 1981), 183–238, 285–322. Concerning the Japanese public sector, see Sandford Borins, 'Management of the Public Sector in Japan: Are There Lessons to Be Learned?' *Canadian Public Administration* 29, 3 (Summer 1986): 175–96. Central agencies and co-ordination in the Japanese government are discussed on pp. 188–93.

4 Shoshana Zuboff, *In the Age of the Smart Machine: The Future of Work and Power* (New York: Basic Books, 1988).

5 Alain Pinsonneault and Kenneth Kraemer, 'The Impact of Information Technology on Middle Managers,' *MIS Quarterly* 17, 3 (1993): 271–92.

6 Colin Campbell, *Governments under Stress*, 77–99, 147–63, 221–7, 351–5; French, *How Ottawa Decides*, 1–58; James Gillies, *Where Business Fails* (Montreal: Institute for Research on Public Policy, 1981), 81–101; Peter Aucoin, 'The Machinery of Government: From Trudeau's Rational Management to Mulroney's Brokerage Politics,' in Pal and Taras, eds., *Prime Ministers and Premiers*, 50–68. For a strong expression of a cabinet minister's dissatisfaction with powerful central agencies, see Donald Johnston, *Up the Hill* (Montreal: Optimum Publishing, 1986), 53–73.

7 The Government of Canada, *Public Service 2000: The Renewal of the Public Service of Canada* (Ottawa: Supply and Services Canada, 1990), especially 32–4 and 56–61, and Ian Clark, 'Restraint, Renewal, and the Treasury Board Secretariat,' *Canadian Public Administration* 37, 2 (Summer 1994): 209–48.

8 See David Osborne and Ted Gaebler, *Reinventing Government* (Reading, MA: Addison-Wesley, 1992), 250–79; David Osborne and Peter Plastrick, *Banishing Bureaucracy* (Reading, MA: Addison-Wesley, 1997), 203–40; and Al Gore, *Creating a Government That Works Better and Costs Less: Report of the National Performance Review* (New York: Random House, 1993), 65–72.

9 OECD, *Governance in Transition: Public Management Reforms in OECD Countries* (Paris: OECD, 1995), 73–5.

10 Edward Stewart, *Cabinet Government in Ontario*, 11–24.

11 Charles Lindblom, *The Intelligence of Democracy* (New York: Free Press, 1965), 21–34 and 117–43.

12 I served in that position between 1962 and 1964 in Woodrow Lloyd's government.
13 See David Lax and James Sebenius, *The Manager as Negotiator: Bargaining for Cooperation and Competitive Gain* (New York: Free Press, 1986), 61. Lax and Sebenius also argue that skilled managers will first act as mediators in helping subordinates resolve their disputes among themselves, before becoming arbitrators and imposing a solution (see 175–6).
14 Osbaldeston, *Keeping Deputy Ministers Accountable*, 69–71, describes formal and informal methods of co-ordination in Ottawa. Central agencies still play a larger role than in a small provincial government, and while informal methods are recognized as important, they are harder to achieve in a larger bureaucracy. For another discussion of interdepartmental co-ordination in Ottawa, see Kernaghan and Siegel, *Public Administration in Canada*, 393–9.
15 Blakeney, 'The Relationship Between Provincial Ministers and Their Deputies,' 44. See also Arthur Kroeger, 'On Being a Deputy Minister,' *Policy Options* 13, 4 (May 1992): 3–6.
16 Stewart, *Cabinet Government in Ontario*, 49.
17 H.J. Michelmann and J.S. Steeves, 'The 1982 Transition in Power in Saskatchewan: The Progressive Conservatives and the Public Service,' *Canadian Public Administration* 28, 1 (Spring 1985): 1–23, discusses the transition from Thatcher to Blakeney (see 3–4); see also Gruending, *Promises to Keep*, 87.
18 Osbaldeston, *Keeping Deputy Ministers Accountable*, 121–2, 139–52, 172–3.
19 Borins, 'Management of the Public Sector in Japan,' 194.

9: Central Agencies: Only the Minimum

1 Gruending, *Promises to Keep*, 86–9.
2 Howard Leeson, 'The Intergovernmental Affairs Function in Saskatchewan, 1960–1983,' *Canadian Public Administration* 30, 3 (Fall 1987): 399–420. See page 407.
3 French, *How Ottawa Decides*, 22, 75–85.
4 A.W. Johnson, 'Biography of a Government,' 299–303; R.I. McLaren, 'Serving Saskatchewan: A Study of the Saskatchewan Public Service' (unpublished manuscript, 1991), 135–9; George Cadbury, 'Planning in Saskatchewan,' in L. LaPierre, J. McLeod, C. Taylor, and W. Young, eds., *Essays on the Left: Essays in Honour of T.C. Douglas* (Toronto: McClelland and Stewart, 1971), 51–64; and Robert McLaren, 'George Woodall Cadbury: The Fabian Catalyst in Saskatchewan's "Good Public Administration,"' *Canadian Public Administration* 38, 3 (Fall 1995): 471–80.
5 Johnson, 'Biography of a Government,' 302.
6 Ibid., 308–22.
7 Ibid., 398–9, 548–9.

8 The Budget Bureau was established in 1946 and was originally part of the EAPB. Because a budget must be presented to cabinet and the Legislature by a minister, this bureau was moved from EAPB (which was chaired by an adviser) to the Treasury in 1948. The work of the Budget Bureau in its early years is described in McLaren, 'Serving Saskatchewan,' 143–6, and Johnson, 'Biography of a Government,' 324–32.

9 See Johnson, 'Biography of a Government,' 332–6, and McLaren, 'Serving Saskatchewan,' 105–17.

10 See Escott Reid, 'The Saskatchewan Liberal Machine before 1929,' in N. Ward and D. Spafford, eds., *Politics in Saskatchewan* (Toronto: Longmans, 1968), 93–104.

11 See McLaren, 'Serving Saskatchewan,' p. 131, and Michelmann and Steeves, 'The 1982 Transition in Power in Saskatchewan,' 8–9.

12 See Leeson, 'The Intergovernmental Affairs Function in Saskatchewan,' 399–420.

10: Financial Management 1: The Budget Process

1 We have chosen to use the popular term 'budgeting' or 'government budgeting' to refer to the decisions made by Treasury Board about public spending. Purists might distinguish between a government's budget – its global statement of tax policies and aggregate spending and revenue – and its estimates, which are detailed statements of departmental spending plans. We feel this is not necessary, since we are only discussing the latter. In addition, the unit within Saskatchewan's Treasury (after 1972, the Department of Finance) that handled the estimates is known as the Budget Bureau.

For a general description of provincial government budgeting in Canada, see C. Lloyd Brown-John, André LeBlond, and D. Brian Marson, *Public Financial Management: A Canadian Text* (Toronto: Nelson, 1988), 456–532. For a discussion of federal government budgeting that is quite pessimistic about the ability of the federal government to control its spending, see Donald Savoie, *The Politics of Public Spending in Canada* (Toronto: University of Toronto Press, 1990).

2 This practice began with the Douglas government and continued in the Lloyd government. See Bryden, 'Cabinets,' in Bellamy et al., *The Provincial Political Systems*, 311; Eager, *Saskatchewan Government*, 178; and Johnson, 'Biography of a Government,' 400.

3 Eager, *Saskatchewan Government*, 178–9.

4 Osbaldeston, *Keeping Deputy Ministers Accountable*, 122–6, stresses the importance of the deputy minister finding opportunities for officials to meet with their minister, in order to understand his or her thinking better.

5 D.M. Wallace, 'Budget Reform in Saskatchewan: A New Approach to Program-based Management,' *Canadian Public Administration* 17, 4 (Winter 1974): 586–99.

6 Borins, 'Management of the Public Sector in Japan,' 185. Hugh Heclo and Aaron
   Wildavsky, *The Private Government of Public Money: Community and Policy
   Inside British Politics*, 2nd ed. (London: Macmillan, 1981), 93–4. For an overview
   of the role of the federal Treasury Board Secretariat in an era of budget restraint,
   see Ian Clark, 'Restraint, Renewal, and the Treasury Board Secretariat.'
7 See Wallace, 'Budget Reform in Saskatchewan,' 588–91, for a discussion of the
   process of budget reform.
8 A.W. Johnson, 'Biography of a Government,' 274–5, 324–8.
9 Heclo and Wildavsky, *The Private Government of Public Money*, 91–2, and
   Leonard Reed, 'The Budget Game and How to Win It,' *Washington Monthly*,
   January 1979, 24–33. See p. 30.
10 This is one of the propositions that are part of the theory of public choice which,
   broadly, states that politicians are rational actors who attempt to maximize their
   chances of gaining or retaining power. See Conrad Winn, 'Ministerial Roles in
   Policy Making: Vote Seeker, Shaman, and Other Incarnations,' in André Blais, ed.,
   Industrial Policy (Toronto: University of Toronto Press, for the Royal Commission
   on the Economic Union and Development Prospects for Canada, 1986), 219–58;
   Sandford Borins, 'Public Choice: "Yes Minister" Made It Popular, But Does
   Winning the Nobel Prize Make It True?' *Canadian Public Administration* 31, 1
   (Spring 1988): 12–26; and Iain McLean, *Public Choice: An Introduction* (London:
   Blackwell, 1987), 45–61, 103–21.
11 For discussions of public sector budgeting as an ongoing public service indoor
   sport, see Heclo and Wildavsky, *The Private Government of Public Money*, 76–
   128, and Sandford Borins and David Good, *Spenders, Guardians, and Policy
   Analysts: A Game of Budgeting under the Policy and Expenditure Management
   System* (Toronto: Institute of Public Administration of Canada, 1984). For a
   discussion of public sector budgeting as an ongoing political game, see Heclo and
   Wildavsky, *The Private Government of Public Money*, 129–96, and Paul Leger,
   *Resource Allocation in a Provincial Government: The Frustration of Respecting
   Global Expenditure Levels* (Toronto: Institute of Public Administration of Canada,
   1984).
12 See Greenspon and Wilson-Smith, *Double Vision*, 119–36, 195–205, 269–78.
13 Rae, *From Protest to Power*, 204–8.
14 Evert Lindquist and Karen Murray, 'Appendix: A Reconnaissance of Canadian
   Administrative Reform during the Early 1990s,' *Canadian Public Administration*
   37, 3 (Fall 1994): 468–89, and Kathy Langlois, 'A Saskatchewan Vision for
   Health: Who Really Makes the Decisions?' in Robin Ford and David Zussman,
   Alternative Service Delivery: Sharing Goverance in Canada (Toronto: Institute of
   Public Administration of Canada, 1997), 173–87.
15 See Clark, 'Restraint, Renewal, and the Treasury Board Secretariat,' 219–20 and

OECD, *Governance in Transition: Public Management Reforms in OECD Countries*, 30–1.

16 See G.B. Reschenthaler and Fred Thompson, 'The Information Revolution and the New Public Management,' *Journal of Public Administration Research and Theory* 6, 1 (January 1996): 125–43.

17 See A.W. Johnson, 'Biography of a Government,' 328–9, 381–5.

11: Financial Management 2: Government Enterprise

1 Johnson, 'Biography of a Government,' 303–8; T.H. McLeod, 'Public Enterprise in Saskatchewan: The Development of Public Policy and Administrative Controls,' (PhD diss., Harvard University, 1959), 129–32; and Robert McLaren, 'George Woodall Cadbury.'

2 See Johnson, 'Biography of a Government,' 189–200, and McLeod and McLeod, *Tommy Douglas*, 123–4. Johnson (p. 198) quotes 'corridor gossip' that Phelps made some of these investments before they had cabinet approval.

3 See Allan Blakeney, 'Saskatchewan's Crown Corporations: A Case Study,' in Philip Clark, ed., *Proceedings of the Fifth Annual Conference of the Institute of Public Administration of Canada* (Toronto: Institute of Public Administration of Canada, 1954), 413–20, and Allan Blakeney, 'Saskatchewan Crown Corporations,' in W. Friedmann, ed., *The Public Corporation: A Comparative Symposium* (Toronto: Carswell, 1954), 93–107.

4 These were moved from the purview of the Government Finance Office to that of the Treasury in 1950. See Johnson, 'Biography of a Government,' 406, and McLeod, 'Public Enterprise in Saskatchewan,' 136–7.

5 See Johnson, 'Biography of a Government,' 406–7, and McLeod, 'Public Enterprise in Saskatchewan,' 214–17.

6 See Blakeney, 'Saskatchewan's Crown Corporations: A Case Study,' 418–19, and Blakeney, 'Saskatchewan's Crown Corporations,' 102–3, for discussions of the advantages of a Crown Corporation holding company, particularly in gathering and using comparative information.

7 Alfred Chandler, in *Strategy and Structure: Chapters in the History of the American Industrial Enterprise*, describes the evolution in the specific cases mentioned, as well as the spread of the multidivisional form throughout the American economy (see 324–82). It is unfortunate that Chandler focused on the American private sector. Had he carried his research farther afield, he might have discovered the Saskatchewan government following the same approach. Oliver Williamson, in *Markets and Hierarchies: Analysis and Antitrust Implications* (New York: Free Press, 1975), 132–75, presents theoretical arguments about why this structure is more efficient than conceivable alternatives.

8 Johnson, 'Biography of a Government,' 435–6.

9 McLeod and McLeod, *Tommy Douglas*, 50.

10 Ibid., 188–90.

11 The management of Crown corporations in the Saskatchewan government is discussed in Douglas Stevens, 'Corporate Autonomy and Institutional Control: The Crown Corporation as a Problem in Organizational Design,' *Canadian Public Administration* 34, 2 (Summer 1991): 286–312. See 304–10.

12 McLeod and McLeod, *Tommy Douglas*, 172.

13 An example of this was some experimentation with industrial democracy in the Potash Corporation of Saskatchewan. This is described in Don Ching, 'Industrial Democracy: Some Practical Observations,' in J. Richards and D. Kerr, eds., *Canada: What's Left?* (Edmonton: NeWest Publishing, 1986), 183–9.

14 For an overview of the Devine government's experience, see Pitsula and Rasmussen, *Privatizing a Province*, 63–9, and David Roberts, 'Devine's Tories Accused of Squandering Millions,' *Globe and Mail*, 16 February 1991, A4.

15 Pitsula and Rasmussen, *Privatizing a Province*, 266–71.

16 Ibid., 276–80.

17 Ibid., 64.

18 Miro Cernetig, 'Alberta Misadventures Approach $1 billion,' *Globe and Mail*, 4 April 1991, A1; Miro Cernetig, 'Albertans Stuck with Smelter Loans,' ibid., 12 April 1991, A1; Terence Corcoran, 'Alberta Inc. Industrial Policy Misses Mark,' ibid., 6 May 1991, B2; Cathryn Motherwell, 'Taxpayers Lose Big as Myrias Sold Cheap,' ibid., 6 June 1991, B1; and Cathryn Motherwell, 'Vencap Anticipates More Losses,' ibid., 8 August 1991, B13.

19 Johnson, 'Biography of a Government,' pp. 355–8; McLeod and McLeod, *Tommy Douglas*, 170–2.

20 Michael Trebilcock, Marsha Chandler, Morley Gunderson, Paul Halpern, and Jack Quinn, *The Political Economy of Business Bailouts* (Toronto: Ontario Economic Council, 1985), see especially 245–68.

21 See Rae, *From Protest to Power*, 137–45, and William Pullen, *The Spruce Falls Power and Paper Company* (Ottawa: Canadian Centre for Management Development, 1992).

22 Sandford Borins with Lee Brown, *Investments in Failure: Five Government Corporations That Cost the Canadian Taxpayer Billions* (Toronto: Methuen, 1986), 19–28, 67–91.

23 See Rae, *From Protest to Power*, 222–3.

24 Borins with Brown, *Investments in Failure*, 155–7.

25 Johnson, 'Biography of a Government,' 502–4.

26 Richards and Pratt, *Prairie Capitalism*, 119–20. Philip Mathias, *Forced Growth: Five Studies of Government Involvement in the Development of Canada* (Toronto: James Lewis and Samuel, 1971), 81–102.

12: Human Resource Management

1 See Johnson, 'Biography of a Government,' 201–3, 210–11, and Meyer Brownstone, 'The Douglas–Lloyd Governments: Innovation and Bureaucratic Adaptation,' 65–80 in L. LaPierre, J. McLeod, C. Taylor, and W. Young, eds., *Essays on the Left: Essays in Honour of T.C. Douglas* (Toronto: McClelland & Stewart, 1971), 70–3.

2 Johnson, 'Biography of Government,' 279, and Brownstone, 'Innovation and Bureaucratic Response,' 73.

3 The Public Service Act of 1947, which established a merit-based public service, is discussed in Johnson, 'Biography of a Government,' 332–4, and Robert I. McLaren, 'Serving Saskatchewan: A Study of the Saskatchewan Public Service' (unpublished manuscript, 1991), 111–15.

4 McLaren, 'Serving Saskatchewan,' 110–11, makes the point that the hiring of high-fliers through the Budget Bureau was a career employment system, which co-existed with a position classification personnel system, in which the best person would be hired for any given job, which is a characteristic of a merit-based public service. Ultimately, anyone joining the management level, whether through the Budget Bureau system or by moving up in the ranks, had to meet the same standards.

5 Johnson, 'Biography of a Government,' 553–4, describes the development of the educational leave program between 1952 and 1959.

6 See Sandford Borins, 'Public Management in Japan,' *Canadian Public Administration* 29, 3 (Summer 1986): 178–83; William Ouchi, *Theory Z*, 17–37; Pascale and Athos, *The Art of Japanese Management*, 76–86; Peters and Waterman, *In Search of Excellence*, 235–78; David Brown, 'Careers in Whitehall,' *Institute of Public Administration of Canada Bulletin*, May/June 1988, 3, 5, 6, 8, 9; and Stan Sesser, 'A Reporter at Large (Singapore),' *The New Yorker*, 13 January 1992, 49.

7 A Royal Institute of Public Administration working group paper provides a fascinating description of succession planning in the British public service as it was practised over twenty years ago. Cabinet Secretary Sir William Armstrong is quoted as follows: 'I tried to look several years ahead. I did a great deal of it personally, starting in 1968. I built up a big chessboard, with departments listed on one side, using counters for people and moving them around to see what could happen ... I started looking at the Deputy Secretaries. But often the Deputy Secretaries were failed Permanent Secretaries, and not all that hot. So I had to look down to the Under Secretary level. But there were some hundreds of them. I asked each Permanent Secretary to rank the Under Secretaries in his department – promotable immediately, promotable in time, not promotable ... I would then bring all this information to my chessboard, and move the counters around. First I would say, in a year's time these people will have retired, and there would be so many

spaces to fill. Then I would look at the people, and move the counters in different ways to fill the spaces, until I had a number of pictures of what might happen one year ahead, two years ahead, and so on. In some cases, where a Permanent Secretary was 58 and might be replaced in two years by someone of 55, I would think seven years ahead to who might replace him.'

See Royal Institute of Public Administration, *Top Jobs in Whitehall* (London: Royal Institute of Public Administration, 1987), 28. Osbaldeston, in *Keeping Deputy Ministers Accountable,* noted that 'by comparison with the private sector, the federal government engages in little career or succession planning for deputy ministers,' and urged the Prime Minister and Clerk of the Privy Council to take the lead in improving succession planning for the senior public service (178–81).

8 Information about this program can be found on the Public Service Commission's website: www.psc-cfp.gc.ca/mtp/index.htm.

9 See A.H. Maslow, *Motivation and Personality* (New York: Harper and Row, 1970).

10 Gruending, *Promises to Keep,* 186–7.

11 Jerry Hammersmith and Bob Hauk, 'Indian and Native Policy in Southern Saskatchewan,' pp. 101–18, in Eleanor Glor, ed., *Policy Innovation in the Saskatchewan Public Sector, 1971–82.*

12 See Ken Norman, 'Saskatchewan,' in Willam A.W. Neilson, ed., *Getting the Pink Slip: Severances and Firings in the Senior Public Service* (Toronto: Institute of Public Administration of Canada, 1990), 120–9, and Pitsula and Rasmussen, *Privatizing a Province,* 41–4.

13 Michelmann and Steeves, 'The 1982 Transition in Power in Saskatchewan,' 14–18.

14 Ibid., 8.

15 Brownstone, 'Innovation and Bureaucratic Adaptation,' pp. 74–8.

16 The classic study of patronage in Saskatchewan is Reid, 'The Saskatchewan Liberal Machine.' McLeod and McLeod, in *Tommy Douglas,* 129, show that in the year before Douglas was elected, the civil service had 197 resignations, 25 retirements, and 1 dismissal. In Douglas's first year in office there were 193 resignations, 69 retirements, and 18 dismissals. The only department with a substantial number of dismissals at senior levels was Natural Resources; in most of the others, deputy ministers were retained, and when new deputy ministers were appointed, it was often by the promotion of branch heads in the same ministry. Lipset, *Agrarian Socialism,* 313–24, makes the point that the government disappointed its supporters, who expected the top ranks to be purged. On the other hand, change was achieved because sympathetic experts were brought in for some key positions and because the senior civil servants who stayed co-operated with the new government.

17 David Zussman and Jak Jabes, *The Vertical Solitude: Managing in the Public Sector* (Halifax: Institute for Research on Public Policy, 1989).

18 Jak Jabes, Nick Jans, Judy Frazer-Jans, and David Zussman, 'Managing in the Canadian and Australian Public Sectors: A Comparative Study of the Vertical Solitude,' *International Review of Administrative Sciences* 58, 1 (March 1992): 5–21.

19 The literature on the new public management is large and rapidly growing. For definitions, see Michael Barzelay, *Breaking through Bureaucracy* (Berkeley: University of California Press, 1992); Sandford Borins, 'A New Paradigm in Public Administration,' in Commonwealth Association for Public Administration and Management, *Government in Transition* (Toronto: University of Toronto Press, 1995), 3–23; Commonwealth Secretariat, *Current Good Practices and New Developments in Public Service Management* (London: Commonwealth Secretariat, 1996); OECD, *Governance in Transition*; and Osborne and Gaebler, *Reinventing Government*. Regarding the United States, the National Performance Review has issued the following major reports by Al Gore: *Creating a Government That Works Better and Costs Less*; *Common Sense Government Works Better and Costs Less* (New York: Random House, 1995); and *The Best Kept Secrets in Government* (Washington: U.S. Government Printing Office, 1996). New Zealand has been on the leading edge of the new public management, and the definitive book about its experience is J. Boston, J. Martin, J. Pallot, and P. Walsh, *Public Management: The New Zealand Model* (New York: Oxford, 1996). Comparative studies include Osborne and Plastrik, *Banishing Bureaucracy*, and Peter Aucoin, *The New Public Management: Canada in Comparative Perspective* (Montreal: Institute for Research on Public Policy, 1995).

20 Sandford Borins, 'The New Public Management Is Here to Stay,' *Canadian Public Administration* 38, 1 (Spring 1995): 122–32, and Ian Clark, 'Global Economic Trends and Pressures on Governments,' *Canadian Public Administration* 39, 4 (Winter 1996): 447–56.

21 F. Leslie Seidle, *Rethinking the Delivery of Public Services to Citizens* (Montreal: Institute for Research on Public Policy, 1995).

22 Government of the United Kingdom, *The Citizen's Charter: Raising the Standard* (London: Her Majesty's Stationery Office, command 1599, 1991).

23 OECD, *Integrating People Management into Public Service Reform* (Paris: OECD, 1996).

13: Intergovernmental Relations

1 See Roy Romanow, John Whyte, and Howard Leeson, *Canada ... Notwithstanding. The Making of the Canadian Constitution, 1976–1982* (Toronto: Carswell Methuen, 1984), and Robert Sheppard and Michael Valpy, *The National Deal: The Fight for a Canadian Constitution* (Toronto: Fleet Books, 1982), 192.

2 This became more important over time, and in 1978 we ultimately established a

small Ministry of Intergovernmental Affairs. I was the minister for the first six months, and then I assigned the responsibility to Roy Romanow. This office did not have sole responsibility for intergovernmental affairs, and the Department of Finance and Crown Investments Corporation also were involved. See Howard Leeson, 'The intergovernmental Affairs Function in Saskatchewan,' *Canadian Public Administration* 30, 3 (Fall 1987): 399–420.

3 See Richard Simeon, *Federal–Provincial Diplomacy: The Making of Recent Policy in Canada* (Toronto: University of Toronto Press, 1972), 215.

4 Ibid., 72–3, 223.

5 A common Canadian position that is advanced by the federal government and all interested provinces will be much more influential in Washington. See Gotlieb, *'I'll Be with You in a Minute, Mr. Ambassador,'* 130.

6 Gruending, *Promises to Keep*, 145.

7 See Sheppard and Valpy, *The National Deal*, 192.

8 The Continuing Committee on Ministers on the Constitution performed this function for several years prior to the 1980–2 constitutional negotiations. See Romanow, Whyte, and Leeson, *Canada ... Notwithstanding*, 21–4.

9 Simeon, *Federal–Provincial Diplomacy*, 134–7, 287–8.

10 Roger Fisher and William Ury, *Getting to Yes: Negotiating Agreement without Giving In* (Boston: Houghton Mifflin, 1981), 17–40.

11 Simeon, *Federal–Provincial Diplomacy*, 130. The federal and provincial opening statements at the 1981 constitutional conference are discussed in Sheppard and Valpy, *The National Deal*, 268–9, and Romanow, Whyte, and Lesson, *Canada ... Notwithstanding*, 193–5.

12 Simeon, *Federal–Provincial Diplomacy*, 220.

13 Fisher and Ury, *Getting to Yes*, 101–11.

14 Lax and Sebenius, in *The Manager as Negotiator*, 55–6, present a fascinating example of a negotiator improving its alternatives to a negotiated outcome. In the early 1960s, Kennecott Copper anticipated that the Chilean government would attempt to expropriate one of its major copper mines. It prepared for this by getting numerous other parties involved on its side – for example, it established long-term contracts with Asian and European customers for the mine's output, and it sought loan guarantees and insurance. Though Chile ultimately expropriated the mine, Kennecott emerged stronger than it would have had it not taken these actions.

15 Simeon, *Federal–Provincial Diplomacy*, 115–23.

16 Sheppard and Valpy, *The National Deal*, 241–4; Romanow, Whyte, and Leeson, *Canada ... Notwithstanding*, 163–85.

17 These were outlined in the 'Kirby memorandum.' See Sheppard and Valpy, *The National Deal*, 55–8, and Romanow, Whyte, and Leeson, *Canada ... Notwithstanding*, 94–5.

18 The federal government's use of the referendum option at the constitutional conference is discussed in Sheppard and Valpy, *The National Deal*, 265–6 and Romanow, Whyte, and Leeson, *Canada ... Notwithstanding*, 106–7, 198–9, 204–6.

19 See Romanow, Whyte, and Leeson, *Canada ... Notwithstanding*, 8–10, 43–5, 234–6, 242–6.

20 Fisher and Ury, *Getting to Yes*, 118–22.

21 Sheppard and Valpy, *The National Deal*, 50–1, 300.

22 Romanow, Whyte, and Leeson, *Canada ... Notwithstanding*, 24, 117–19, 273–5.

14: Lobbying: Advice to the Private Sector

1 W.T. Stanbury, *Business–Government Relations in Canada* (Toronto: Methuen, 1986), 343.

2 See Sandford Borins, 'Action Learning About Lobbying: Establishing the Ontario Centre for International Business,' *Proceedings of the 1990 Annual Conference of the Administrative Sciences Association of Canada, Policy Division*, 5–14.

3 Stanbury, *Business–Government Relations in Canada*, 400–5.

4 Allison, *Essence of Decision: Explaining the Cuban Missile Crisis*, 175–6.

5 Stanbury, *Business–Government Relations in Canada*, 391–5.

6 Gotlieb, *'I'll Be with You in a Minute, Mr. Ambassador'*, 129–30, emphasizes the importance of timing in Canadian efforts to influence American legislators, and concludes that 'in lobbying, timing is everything.'

7 Richards and Pratt, *Prairie Capitalism*, 260–3.

8 Ibid., 296–8.

9 Ibid., 264–6; Gruending, *Promises to Keep*, 142.

10 Gruending, *Promises to Keep*, 149; Richards and Pratt, *Prairie Capitalism*, 271–2.

11 Richards and Pratt, *Prairie Capitalism*, 271, 297–300.

12 Stanbury, *Business–Government Relations in Canada*, 364–70.

13 Ontario Ministry of Consumer and Commercial Relations, *Used Vehicle Information Package*, response to questionnaire on public sector innovation in Canada, August 1995.

14 Readers interested in program implementation – a topic we discuss at greater length in chapter 16 – may wonder how private sellers were induced to report the fair market value of their cars. The UVIP requires them to pay sales tax on at least the wholesale value of their make and age of car as published in the 'Canadian Red Book.'

15 Gruending, *Promises to Keep*, 141; Richards and Pratt, *Prairie Capitalism*, 262.

16 Gotlieb, *'I'll Be with You in a Minute, Mr. Ambassador'*, 53–8.

17 Calvin Woodward, 'U.S. Lumber Dealers on Canada's Aide,' *Globe and Mail*, 25 March 1992, B7.

18 Gruending, *Promises to Keep*, 147.

19 John Burton, 'Resource Rent and Taxation – Application of New Principles and Approaches in Saskatchewan,' 59–77, in Glor, ed., *Policy Innovation in the Saskatchewan Public Sector, 1971–1982*.

20 A. Freeman, 'Shopping in U.S. to Get More Expensive Under Ottawa Plan,' *Globe and Mail*, 12 February 1992, A1,2; A. Freeman, 'Post Office Agrees to Collect Duties, GST Before Delivery,' *Globe and Mail*, 3 March 1992, A1.

21 Rae, *From Protest to Power*, 228.

15: Public Consultation

1 Quoted in Kernaghan and Siegel, *Public Administration*, 301.

2 See Janet Smith and Anne Patterson, *Managing a Royal Commission* (Ottawa: Canadian Centre for Management Development, 1994).

3 J.M. Keynes, *The General Theory of Employment, Interest, and Money* (New York: Harcourt, Brace, 1965), 383.

4 Sandford Borins, *The Language of the Skies: The Bilingual Air Traffic Control Conflict in Canada* (Montreal: McGill-Queen's University Press, 1983).

5 Patterson, Anne, R.A. Lohin, and D.S. Ferguson, *Consultation: When the Goal Is Good Decisions* (Ottawa: Canadian Centre for Management Development, 1992).

6 Hajo Versteeg, *A Case Study in Multi-Stakeholder Consultation* (Ottawa: Canadian Centre for Management Development, 1992).

16: Managing Change

1 See Eleanor Glor, 'What Makes Innovation Possible,' in Glor, ed. *Policy Innovation in the Saskatchewan Public Sector, 1971–82*, 3–26.

2 Cowley, 'The Art of the Possible,' 32.

3 French, *How Ottawa Decides*, 75–85.

4 Taylor, *Health Insurance and Canadian Public Policy*, 98–9; McLeod and McLeod, *Tommy Douglas*, 151.

5 Peters and Waterman, *In Search of Excellence*, 75.

6 A. Johnson, 'Public Policy: Creativity and Bureaucracy,' *Canadian Public Administration* 22, 1 (Spring 1978): 1–15.

7 Peters and Waterman, *In Search of Excellence*, 200–13. See also Tom Peters and Nancy Austin, *A Passion for Excellence: The Leadership Difference* (New York: Random House, 1985), 135–45.

8 Anthony Downs, *Inside Bureaucracy* (Boston: Little, Brown, 1967), 102–10.

9 Sandford Borins, 'Public Management Innovation in Canada: Evidence from the IPAC Competition,' *Optimum* 22, 3 (Winter 1991): 9.

10 Gruending, *Promises to Keep*, 116–17.
11 Allan Blakeney, 'Reflections on Innovations I Hoped to See,' in E. Glor, ed., *Policy Innovation in the Saskatchewan Public Sector, 1971–82*, 253–70.
12 Borins, *The Language of the Skies*, 191–205.
13 Steve Wolfson, 'Use of Paraprofessionals: The Saskatchewan Dental Plan,' in Glor, ed., *Policy Innovation in the Saskatchewan Public Sector, 1971–82*, 126–39.
14 Paul Barker, 'Decision Making in the Blakeney Years,' *Prairie Forum* 19, 1 (Spring 1994).
15 Robert Sass, 'Self-Enforcement of a Rights-Based Approach to Workplace Health and Safety,' in Glor, ed., *Policy Innovation in the Saskatchewan Public Sector, 1971–82*, 150–66.
16 See Gruending, *Promises to Keep*, 104–13; Cowley, 'The Art of the Possible,' 24–8; and Blakeney, 'Reflections on Innovations I Hoped to See,' 258.
17 Pitsula and Rasmussen, *Privatizing a Province*, 44–6.
18 See Chapter 6, 'Single Window Delivery of Public Services in Canada,' in Seidle, *Rethinking the Delivery of Services to Citizens*.

17: Crises and the Media

1 Robert Williamson, 'Cool Head Helps Cold Buster,' *Globe and Mail*, 16 January 1992, B1, B13.
2 Two examples of guidebooks are, for the federal public service, Privy Council Office, *Crisis Management* (Ottawa: Supply and Services Canada, 1989), and Department of Public Affairs, University of Toronto, *Dealing with the Media: A Guide to Better Media Relations* (Toronto: University of Toronto Press, 1992).
3 Taylor, *Health Insurance and Canadian Public Policy*, 298–9; Robin Badgley and Samuel Wolfe, *Doctors' Strike: Medical Care and Conflict in Saskatchewan* (Toronto: Macmillan, 1967), 67–8.
4 Taylor, *Health Insurance and Canadian Public Policy*, 317.
5 Ibid., 317–23; Badgley and Wolfe, *Doctors' Strike*, 71–2; J.L. Granatstein, *Canada, 1957–1967: The Years of Uncertainty and Innovation* (Toronto: McClelland and Stewart, 1986), 189–91; and E.A. Tollefson, *Bitter Medicine: The Saskatchewan Medicare Feud* (Saskatoon: Modern Press, 1963), 113.
6 Michael Brecher with Benjamin Geist, *Decisions in Crisis: Israel, 1967 and 1973* (Berkeley: University of California Press, 1980), 341–406.
7 Allison, *Essence of Decision*, pp. 57, 123–4, 193–210.
8 Ibid., 127–32.
9 Ibid., 178.
10 J.W. Pullen, *The St. Louis Bridge Incident* (Ottawa: Canadian Centre for Management Development, 1989).

11 S. Borins and L. St Laurent, *The Four Million Dollar Typo: A Case about Account-ability* (Toronto: Institute of Public Administration of Canada, 1984).

18: Managing a Change of Government

1 Rae, *From Protest to Power*, 129.
2 Greenspon and Wilson-Smith, *Double Vision*, 7. See also 8, 22, 34, and 165.
3 Graham White, 'Traffic Pile-ups at Queen's Park: Recent Ontario Transitions,' in Donald Savoie, ed., *Taking Power: Managing Government Transitions* (Toronto: Institute of Public Administration of Canada, 1993), 115–43.
4 Sandford Borins, *High Level Seminar for Cabinet Secretaries: A Report* (Toronto: Commonwealth Association for Public Administration and Management, 1997).
5 Madeline Drohan, 'Blair's Blazing Pace Startles Staid U.K.: PM makes the Most of First 100 Days,' *Globe and Mail*, 2 August 1997, A1, A9.
6 'SaskPower Chief Fired by NDP,' *Globe and Mail*, 15 November 1991, A5.
7 Graham White, 'Transition: The Tories Take Power,' in Sid Noel, ed., *Revolution at Queen's Park: Essays on Governing Ontario* (Toronto: Lorimer, 1997), 139–50.

Conclusion

1 A good introduction to action learning is C.J. Margerison, 'Action Learning and Excellence in Management Development,' *Journal of Management Development* 7, 5 (October 1988): 43–53.

Bibliography

Allison, Graham T. *Essence of Decision: Explaining the Cuban Missile Crisis.* Boston: Little, Brown, 1971.

Atkinson, Michael M., and Kim Richard Nossal. 'Bureaucratic Politics and the New Fighter Aircraft Decisions.' *Canadian Public Administration* 24, 4 (Winter 1981): 531–62.

Aucoin, Peter. *The New Public Management: Canada in Comparative Perspective.* Montreal: Institute for Research on Public Policy, 1995.

– 'The Machinery of Government: From Trudeau's Rational Management to Mulroney's Brokerage Politics,' pp. 50–68. In Leslie Pal and David Taras, eds., *Prime Ministers and Premiers: Political Leadership and Public Policy in Canada.* Toronto: Prentice-Hall, 1988.

Aucoin, Peter, and Herman Bakvis. 'Consolidating Cabinet Portfolios: Australian Lessons for Canada.' *Canadian Public Administration* 36, 3 (Fall 1993): 392–420.

Axworthy, Thomas. 'Of Secretaries to Princes.' *Canadian Public Administration* 31, 2 (Summer 1988): 247–64.

Badgley, Robin, and Samuel Wolfe. *Doctors' Strike: Medical Care and Conflict in Saskatchewan.* Toronto: Macmillan, 1967.

Banks, Margaret. 'Privy Council, Cabinet, and Ministry in Britain and Canada: A Story of Confusion.' *Canadian Journal of Economics and Political Science* 31, 2 (May 1965): 193–205.

Barker, Paul F. 'Decision Making in the Blakeney Years.' *Prairie Forum* 19, 1 (Spring 1994): 65–79.

– 'The Formulation and Implementation of the Saskatchewan Dental Plan.' PhD diss. University of Toronto, 1985.

Barzelay, Michael. *Breaking through Bureaucracy.* Berkeley: University of California Press, 1992.

Berle, A.A., and G.C. Means. *The Modern Corporation and Private Property.* New York: Harcourt, Brace and World, 1932.

Blakeney, Allan. 'Reflections on Innovations I Hoped to See.' pp. 253–70. In E. Glor, ed, *Policy Innovation in the Saskatchewan Public Sector, 1971–82.* North York: Captus Press, 1997.

– 'Goal-setting: Politicians' Expectations of Public Administrators.' *Canadian Public Administration* 24, 1 (Spring 1981): 1–7.

– 'The Relationship between Provincial Ministers and Their Deputy Ministers.' *Canadian Public Administration* 15, 1 (Spring 1972): 42–5.

– 'Saskatchewan Crown Corporations,' pp. 93–107. In W. Friedmann ed., *The Public Corporation: A Comparative Symposium.* Toronto: Carswell, 1954.

– 'Saskatchewan's Crown Corporations: A Case Study,' 413–20. In Philip Clark, ed., *Proceedings of the Fifth Annual Conference of the Institute of Public Administration of Canada.* Toronto: Institute of Public Administration of Canada, 1954.

Borins, Sandford. 'Innovating for High Performance.' Unpublished manuscript, 1998.

– *Innovating with Integrity: How Local Heroes Are Transforming American Government.* Washington: Georgetown University Press, 1998.

– *High Level Seminar for Cabinet Secretaries: A Report.* Toronto: Commonwealth Association for Public Administration and Management, 1997.

– 'A New Paradigm in Public Administration,' pp. 3–23. In Commonwealth Association for Public Administration and Management, *Government in Transition.* Toronto: University of Toronto Press, 1995.

– 'The New Public Management Is Here to Stay.' *Canadian Public Administration* 38, 1 (Spring 1995): 122–32.

– 'Public Management Innovation in Canada: Evidence from the IPAC Competition.' *Optimum* 22, 3 (Winter 1991): 5–16.

– 'Action Learning about Lobbying: Establishing the Ontario Centre for International Business,' pp. 5–14. In *Proceedings of the 1990 Annual Conference of the Administrative Sciences Association of Canada, Policy Division.* 2–5 June 1990.

– 'Public Choice: "Yes Minister" Made It Popular, But Does Winning the Nobel Prize Make It True?' *Canadian Public Administration* 31, 1 (Spring 1988): 12–26.

– 'Management of the Public Sector in Japan: Are There Lessons to Be Learned?' *Canadian Public Administration* 29, 3 (Summer 1986): 175–96.

– *The Language of the Skies: The Bilingual Air Traffic Control Conflict in Canada.* Montreal: McGill-Queen's University Press, 1983.

Borins, Sandford, with Lee Brown. *Investments in Failure: Five Government Corporations That Cost the Canadian Taxpayer Billions.* Toronto: Methuen, 1986.

Borins, Sandford, and David Good. *Spenders, Guardians, and Policy Analysts: A Game of Budgeting under the Policy and Expenditure Management System.* Toronto: Institute of Public Administration of Canada, 1984.

Borins, Sandford, and Laurence St. Laurent. *The Four Million Dollar Typo: A Case about Accountability.* Toronto: Institute of Public Administration in Canada, 1984.

Boston, Jonathan, John Martin, June Pallot, and Pat Walsh. *Public Management: The New Zealand Model.* New York: Oxford, 1996.

Brecher, Michael, with Benjamin Geist. *Decisions in Crisis: Israel, 1967 and 1973.* Berkeley: University of California Press, 1980.

Brown, David. 'Careers in Whitehall.' *Institute of Public Administration of Canada Bulletin* 12, 2 (May/June 1988): 3ff.

Brownstone, Meyer. 'The Douglas–Lloyd Governments: Innovation and Bureaucratic Adaptation,' pp. 65–80. In L. LaPierre, J. McLeod, C. Taylor, and W. Young, eds., *Essays on the Left: Essays in Honour of T.C. Douglas.* Toronto: McClelland and Stewart, 1971.

Brown-John, C. Lloyd, André LeBlond and Brian D. Marson. *Public Financial Management: A Canadian Text.* Toronto: Nelson, 1988.

Bryden, Kenneth. 'Cabinets,' pp. 310–22. In David Bellamy, Jon Pammet, and Donald Rowat eds., *The Provincial Political Systems: Comparative Essays.* Toronto: Methuen, 1976.

Burton, John. 'Resource Rent and Taxation – Application of New Principles and Approaches in Saskatchewan.' pp. 59–77. In E. Glor, ed., *Policy Innovation in the Saskatchewan Public Sector, 1971–1982.* North York: Captus Press, 1997.

Cadbury, George. 'Planning in Saskatchewan.' In L. LaPierre, J. McLeod, C. Taylor, and W. Young, eds., *Essays on the Left: Essays in Honour of T.C. Douglas.* Toronto: McClelland and Stewart, 1971.

Campbell, Colin. *Governments under Stress: Political Executives and Key Bureaucrats in Washington, London, and Ottawa.* Toronto: University of Toronto Press, 1983.

Campbell, Colin, and George Szablowski. *The Super-bureaucrats: Structure and Behaviour in Central Agencies.* Toronto: Macmillan, 1979.

Cernetig, Miro. 'Alberta Misadventures Approach $1 Billion.' *Globe and Mail,* 4 April 1991, A1.

– 'Albertans Stuck with Smelter Loans.' *Globe and Mail,* 12 April 1991, A1.

Chandler, Alfred. *Strategy and Structure: Chapters in the History of the American Industrial Enterprise.* Cambridge: MIT Press, 1962.

Chenier, John. 'Ministers of State to Assist: Weighing the Costs and Benefits.' *Canadian Public Administration* 28, 3 (Fall 1985): 397–412.

Ching, Don. 'Industrial Democracy: Some Practical Observations,' pp. 183–9. In J. Richards and D. Kerr, eds., *Canada: What's Left?* Edmonton: NeWest Publishing, 1986.

Clark, Ian. 'Global Economic Trends and Pressures on Governments.' *Canadian Public Administration* 39, 4 (Winter 1996): 447–56.

– 'Restraint, Renewal, and the Treasury Board Secretariat.' *Canadian Public Administration* 37, 2 (Summer 1994: 209–48.

Commonwealth Secretariat. *Current Good Practices and New Developments in Public Service Management.* London: Commonwealth Secretariat, 1996.

Corcoran, Terence. 'Alberta Inc. Industrial Policy Misses Mark.' *Globe and Mail,* 6 May 1991, B2.

Cowley, Elwood. 'The Art of the Possible,' pp. 24–33. In J. Richards and D. Kerr, eds., *Canada: What's Left?* Edmonton: NeWest Publishers, 1986.

Crittenden, Guy. 'The Harris Kremlin: Inside Ontario's Revolutionary Politburo.' *Globe and Mail.* 1 November 1997. D1, D9.

Crossman, Richard H.S. *The Myths of Cabinet Government.* Cambridge: Harvard University Press, 1972.

Department of Public Affairs, University of Toronto. *Dealing with the Media: A Guide to Better Media Relations.* Toronto: University of Toronto Press, 1992.

Doern, G. Bruce, and Brian W. Tomlin. *Faith and Fear: The Free Trade Story.* Toronto: Stoddard, 1991.

Doern, G. Bruce, and Glen Toner. *The Politics of Energy: The Development and Implementation of the NEP.* Toronto: Methuen, 1985.

Downs, Anthony. *Inside Bureaucracy.* Boston: Little, Brown, 1967.

Drohan, Madeline. 'Blair's Blazing Pace Startles Staid UK: PM Makes the Most of First 100 Days.' *Globe and Mail,* 2 August 1997, A1, A9.

Dunn, Christopher. *The Institutionalized Cabinet: Governing the Western Provinces.* Montreal: McGill–Queen's University Press, 1995.

– 'Changing the Design: Cabinet Decision-making in Three Provincial Governments.' *Canadian Public Administration* 34, 4 (Winter 1991): 621–40.

Eager, Evelyn. *Saskatchewan Government: Politics and Pragmatism.* Saskatoon: Western Producer Prairie Books, 1980.

Fisher, Roger, and William Ury. *Getting to Yes: Negotiating Agreement without Giving In.* Boston: Houghton Mifflin, 1981.

Freeman, A. 'Post Office Agrees to Collect Duties, GST Before Delivery.' *Globe and Mail,* 3 March 1992, A1.

– 'Shopping in U.S. to Get More Expensive Under Ottawa Plan. *Globe and Mail,* 12 February 1992, A1, A2.

French, Richard. *How Ottawa Decides: Planning and Industrial Policy Making, 1968– 1984.* 2nd ed. Toronto: Lorimer, 1984.

Gagnon, Georgette, and Dan Rath. *Not Without Cause: David Peterson's Fall from Grace.* Toronto: HarperCollins, 1991.

Galbraith, J.K. *The New Industrial State*. Boston: Houghton Mifflin, 1967.

Gillies, James. *Boardroom Renaissance: Power, Morality, and Performance in the Modern Corporation*. Toronto: McGraw-Hill Ryerson, 1992.

– *Where Business Fails*. Montreal: Institute for Research on Public Policy, 1981.

Glor, E. ed. *Policy Innovation in the Saskatchewan Public Sector, 1971–82*. North York: Captus Press, 1997.

Gore, A. *The Best Kept Secrets in Government*. Washington: U.S. Government Printing Office, 1996.

– *Common Sense Government Works Better and Costs Less*. New York: Random House, 1995.

– *Creating a Government That Works Better and Costs Less: Report of the National Performance Review*. New York: Random House, 1993.

Gotlieb, Allan. *'I'll Be with You in a Minute, Mr. Ambassador': The Education of a Canadian Diplomat in Washington*. Toronto: University of Toronto Press, 1991.

Government of Canada. *Public Service 2000: The Renewal of the Public Service of Canada*. Ottawa: Supply and Services Canada, 1990.

Government of the United Kingdom. *The Citizen's Charter: Raising the Standard*. London: Her Majesty's Stationery Office Command 1599, 1991.

Graham, Katherine. 'Discretion and the Governance of Canada: The Buck Stops Where?' pp. 1–24. In Katherine Graham, ed., *How Ottawa Spends: 1989–90*. Ottawa: Carleton University Press, 1989.

Granatstein, J.L. *Canada, 1957–1967: The Years of Uncertainty and Innovation*. Toronto: McClelland and Stewart, 1986.

– *The Ottawa Men: The Civil Service Mandarins, 1935–1957*. 2nd ed. Toronto: University of Toronto Press, 1998.

Gray, Charlotte. 'Caucus Charisma.' *Saturday Night*, July/August 1990, 15–18.

Greenspon, Edward, and Anthony Wilson-Smith. *Double Vision: The Inside Story of the Liberals in Power*. Toronto: Seal, 1997.

Gruending, Dennis. *Promises to Keep: A Political Biography of Allan Blakeney*. Saskatoon: Western Producer Prairie Books, 1990.

Hammersmith, Jerry, and Bob Hauk. 'Indian and Native Policy in Southern Saskatchewan,' pp. 101–18. In Eleanor Glor, ed., *Policy Innovation in the Saskatchewan Public Sector, 1971–82*. North York: Captus Press, 1997.

Harcourt, Mike, with Wayne Skene. *Mike Harcourt: A Measure of Defiance*. Vancouver: Douglas and McIntyre, 1996.

Heclo, Hugh, and Aaron Wildavsky. *The Private Government of Public Money: Community and Policy Inside British Politics*. 2nd ed. London: Macmillan, 1981.

Hodgetts, J.E. *The Canadian Public Service: A Physiology of Government, 1867–1970*. Toronto: University of Toronto Press, 1973.

Jabes, J., N. Jans, J. Frazer-Jans, and D. Zussman. 'Managing in the Canadian and Australian Public Sectors: A Comparative Study of the Vertical Solitude. *International Review of Administrative Sciences* 58, 1 (March 1992): 5–21.

Jennings, Ivor. *Cabinet Government.* 3rd ed. Cambridge: Cambridge University Press, 1959.

Johnson, Albert W. 'Public Policy: Creativity and Bureaucracy.' *Canadian Public Administration* 22, 1 (Spring 1978): 1–15.

– 'Biography of a Government: Policy Formulation in Saskatchewan, 1944–1961.' PhD diss., Harvard University, 1963.

– 'Efficiency in Government and Business.' *Canadian Public Administration* 6, 3 (1963): 245–60.

Johnston, Donald. *Up the Hill.* Montreal: Optimum Publishing, 1986.

Kernaghan, Kenneth, and David Siegel. *Public Administration in Canada: A Text.* 3rd ed. Toronto: Nelson, 1995.

Keynes, J.M. *The General Theory of Employment, Interest, and Money.* New York: Harcourt, Brace, 1965.

Kroeger, Arthur. 'On Being a Deputy Minister.' *Policy Options* 13, 4 (May 1992): 3–6.

Langlois, Kathy. 'A Saskatchewan Vision for Health: Who Really Makes the Decisions?', pp. 173–87 in R. Ford and D. Zussman, eds., *Alternative Service Delivery: Sharing Governance in Canada* (Toronto: Institute of Public Administration of Canada, 1997).

Lax, David, and James Sebenius. *The Manager as Negotiator: Bargaining for Cooperation and Competitive Gain.* New York: Free Press, 1986.

Leeson, Howard. 'The Intergovernmental Affairs Function in Saskatchewan, 1960–1983.' *Canadian Public Administration* 30, 3 (Fall 1987): 399–420.

Leger, Paul. *Resource Allocation in a Provincial Government: The Frustration of Respecting Global Expenditure Levels.* Toronto: Institute of Public Administration of Canada, 1984.

Leighton, David, and Donald Thain. *Making Boards Work: What Directors Must Do to Make Canadian Boards Effective.* Toronto: McGraw-Hill Ryerson, 1997.

Lindblom, Charles. *The Intelligence of Democracy.* New York: Free Press, 1965.

Lindquist, Evert, and Karen Murray. 'Appendix: A Reconnaissance of Canadian Administrative Reform during the Early 1990s.' *Canadian Public Administration* 37, 3 (Fall 1994): 468–89.

Lindquist, Evert, and Graham White. 'Analyzing Canadian Cabinets: Past, Present, and Future,' pp. 113–38, in Mohamed Charih and Arthur Daniels, eds., *New Public Management and Public Administration in Canada* (Toronto: Institute of Public Administration of Canada, 1997).

Lipset, S.M. *Agrarian Socialism: The Cooperative Commonwealth Federation in Saskatchewan. A Study in Political Sociology.* New York: Doubleday Anchor, 1968.

Lynn, Jonathan, and Anthony Jay. *Yes Prime Minister: The Diaries of the Right Hon. James Hacker.* 2 vols. London: BBC Books, 1986–7.

Margerison, C.J. 'Action Learning and Excellence in Management Development.' *Journal of Management Development,* 7, 5 (October 1988): 43–53.

Maslow, A.H. *Motivation and Personality.* New York: Harper and Row, 1970.

Mathias, Philip. *Forced Growth: Five Studies of Government Involvement in the Development of Canada.* Toronto: James Lewis and Samuel, 1971.

McLaren, Robert I. 'George Woodall Cadbury: The Fabian Catalyst in Saskatchewan's "Good Public Administration."' *Canadian Public Administration* 38, 3 (Fall 1995): 471–80.

– 'Serving Saskatchewan: A Study of the Saskatchewan Public Service.' Unpublished paper, 1991.

McLean, Iain. *Public Choice: An Introduction.* London: Blackwell, 1987.

McLeod, T.H. 'Public Enterprise in Saskatchewan: The Development of Public Policy and Administrative Controls.' PhD diss., Harvard University, 1959.

McLeod, T.H., and I. McLeod. *Tommy Douglas: The Road to Jerusalem.* Edmonton: Hurtig, 1987.

Michelmann, H.J., and J.S. Steeves. 'The 1982 Transition in Power in Saskatchewan: The Progressive Conservatives and the Public Service.' *Canadian Public Administration* 28, 1 (Spring 1985): 1–23.

Mitchell, William Ormond. *Who Has Seen the Wind.* Toronto: Macmillan, 1947.

Morgan, Gareth. *Images of Organization.* Beverly Hills: Sage, 1986.

Mortimer, John. *Titmuss Regained.* New York: Viking, 1990.

Motherwell, Cathryn. 'Taxpayers Lose Big as Myrias Sold Cheap.' *Globe and Mail,* 6 June 1991, B1.

– 'Vencap Anticipates More Losses.' *Globe and Mail,* 8 August 1991, B13.

Mottram, Richard, Permanent Under-Secretary of State for Defence (United Kingdom), in letter to Sandford Borins, 28 October 1997.

Norman, Ken. 'Saskatchewan,' pp. 120–9. In A.W. Neilson, ed., *Getting the Pink Slip: Severances and Firings in the Senior Public Service.* Toronto: Institute of Public Administration of Canada, 1990.

Nossal, Kim Richard. 'Allison Through the (Ottawa) Looking Glass: Bureaucratic Politics and Foreign Policy in a Parliamentary System.' *Canadian Public Administration* 22, 4 (Winter 1979): 610–26.

OECD. *Integrating People Management into Public Service Reform.* Paris: OECD, 1996.

– *Governance in Transition: Public Management Reform in OECD Countries.* Paris: OECD, 1995.

Ontario Ministry of Consumer and Commercial Relations. *Used Vehicle Information Package.* August 1995.

Osbaldeston, Gordon. *Organizing to Govern*. Toronto: McGraw-Hill Ryerson, 1992.
– *Keeping Deputy Ministers Accountable*. Toronto: McGraw-Hill Ryerson, 1989.
Osborne, D., and T. Gaebler. *Reinventing Government: How the Entrepreneurial Spirit Is Transforming the Public Sector*. Reading, MA: Addison-Wesley, 1992.
Osborne, D., and P. Plastrick. *Banishing Bureaucracy*. Reading, MA: Addison-Wesley, 1997.
Ouchi, William. *Theory Z: How American Business Can Meet the Japanese Challenge*. Reading, MA: Addison-Wesley, 1981.
Paquet, Gilles, and Robert Shepherd. 'The Programme Review Process: A Deconstruction,' pp. 39–72. In G. Swimmer, ed., *How Ottawa Spends, 1996–97: Life Under the Knife*. Ottawa: Carleton University Press, 1996.
Pascale, Richard, and Anthony Athos. *The Art of Japanese Management: Applications for American Executives*. New York: Simon and Schuster, 1981.
Patterson, Anne, Rod Lohin, and Scott Ferguson. *Consultation: When the Goal Is Good Decisions*. Ottawa: Canadian Centre for Management Development, 1992.
Peters, Tom, and Nancy Austin. *A Passion for Excellence: The Leadership Difference*. New York: Random House, 1985.
Peters, Thomas J., and Robert H. Waterman. Jr. *In Search of Excellence: Lessons from America's Best-Run Companies*. New York: Harper and Row, 1982.
Pinsonneault, Alain, and Kenneth Kraemer. 'The Impact of Information Technology on Middle Managers.' *MIS Quarterly* 17, 3 (1993): 271–92.
Pitsula, James, and Ken Rasmussen. *Privatizing a Province: The New Right in Saskatchewan*. Vancouver: New Star Books, 1990.
Plumptre, T.W. *Beyond the Bottom Line: Management in Government*. Halifax: Institute for Research on Public Policy, 1988.
Privy Council Office. *Crisis Management*. Ottawa: Supply and Services Canada, 1989.
Pullen, J.W. *The Spruce Falls Power and Paper Company*. Ottawa: Canadian Centre for Management Development, 1992.
– *The St. Louis Bridge Incident*. Ottawa: Canadian Centre for Management Development, 1989.
Rae, Bob. *From Protest to Power: Personal Reflections on a Life in Politics*. Toronto: Viking, 1996.
Reed, Leonard. 'The Budget Game and How to Win It.' *Washington Monthly*, January 1979, 24–33.
Reich, Robert. *Locked in the Cabinet*. New York: Knopf, 1997.
Reid, Escott. 'The Saskatchewan Liberal Machine before 1929,' pp. 93–104. In N. Ward, and D. Spafford, eds., *Politics in Saskatchewan*. Toronto: Longmans, 1968.
Reschenthaler, G.B., and F. Thompson. 'The Information Revolution and the New Public Management.' *Journal of Public Administration Research and Theory* 6, 1 (January 1996): 125–43.

Richards, J., and L. Pratt. *Prairie Capitalism: Power and Influence in the New West.* Toronto: McClelland and Stewart, 1979.

Ritchie, Gordon. *Wresting with the Elephant: The Inside Story of the Canada–US Trade Wars.* Toronto: Mcfarlane Walter and Ross, 1997.

Roberts, David. 'Devine's Tories Accused of Squandering Millions.' *Globe and Mail,* 16 February 1991, A4.

Romanow, Roy, John Whyte, and Howard Leeson. *Canada ... Notwithstanding. The Making of the Canadian Constitution, 1976–1982.* Toronto: Carswell Methuen, 1984.

Rose, Richard. *Ministers and Ministries: A Functional Analysis.* Oxford: Oxford University Press, 1987.

Royal Institute of Public Administration. *Top Jobs in Whitehall.* London: Royal Institute of Public Administration, 1987.

Sallot, Jeff. 'Top Court Becomes Supreme Player.' *Globe and Mail,* 6 April 1992, A1, A4.

'SaskPower Chief Fired by NDP.' *Globe and Mail,* 15 November, 1991, A5.

Sass, Robert. 'Self-Enforcement of a Rights-Based Approach to Workplace Health and Safety,' pp. 150–66. In E. Glor, ed., *Policy Innovation in the Saskatchewan Public Sector, 1971–82.* North York: Captus Press, 1997.

Savoie, Donald. *The Politics of Public Spending in Canada.* Toronto: University of Toronto Press, 1990.

Seidle, F. Leslie. *Rethinking the Delivery of Public Services to Citizens.* Montreal: Institute for Research on Public Policy, 1995.

Sesser, Stan. 'A Reporter at Large (Singapore).' *The New Yorker,* 13 January 1992, p. 49.

Sheppard, Robert, and Michael Valpy. *The National Deal: The Fight for a Canadian Constitution.* Toronto: Fleet Books, 1982.

Simeon, Richard. *Federal–Provincial Diplomacy: The Making of Recent Policy in Canada.* Toronto: University of Toronto Press, 1972.

Smishek, Walter. 'Relations between Treasury Board and Outside Agencies or Interests.' Blakeney Papers, Collection R-800, file XXXII, 89. 18 August 1977.

Smith, David. *Prairie Liberalism: The Liberal Party in Saskatchewan.* Toronto: University of Toronto Press, 1975.

Smith, Janet, and Anne Patterson, *Managing a Royal Commission.* Ottawa: Canadian Centre for Management Development, 1994.

Snow, C.P. *Corridors of Power,* pp. 1–279. In C.P. Snow, *Strangers and Brothers.* Vol. 3. Harmondsworth: Penguin, 1984.

Stanbury, W.T. *Business–Government Relations in Canada.* Toronto: Methuen, 1986.

Stevens, Douglas. 'Corporate Autonomy and Institutional Control: The Crown Corporation as a Problem in Organizational Design.' *Canadian Public Administration* 34, 2 (Summer 1991): 286–312.

Stewart, Edward. *Cabinet Government in Ontario: A View from Inside.* Halifax: Institute for Research on Public Policy, 1989.

Taylor, Malcolm. *Health Insurance and Canadian Public Policy.* 2nd ed. Montreal: McGill-Queen's University Press, 1987.

Tollefson, E.A. *Bitter Medicine: The Saskatchewan Medicare Feud.* Saskatoon: Modern Press, 1963.

Trebilcock, Michael, Marsha Chandler, Morley Gunderson, Paul Halpern, and Jack Quinn. *The Political Economy of Business Bailouts.* Toronto: Ontario Economic Council, 1985.

Trudeau, Pierre, and Thomas Axworthy. *Towards a Just Society: The Trudeau Years.* Markham, ON: Viking, 1990.

Versteeg, Hajo. *A Case Study in Multi-Stakeholder Consultation.* Ottawa: Canadian Centre for Management Development, 1992.

Walker, Patrick Gordon. *The Cabinet: Political Authority in Britain.* New York: Basic Books, 1970.

Wallace, D.M. 'Budget Reform in Saskatchewan: A New Approach to Program-based Management.' *Canadian Public Administration* 17, 4 (Winter 1974): 586–99.

Waller, Tom. 'Framework for Economic Development: The Role of Crown Corporations and the Crown Investments Corporation of Saskatchewan,' pp. 29–48. In Eleanor Glor, ed., *Policy Innovation in the Saskatchewan Public Sector, 1971–82.* North York: Captus Press, 1997.

White, Graham. 'Transition: The Tories Take Power,' pp. 139–50. In Sid Noel, ed. *Revolution at Queen's Park: Essays on Governing Ontario.* Toronto: Lorimer, 1997.

– 'Traffic Pile-ups at Queen's Park: Recent Ontario Transitions,' pp. 115–44. In Donald Savoie, ed., *Taking Power: Managing Government Transitions.* Toronto: Institute of Public Administration of Canada, 1993.

– 'Big Is Different from Little: On Taking Size Seriously in the Analysis of Canadian Governmental Institutions.' *Canadian Public Administration* 33, 4 (Winter 1990): 534–40.

Williamson, Oliver. *Markets and Hierarchies: Analysis and Antitrust Implications.* New York: Free Press, 1975.

Williamson, Robert. 'Cool Head Helps Cold Buster.' *Globe and Mail,* 16 January 1992, B1, B13.

Wilson, Harold. *The Governance of Britain.* New York: Harper and Row, 1976.

Winn, Conrad. 'Ministerial Roles in Policy Making: Vote Seeker, Shaman, and Other Incarnations,' pp. 219–58. In André Blais, ed., *Industrial Policy.* Toronto: University of Toronto Press, for the Royal Commission on the Economic Union and Development Prospects for Canada, 1986.

Winsor, Hugh, and Edward Greenspon. 'PM bets on familiar faces.' *Globe and Mail,* June 1997, A1, A5.

Wolfe, David. 'Queen's Park Policy-Making Systems,' pp. 151–64. In Sid Noel, ed., *Revolution at Queen's Park: Essays on Governing Ontario.* Toronto: Lorimer, 1997.

Wolfson, Steve. 'Use of Paraprofessionals: The Saskatchewan Dental Plan,' pp. 126–39. In E. Glor, ed., *Policy Innovation in the Saskatchewan Public Sector, 1971–82.* North York: Captus Press, 1997.

Woodward, Calvin. 'U.S. Lumber Dealers on Canada's Side.' *Globe and Mail,* 25 March 1992, B7.

Zuboff, Shoshana. *In the Age of the Smart Machine: The Future of Work and Power.* New York: Basic Books, 1988.

Zussman, David. Personal communication with Sandford Borins, 25 October 1997.

Zussman, David, and Jak Jabes. *The Vertical Solitude: Managing in the Public Sector.* Halifax: Institute for Research on Public Policy, 1989.

Index